KU-033-426

Steve Levy has an itch for the Bible and he's itching to get the Bible into your blood. Sometimes you will feel like he's dragging you – but it's for your good. He holds that the Bible delights in Jesus – and he can't wait for you to share that delight. Steve has a fever for the Bible and is desperate to infect you! Let him.

Dale Ralph Davis

My prayer is that the Holy Spirit will use this lively and stimulating book by Steve Levy to remove the veil from many minds. How different (and how thankful!) they will be when they see that Christ is in *all* the Scriptures!

Stuart Olyott
Pastoral Director of the Evangelical Movement of Wales

That it is well-written and easy to read is good for starters; but the heart of the situation is the sheer happiness of meeting someone who is so in love with the Bible, so sensible in his approach, so clear that the Bible is all about Jesus, and so sure every believing reader will be led to a true understanding of what God himself has written for our learning.

Alec Motyer

The glory of Christ is *the* goal of all time and eternity. The purpose of the *Bible*, from beginning to end, is to reveal that glory to us, that we too might worship him. Jesus tells us that plainly, and Steve Levy wants to show us, just as plainly, how this is so. With an evident love for the task, and with a delightfully light touch, he'll give you a lot of help in that direction, and plenty of fun along the way!

William J U Philip
Minister, St George's-Tron Church, Glasgow

Some years ago the Marcions landed, turning the world of the Bible into a howling wasteland of disconnected irrelevances. In this book Steve Levy fights back to reclaim a thrilling Bible that from beginning to end speaks of Jesus. If you want more joy in your Bible reading, if you want to love Christ more, read it!

Michael Reeves
Theological Adviser, UCCF

Although there are plenty of Bible overview books and resources available today, many of them overlook Old Testament passages that show that saving faith has always looked to God's Son. Steve's book will not only leave you with a much clearer understanding about what the whole Bible is about, it will also ignite your passion for God's Word.

Martin Downes

Bible Overview

Steve Levy

Foreword by Richard Bewes

CHRISTIAN
FOCUS

In memory of the eternal life of Simon James.

Unless otherwise indicated, all Scripture quotations taken from the *Holy Bible, New International Version.* Copyright © 1973, 1978, 1984 by International Bible Society. Used by permission of Hodder & Stoughton Publishers, A member of the Hodder Headline Group. All rights reserved. "NIV" is a registered trademark of International Bible Society. UK trademark number 1448790.

Scripture quotations marked esv are from *The Holy Bible, English Standard Version*, copyright © 2001 by Crossway Bibles, a division of Good News Publishers. Used by permission. All rights reserved.

Scripture quotations marked kjv are taken from the King James Version

© Steve Levy 2008

ISBN 978-1-84550-378-9

First published in 2008
by
Christian Focus Publications Ltd.,
Geanies House, Fearn,
Ross-shire, Scotland, UK, IV20 1TW
www.christianfocus.com

Edited by Paul Blackham
Cover design by moose77.com
Printed by Norhaven A/S, Denmark

Contents

Foreword

The eighteenth - century evangelist George Whitefield was once preaching on Blackheath. A man and his wife saw the crowd of thirty thousand, and went up to investigate. Then the man said, 'Come on Mary, we won't stop any longer; he's talking about something that happened eighteen hundred years ago. What's that to us?'

However, in spite of themselves, the two stayed on, and were so fascinated by what they heard that they went home and dusted down the Bible that was lying on a shelf, and said, 'Is it possible that these old truths have been here so long, and we've not known it?'

I confidently predict that *Bible Overview* is going to have a similar effect upon thousands of readers. This is a page-turner of a book! I truly cannot think of a better way of introducing someone to the Bible than through these wonderfully luminous chapters that you have before you.

Steve Levy writes in crisp, short sentences, with an infectious love for the Scriptures – and for the pivotal figure of all history about whom they are concerned. The Bible is about to come *alive*, as you turn now to the very first page!

Richard Bewes O.B.E.
West London

Acknowledgements

Nearly five years ago Paul Blackham suggested I write this book. I must confess on many occasions the project was nearly shelved – but here it is.

I owe Paul an enormous debt for editing and advising and quite often correcting. I also have to say how gracious he has been because when we have disagreed, it is my opinion that has remained in the book. That means if there are parts that are wrong it my fault and mine alone.

The second great influence is my wife Clare. Thank you for your patience in taking a book written with the skill of a junior school child and turning it into the finished product – even if at times I can't recognise what I've written – that simply gives credit to your abilities.

There is no way this would have been written without you both enduring my stubbornness.

Paul Tucker, my pastor, laid the foundation of what the Bible teaches long before I was able to appreciate his help. Both Paul Blackham and I owe an enormous debt to DN Jones, whose teaching clarified so much of the Bible to us.

Thanks also to Disco Stu, Matt and all the apprentices for their research and questioning. I do find it stimulating when you disagree even if I don't always show it.

Lastly, I want to thank God for Simon. One of his last comments to me punctured my pride when he told me the book had to be published when I was about to give up. He also told me to get rid of the diagrams – I have!

This and his great friendship are the reasons I am dedicating this book to him. I will see you soon.

In memory of the eternal life of Simon James.

Preface

When I first became a Christian at the age of eleven I knew I had to read the Bible. I bought myself a big black leather King James Version and every night I read a chapter at a time, hoping against all hope that it would be one of those shortish ones. Reading Psalms with its small chapters was fine, but I still remember the shock of seeing Psalm119 for the first time!

It did me good, but often I couldn't remember what I'd read the night before. In fact often I couldn't remember what I'd read five minutes before. I was very grateful for the string that marked my place.

Wading through the Old Testament I would think, 'If I'd been to Israel, I might understand, or at least know how to pronounce, "Pi-hahiroth" or "Baal-zephon" or 'Migdol'. 'If I was good at maths I might be able to understand what the ark or the temple looked like. After all, what on earth is a cubit?! If only I could speak Hebrew or Greek like the preachers I heard. But they seemed to complicate matters in my mind and anyway I couldn't even cope with French in school. What hope could there be for me?

All this made me despair of understanding all of the Bible, so I started to have favourite bits, and distinctly un-favourite bits – most of it.

I persevered without grasping much at all because I knew from my parents that all of the Bible was God's Word but it was not until years later, listening to the preaching of Paul Tucker, that I discovered the key to understanding it all.

Once I saw this, and the light was switched on, I saw the whole Bible could be understood and enjoyed.

By the way, when I say 'all', I don't mean when my father made me eat 'all' of a slightly off-looking cheese sandwich at an old lady's house – not wanting to cause offence but struggling to force down each mouthful. The Bible is not like that. I mean the 'all' of a huge chocolate sundae at Joe's ice-cream parlour, where only a fool would leave even a melted drop left – hardly a duty!

If you don't believe me, read what the Bible says about itself, 'How sweet are your words to my taste, sweeter than honey to my mouth!' (Ps. 119:103).

The Bible promises to give great experiences.

It makes me understand myself.
It makes me understand the world.
It is my light, my life, my hope, my guide, my joy.
It shows me how to clean up the mess I make of my life at times.
It gives advice in all circumstances.
It gives me strength when I feel weak.
It gives comfort.
It makes sense of my suffering.
It gives purpose to my existence.
It saves my life.
It makes me wise.
It saves from my enemies.
It makes me cry, and it is my delight.
It makes me solid as a Christian.
And it teaches me to praise.

The purpose of this book is not to kick-start daily Bible reading, or to get you to read commentaries or other Christian books, as useful as they might be. I want to be far more daring than that.

I want you to delight in the Bible, so that when someone asks you how your daily reading is going, you'll answer, 'I wouldn't miss it for the world, it's delicious.' I want you to hunger to devour it, not in bite-size chapters, but setting time aside to read each book of the Bible through from beginning to end, as in fact they were originally meant to be read.

My hope is that whatever your upbringing, intelligence or church background, you will thirst after reading God's Word, all of it, and delight in every single bit.

Introduction:
Who will show me what the Bible says?

It explains itself

I had been invited to speak at a Christian Union house party and unusually for me I had turned up early. As I entered the room I heard an animated discussion taking place about the impending visiting preacher and his somewhat controversial views:

> 'Steve Levy said this…'
> 'He didn't…'
> 'Well I think that's outrageous.'
> 'Well I think he's got a point.'
> 'Maybe he meant this…'

The discussion was becoming increasingly heated. Eventually one of the students, sweet but a little over-smiley, noticed me looking bemused and assumed I was a mature student. He asked me who I was and what did I think of everything that had been said. I took great delight with my reply.

> 'My name's Steve Levy. By the way, I'm pretty sure I know what I said and meant on this issue.'

After the slightly embarrassed silence, we had a laugh over the incident but it still stands out in my mind. To find out what I thought, they only had to ask me.

There are a lot of conflicting views about the Bible but I don't care to know what *you think* the meaning of a particular book or verse is. I want to know what the Bible says about itself.

Who better to ask than the author?

There are times when I forget things. There are times when I change my mind. God is not like that. He is altogether different to us. He never forgets. He created the universe and he will be there long after history has ended. Every fact is always before Him. He has numbered every hair of our heads.

He appoints the day of my birth and the day of my death. He knows where I am sitting as I am reading this book and He knows when I will stop.

Being the infinite God, when He inspired the Scriptures, He had you, the reader, in mind and your church. This is a book by God.[1] He cannot lie. He knows what He means and He always means what He says.

So how do we interpret the Bible? When you read it you realize you don't have to, that *it interprets itself*. This is true throughout the Bible but is startlingly clear in the New Testament, where verses from the Old Testament are quoted with an explanation following.

The best interpreter of the Bible is the Bible itself and the job of the preacher and Bible teacher is simply to proclaim the explanation.

Over and again the Bible says our contempt for God is the problem. We try to replace God or to ignore Him, preferring the opinions of human beings, instead of simply trusting and obeying the words of the living God.

> 'Why do you say, O Jacob,
> and complain, O Israel,
> "My way is hidden from the Lord;
> my cause is disregarded by my God"?
> Do you not know?
> Have you not heard?
> The Lord is the everlasting God,
> the Creator of the ends of the earth.
> He will not grow tired or weary,
> and his understanding no-one can fathom.

He gives strength to the weary
and increases the power of the weak.
Even youths grow tired and weary,
and young men stumble and fall;
but those who hope in the Lord
will renew their strength.
They will soar on wings like eagles;
they will run and not grow weary,
they will walk and not be faint' (Isa. 40:27-31).

God never disregards you. He knows you better than you know yourself. Come to him weak. Come to him when you are tired, and He will lift you up.

Making sense of all the books
As a boy my earliest introduction to the Bible as a whole came through a particularly long song:

Sixty-six books in God's holy word,
telling the story of Jesus my Lord.
The books of the Bible I love to tell,
the books of the Bible, I know so well.
Genesis, Exodus, Leviticus…

We were made to sing it over and over until we had learnt it by heart. Needless to say it was quite traumatic! However when the preacher announced his text from Zephaniah and people were hastily fumbling through their Bibles trying to find it, I would just burst into song, quietly and under my breath of course. The only disadvantage being that by the time I got to Zephaniah the reading had finished!

Most of us have been there I'm sure. When faced with this long list of Bible books, how do we make sense of them? How did Jesus and the apostles make sense of them? How did they fit them together? How does the Bible fit them together?

The contents page

Let's start with the contents page. You might be thinking, 'that's the one page I do understand', but trust me on this one. What do you see – two books, the Old and New Testaments or 66 individual books all saying different things by different authors?

In Ephesians, Paul says that the Bible is one book, the 'foundation' laid through the 'apostles and prophets' (Eph. 2:20). Apostles were men 'sent' by Jesus Christ and given his special authority to preach and write. Prophets spoke and wrote God's Word. Both sets of men were chosen by God to speak His words (Eph. 4:11).

The Bible, he stresses, is one book with one author – God Himself.

What's all this about 'the Law of Moses, the Prophets and the Psalms'?

Look at the contents page of the Bible again. Our Old Testament starts with the historical books (Genesis to Esther), goes on to the wisdom books (Job to Song of Solomon) and finishes with the prophetic books (Isaiah to Malachi).

But the order of the original Hebrew Bible was different. The Bible Jesus knew started with the law, went on to the prophets and concluded with the writings (Psalms), 'Everything must be fulfilled that is written about me in the Law of Moses, the Prophets and the Psalms' (Luke 24:44).

Sometimes the New Testament writers refer to 'the Prophets', sometimes to 'the Law and the Prophets'. Other times they refer to 'Moses and the Prophets' or to 'the Law, the Prophets and the Psalms'. All very confusing you might think. But look at the chart. When you see these phrases being used you should know exactly which books are being referred to.[2]

At this point though I still wish I could get that dreadful 'Sixty six books' tune out of my head!

The Contents of the Bible

The Law **(Torah - meaning instruction)** Genesis, Exodus, Leviticus, Numbers, Deuteronomy	The first five books of the Bible were written or at least edited by Moses who was the greatest of all the prophets (Deut. 34:10).
The Former Prophets Joshua, Judges, Samuel, Kings	We often think of these books as history books but that is not their main purpose. They are preaching a message to us. They tell of the conquest of the land, the kingship of God's people and the decline to exile.
The Latter Prophets Isaiah, Jeremiah, Ezekiel, Hosea, Joel, Amos, Obadiah, Jonah, Micah, Nahum, Habakkuk, Zephaniah, Haggai, Zechariah, Malachi	These prophets all write either before, during or after the exile. They speak of God's judgment against sin and of the great hope that can be had in Jesus.
The Writings (Psalms) Psalms, Job, Proverbs, Song of Songs, Ruth, Lamentations, Ecclesiastes, Esther, Daniel, Ezra, Nehemiah, Chronicles	This section (named after its biggest book) has many different books, but all of the writings seem to take a step back from what is going on and show us the wise way to live.
Gospels (Good News) Matthew, Mark, Luke, John	All of these books focus on the life, death and resurrection of the Lord Jesus Christ.
Apostolic Writings Acts to Revelation	Acts tells of the work of Jesus through the Holy Spirit and the letters explain the implications of the life, death and resurrection of Jesus for the church. Revelation focuses on the glorified Lord, showing how life and history ought to be seen in the light of His return.

(Endnotes)
[1] 'The God of the Old Testament is not God the Father awaiting the revelation of his Son. Is it not the case that the God of the OT is the Holy Trinity working incognito. One Gospel, one people, one way of salvation, one God.' (Alec Motyer)

[2] 'Jesus uses "the law" as the formal title of Genesis to Deuteronomy, the books of Moses, eg Luke 24:44. In Matthew 17 Jesus mentions the law and the prophets separately but in 5:18, he uses "law" as a comprehensive description of the Scriptures – and can do this because "law" translates Torah, which means "teaching" – God's truth revealed to his redeemed.' (Alec Motyer). The law is the fundamental revelation of God through Moses and is basic to the whole Old Testament.

Part One
What the Bible says about itself

1:1
The Bible's about Jesus

Ever felt you're missing the point?
Somebody decided to buy the Levy family Monopoly. (I cannot think of a more inappropriate present for a family with three boys who only ever played football!) But my sister insisted we should play it with her and so we did.

After an argument, over who would be the dog and the sports car, we started. The rules seemed pretty obvious so we ignored them. Three days later we were still playing. Nobody knew how to win or lose and by now rules were being invented as we argued through each lap of the board.

If only someone could have explained the purpose of the game, it might have been bearable.

I didn't understand what I was playing, or why, and I hated every minute.

What does Jesus say the Bible is about?
Jesus says this, 'Do not think that I have come to abolish the Law or the Prophets; I have not come to abolish them but to fulfil them' (Matt. 5:17).

The word 'fulfil' is not referring to a handful of Old Testament references – a verse predicting where Jesus would be born, a few verses hidden away in Isaiah about the suffering servant.

Jesus is very clear. He didn't come to destroy the Law and the Prophets. He is what they are all about. If we take Jesus out of the Old Testament it is little wonder it confuses us.

> Beginning with Moses and all the Prophets, he explained to them what was said in **all** the Scriptures concerning himself (Luke 24:27).

Not just some, not just bits to be read at Christmas – all. **All** of the Bible is about Jesus. You might be thinking, 'I can't see that'. Then something is wrong with the way you read it. Listen to Jesus again:

> 'This is what I told you while I was still with you: Everything must be fulfilled that is written about me in the Law of Moses, the Prophets and the Psalms.' Then he opened their minds so they could understand the Scriptures. He told them, 'This is what is written: The Christ will suffer and rise from the dead on the third day. And repentance and forgiveness of sins will be preached in his name to all nations' (Luke 24:44-47).

When our eyes are opened, we see that the Law, the Prophets and the Psalms have one message – Jesus' suffering, His death, His resurrection and the offer of the gospel for everyone.

Moses explains Jesus

My eyes were opened to this truth, one humid June afternoon in a London Starbucks. I was deep in conversation with a well-known Bible scholar.

'Jesus explains Moses,' I said with great confidence and feeling very profound (it is amazing how pompous I can be). 'Of course that's true,' he replied, 'but the Bible's emphasis is that Moses explains Jesus.'

Normally I would have started arguing straight away, but two things stopped me. First, as I thought of every text to prove he was wrong, I realized in fact that I was wrong. The second was he had just bought me a huge strawberry and cream something or other and if I were too aggressive he might not buy me another one!

It took me five minutes and a lot of slurping to admit that he was right. I left with considerably better theology.

When you listen to Jesus, Moses and the Prophets have already explained who He is and what He does.

> 'If you believed Moses, you would believe me, **for he wrote about me**' (John 5:46).

Hold on. Isn't the New Testament about Jesus and the Old – well who knows? Listen to this verse:

> 'I am saying **nothing beyond what the prophets and Moses said would happen** – that the Christ would suffer and, as the first to rise from the dead, would proclaim light to his own people and to the Gentiles' (Acts 26:22-23).

Do you see: 'nothing beyond what the prophets and Moses said would happen.' When you are reading any of the Old Testament books, whether Numbers, Leviticus, Kings or Chronicles, you are reading about the gospel of Jesus Christ. You are not reading an illustration of the gospel, you are not reading stories that can be reinterpreted in the light of the gospel. You are reading God's clear word about Jesus. That is how the Bible sees itself.

The Old Testament is not a riddle that no one can make head or tail of until Jesus comes along and unravels it all. If you believe that, it doesn't take long to draw the conclusion (even subconsciously) that there's little point reading the Old, you might as well go straight to the explanation in the New. The Bible simply won't let you do that.

Still confused? Listen to Jesus as He tells the story of the rich man who wants his five brothers saved from hell:

> 'Let him warn them, so that they will not also come to this place of torment.' Abraham replied, 'They have Moses and the Prophets; let them listen to them.'

'No, father Abraham,' he said, 'but if someone from the dead goes to them, they will repent.'

He said to him, 'If they do not listen to Moses and the Prophets, they will not be convinced even if someone rises from the dead'(Luke 16:28b-31).

Moses and the Prophets tell us enough about Jesus to save us from hell. They are more impressive than seeing someone raised from the dead – that makes for pretty essential reading! The glory of the resurrection is seen not only in the gospels, but in all the Scriptures. Jesus Himself tells us that the Old Testament prophecies about Him (and His resurrection) are the most convincing evidence.

Both Peter and Paul use the same argument. If you've read Moses you should understand Jesus and His work:

'But this is how God fulfilled what he had foretold through **all the prophets**, saying that his Christ would suffer. Repent, then, and turn to God, so that your sins may be wiped out, that times of refreshing may come from the Lord, and that he may send the Christ, who has been appointed for you – even Jesus. He must remain in heaven until the time comes for God to restore everything, as he **promised long ago through his holy prophets**. For Moses said, "The Lord your God will raise up for you a prophet like me from among your own people; you must listen to everything he tells you. Anyone who does not listen to him will be completely cut off from among his people.'

Indeed, **all the prophets from Samuel on, as many as have spoken, have foretold these days**' (Acts 3:18-24).

They arranged to meet Paul on a certain day... he explained and declared to them the kingdom of God and **tried to convince them about Jesus from the Law of Moses and from the Prophets** (Acts 28:23).

Paul was able to perform great miracles. He spoke tongues more than any man. He was inspired by the Spirit to write most of the New Testament. He has an opportunity to evangelize a large number of people – so where does he start? Which Bible passage does he use to explain the good news about Jesus? With his Old Testament in one hand, he preaches about the wonderful salvation they can know in Jesus from the 'Law of Moses and from the Prophets'.

An overview of main themes

We have seen that the best interpreter of the Bible is the Bible. We have seen that **all** of the Bible is about Jesus and that the Old Testament explains truths about Jesus. So let's conclude with some of the great truths that are revealed to us about Jesus throughout the Bible:

▷ **Through Jesus the world is made**
(Gen. 1:1-3; John 1:1-3).

▷ **The gospel of Jesus Christ is preached to Abraham**
(Gen. 15:1-4; Gal. 3:8).

▷ **Jesus is the 'I am' who redeems Israel**
(Exod. 3:13-14; John 8:58).

▷ **Jesus gives the inheritance of the land**
(Judg. 2:1-4; Heb. 9:15).

▷ **Jesus is the Son of David who brings a kingdom that will not end**
(Ps. 2:2-7; Luke 1:32-33).

▷ **Jesus is the servant who explains the exile and brings its end**
(Isa. 42:1-9; Matt. 1:17).[1]

▷ **The Spirit of Christ testifies to the prophets about Jesus' suffering and the glories that will follow**
(Isa. 53; 1 Pet. 1:11).[2]

(ENDNOTES)
[1] The Old Testament Scriptures, as Jesus and the apostles knew them, ended with 2 Chronicles, and that book ends with the people still in exile waiting for the Christ.
[2] There is so much more! As the rest of this book will show!

1:2
It's always been about Jesus

I had an interesting conversation once with a man who held quite a position of authority in a Bible-believing church. After the service he took me to one side and said the most remarkable thing.

> 'There are many ways to come to God. You don't have to come through Jesus. In fact I didn't know anything about Jesus when I became a Christian.'

A little taken aback, I explained that there has only ever been one way to God – through Jesus. Sadly he simply shrugged his shoulders

The Bible is explicitly clear. You cannot know God without Jesus.

Many people get confused with the Old Testament believers. They came to God somehow but not as we come now, not directly through Jesus. But look at the texts:

> Jesus answered, 'I am the way and the truth and the life. No-one comes to the Father except through me' (John 14:6).

> 'All things have been committed to me by my Father. No-one knows the Son except the Father, and no-one knows the Father except the Son and those to whom the Son chooses to reveal him' (Matt. 11:27).

To know the Father you need Jesus. If you don't know Jesus you don't know the Father. Jesus does not say that this truth applies from now on. This truth is universal, for all time and eternity. Either we come to God through Jesus or it's not God that we're coming to. And that applies to every single believer in the Old Testament – they came to the Father as we come – through Jesus. John expands on this:

> No-one has ever seen God, but God the one and only, who is at the Father's side, has made him known (John 1:18).

Hang on a minute. No one has ever see God? Hasn't John read the Old Testament? The Lord appears to people all the time. He appears first to Adam in the garden, then to Noah and Abraham, Isaac, Jacob and Moses.

But of course he hasn't got it wrong. The Lord who appears is Jesus. They didn't see the Father – they saw Jesus who made the Father known to them.

What did Jesus do for the Old Testament believers?

The result of knowing Jesus is always the same – as we come to God through Jesus we receive his righteousness and we are put right with God. When the Law and the Prophets speak about righteousness and salvation there is only one place that it can be found.

> But now a righteousness from God, apart from law, has been made known, to which the Law and the Prophets testify (Rom. 3:21).

> 'But my righteousness will last for ever, my salvation through all generations' (Isa. 51:8b).

Salvation has not changed and cannot change. To quote the famous verse:

> Jesus Christ is the same yesterday and today and forever (Heb. 13:8).

Did all of the Old Testament believers know the Jesus we know?
The book of Romans is written to explain the gospel. After giving one of the most detailed explanations of how the gospel of God works in chapter 3, in chapter 4, Paul looks for some genuine examples of saving faith. Where does he turn but to Abraham and David?

These men are examples of how to believe in Jesus – example Christians if you like. On top of Paul's argument in Romans, there are many other instances of the New Testament going back to these Old Testament believers.

Abraham
Jesus knew exactly what Abraham thought about Him:

'Your Father Abraham rejoiced at the thought of seeing my day; **he saw it** and was glad' (John 8:56).

David
Peter explains exactly what David thought about Jesus. David always saw Jesus. David knew and spoke of the resurrection in great detail. David called Jesus 'Lord'.

David said about him: '"I saw the Lord always before me. Because he is at my right hand, I will not be shaken"' (Acts 2:25).

'**Seeing what was ahead, he spoke of the resurrection of the Christ,** that he was not abandoned to the grave, nor did his body see decay' (Acts 2:31).

Jesus knew exactly what David thought about him:

'How is it then that David, speaking by the Spirit, calls him "Lord"?' (Matt. 22:43).

Mark and Luke emphasize the same point in their gospels, it is so important.

Moses

Moses as the writer of the first five books of the Bible towers over the Old Testament. What made him great?

> He regarded disgrace **for the sake of Christ** as of greater value than the treasures of Egypt, because he was looking ahead to his reward (Heb. 11:26).

Moses left everything for Christ. You can't have the kind of impact Moses had without knowing Jesus.

The Israelites

Jesus was with the Israelites in the wilderness day by day as he is with us.

> For I do not want you to be ignorant of the fact, brothers, that our forefathers were all under the cloud and that they all passed through the sea. They were all baptised into Moses in the cloud and in the sea. They all ate the same spiritual food and drank the same spiritual drink; for they drank from the spiritual rock that accompanied them, and that rock was Christ (1 Cor. 10:1-4).

> Now I want to remind you, although you once fully knew it, that Jesus, who saved a people out of the land of Egypt, afterwards destroyed those who did not believe (Jude 5 ESV).

Isaiah and the prophets who followed him

> Isaiah said this because he saw Jesus' glory and spoke about him (John 12: 41).

The gallery of faith

This is why in Hebrews 11 there are so many examples of Christian faith (as if there was any other kind of faith). Believers in the Old Testament had the same relationship with God that you and I have. They are as much our examples of how to live for Jesus as New Testament believers.

So how does that work?

When I was starting out as a preacher (I had preached the sum total of one sermon on a Sunday to a church congregation) I was asked to preach at a communion service. What on earth was I to say? I rang my pastor Paul Tucker for advice.

'Summarize communion as it summarizes our faith.'
'Exactly how would I do that?'

Silence. I could sense his disappointment at one of his many protégées, as he once called us. And then came a sermon well worth stealing.

'We look *back* at the cross of Jesus, we look *up* to the ascended Jesus. We look *forward* to Christ's return.'

I added we look *around* at Jesus' church, so I could feel at least part of it was mine!

The Old Testament believer looked up to the pre-incarnate Christ and on occasions (as we shall see) met with Him. He looked forward to the cross of Jesus and he looked further forward to His return. And he looked around at His gathered church.

Hardly a huge difference!

What did they call Him?

I have been called many names in my lifetime – 'Rabs' (short for Rabbi – the downside of a Jewish surname), 'milkman', 'fat boy', 'Bible-basher', 'vicar', 'Levy' and a few others not repeatable in a Christian book. Some of them describe who I am, others how I look and others, what I do. But if I am with someone who really knows me, they call me by my name, Steve.

In the New Testament Jesus is called many names – 'Immanuel', 'Master', 'Good teacher', 'Son of Man'. All of these names sum up an aspect of His character or person. But His best name, the name we know Him by is the Lord Jesus Christ.

In the Old Testament Jesus also has many names – the 'Angel of the Lord', the 'Commander of the Lord's army', 'Son of Man' and sometimes simply the 'Lord'.

So when reading the Old Testament, should we say it is Jesus speaking and call Him by the name we are most familiar with? God inspired the writer to the Hebrews to do just that (Heb. 2:11-12). Should we say Jesus appeared in the Old Testament? John does just that (John 12:41). Should we refer to the Old Testament people of God as the church? God inspired Stephen to do just that (Acts 7:38).

So let's follow the Bible's example and use names that help us to apply the Bible to our own lives.[1]

There are over 300 titles given to Jesus in the Bible.[2] He doesn't have a different name in the Old Testament. David calls Him 'Lord' and speaks of the resurrection of 'Christ'. Isaiah sees 'Jesus' glory' and Moses gives up everything for his 'Christ'.

The Jesus who saved us from our sins, the Jesus who is the author and finisher of our faith is the same Jesus who spoke in the Old Testament. He wants us to see Him and find Him in all the Scriptures. This is how the Bible talks and God knows best!

If we find studying the Bible hard work at times, it might be because we're missing the point.

'You diligently study the Scriptures because you think that by them you possess eternal life. These are the Scriptures that testify about me, yet you refuse to come to me to have life' (John 5:39-40).

(ENDNOTES)

[1] In the New Testament we translate the Greek word *ekklesia* with the English word 'church'. In the Greek translation of the Hebrew Scriptures from 300 BC, the word *ekklesia* is often used to refer to the assembly of Israel. This means that the people of Jesus' day used the word *ekklesia* to speak about the people of God in the Old Testament. *Ekklesia* ('church') is an Old Testament word! You will find that many older Christian writers often speak of the church in the Old Testament in this way.

[2] See 'Names of Christ' by: T.C. Horton & Charles Hurlburt, published by Moody Press.

1:3
Who is the Bible from and who is it to?

When we first got married we bought a rocking chair which I had to assemble. The packaging was removed and everything including the instructions was dispatched to the bin – after all how hard can it be to assemble a rocking chair?

It was a good three days before I was rummaging through the large bins outside our flat trying to find the stupid instructions (quite why I thought the instructions were stupid when I hadn't even read them is beyond my abilities or memory). But eventually I found them – slightly damp.

I did come to realize that the instructions, even in their smelling state, were of some importance. Without them the chair was never going to be put together. Young men never want advice.

I've now passed that stage and just ask my father to do everything!

The instructions were written by the people who designed and manufactured the chair for people who hadn't the first idea how to assemble it – me. Once I knew their purpose it changed the way I looked at them.

The Bible is not just a book about Jesus. It is written *by* someone *for* someone.

God speaks
How do I know what to believe and how to behave? Is it by doing what feels right? Is it by doing what has always been

done? Is it not wanting to offend anyone or at least doing what offends the least number of people? Is it by trying to always find the middle ground? In a world where there are so many different voices claiming authority, is there a right or wrong way at all?

The Bible gives a clear and resounding answer. God speaks. In fact God speaks a lot.

You only have to read the beginning of the Bible and you see this phrase, 'God said'. As you read on you hear it again and again. In Leviticus you hear it 36 times. Sometimes He just speaks, other times He speaks through men. But it is God speaking.

This is remarkable. The God who knows all things, made all things, made me and knows my end, this God talks and He talks a lot. The God who stands above time and space, who finds the future no problem because He sees all history from the Egyptian empire until the twenty-first century – this God speaks. The God who cannot lie speaks. The God of love speaks.

This must change the way we read the Bible. Family, friends, the media, the opinions of others must fall silent because God speaks. There's one person God wants to speak with authority about and that person is Jesus.

God speaks clearly about Jesus

When I eventually found the instructions for the rocking chair, I found they were written in at least six other languages. All of them showed how to assemble the chair but the only instructions of any use were the ones in English.

Is the Bible only useful in parts – we are to ignore the hard bits because they are beyond our understanding?

There is no doubt there are parts of the Bible that are hard to understand. Look at what Peter says when he is talking about the Scriptures that the apostle Paul wrote:

> His letters contain some things that are hard to understand, which ignorant and unstable people distort, as they do the other Scriptures, to their own destruction (2 Pet. 3:16).

But none of it is impossible. Those who don't understand are not described as slow learners but as 'ignorant and unstable' and will be judged accordingly. So how do you understand the hard bits of the Bible?

> The statutes of the Lord are trustworthy, **making wise the simple** (Ps. 19:7b).

It makes the simple wise, not the wise wiser. What an enormous relief. If you are simple like me, there's hope!

Too simple to understand?

When I took art in school a teacher looked over my shoulder and asked with contempt, 'What is it?' In my panic as I looked down at this terrible mess, not even I could remember – and I'd just been drawing it! He held up the picture and said to the class, 'There really is no hope of Steve ever becoming an artist.' (I was hardly heartbroken!)

But God cannot hold us up if we're believers and say, 'This person is too simple to understand all I have to say about Jesus.' Look at the people He came to save. Look at the church. You'll see there is real hope. He makes simple people wise.

Are you a single mum who didn't finish school? God can make you wiser than Einstein. Are you a Christian who can hardly read? God can make you wiser than the Prime Minister. Come to the Bible like a child and learn about Jesus – the very wisdom of God.

> It is because of him that you are in Christ Jesus, who has become for us wisdom from God (1 Cor. 1:30).

The letters in the New Testament were written to churches made up of ordinary people, including children (Eph. 6:1-3), slaves (Eph. 6:5-8) and even ministers (1 Tim. 1:2)! These were read out loud to everyone and were meant to be understood and put into practice.

Why can't everyone see it?

So why doesn't everyone understand that the Bible is explaining Jesus? Is it because we live in a different era, or we haven't been to Israel, or we don't understand the languages?

Well no. The time span of the Old and New Testaments is over two thousand years, the political changes are many and dramatic and the language changes radical. And yet when Jesus and the apostles quote the Old Testament, not once do they assume their hearers can't understand because they haven't been to that particular spot in the Middle East. Not once do they say to their listeners that if they spoke Hebrew things would make more sense.

It is not intellectual ignorance that blindfolds us and stops understanding.[1]

There is something we are warned about that is far more important if we are to understand the Bible.

> The man without the Spirit does not accept the things that come from the Spirit of God for they are foolishness to him, and he cannot understand them, because they are spiritually discerned (1 Cor. 2:14).

> But their minds were made dull, for to this day the same veil remains when the old covenant is read. It has not been removed, because only in Christ is it taken away. Even to this day when Moses is read, a veil covers their hearts. But whenever anyone turns to the Lord, the veil is taken away (2 Cor. 3:14-16).

The problem of understanding the Bible has nothing to do with languages or geography or archaeology – it is spiritual. If you're not born again you've got problems. If you refuse to see Jesus you've got problems. Look how strong Jesus' language is in condemning those who don't see Him in Scripture. Even to Christians he says:

> 'How foolish you are, and how slow of heart to believe all that the prophets have spoken! Did not the Christ have to suffer these things and then enter his glory?' And beginning with

Moses and all the Prophets, he explained to them what was said
in all the Scriptures concerning himself (Luke 24:25-27).

Not seeing Jesus when reading Moses really is the definition
of spiritual blindness. Something I'm sure we all want to avoid
(John 9:28-41).

> 'You diligently study the Scriptures because you think that
> by them you possess eternal life. These are the Scriptures that
> testify about me, yet you refuse to come to me to have life'
> (John 5:39-40).

We need help

We need our eyes open, even though the truth is staring us in
the face. Jesus says if we can't see it we're dull, slow, hard-hearted
and blind – to shock us into repentance and turn us to Him.

Dr Martyn Lloyd-Jones once gave this illustration:

> If a man says he doesn't like Beethoven he tells me nothing
> about Beethoven but he tells me a great deal about himself.

(This illustration always worries me because I can't stand
Beethoven. But you get the point.) So if you can't see Jesus,
his death and resurrection, then you tell me nothing about the
theme of the Bible but you tell me a great deal about you.

In fact the people who think they are wise or clever are
the ones in most danger of misunderstanding God's Word
(1 Cor. 1:27). In fact many theologians have come up with some
of the most bizarre interpretations imaginable.

To tell the truth about that rocking chair, even though it
had all the appearances of looking right it had a tendency to
creak. People over a certain weight were always encouraged to sit
somewhere else.

Several years later a friend who worked in a furniture store
took it apart and put it together again. Now it doesn't creak and
can take a weight of up to twenty stone – my wife has some
large relatives!

The help of the author

The point is I needed help with the instructions. So it is with the Bible.

> … they are spiritually discerned (1 Cor. 2:14).

Jesus left his Spirit to help us. If you are a Christian you need to pray and ask for the help of the author, whom Jesus has left with believers. It is just 'foolish' to read the Bible without asking for help.

Ask God, accept His authority over your life and you will receive help. He has given his Word. He will help you to understand and give you the power you need to obey.

> 'If you then, though you are evil, know how to give good gifts to your children, how much more will your Father in heaven give the Holy Spirit to those who ask him!' (Luke 11:13).

This help is available for every believer. God is not playing hide-and-seek with you. He longs for you to understand. So we must pray as we read the Bible and be willing to turn to the Lord.

(ENDNOTES)

[1] We are not saying that translators are unimportant. We thank God for the language skills he has given to different members of his church. However, we should not pretend that every member of the body must all possess the same gifts.

1:4
How to know you're reading it properly

God tells me all I need to know
Every Christmas my older brother organizes a football and rugby game after lunch at my parents' house. As he is considerably bigger than me I always use the same line:

'I don't mind watching but don't expect me to join in.'

Many people read the Bible in that way – it has no effect because they're not reading it properly – they're not joining in.

Jesus replied: "'Love the Lord your God with all your heart and with all your soul and with all your mind. This is the first and greatest commandment. And the second is like it: Love your neighbour as yourself." All the Law and the Prophets hang on these two commandments' (Matt. 22:37-40).

The Bible tells us about Jesus so we can love God and love like God. We are meant to join in with all our heart and soul and mind. The Bible is like dynamite – it explodes our old ways of living and thinking.

Not only does the Bible have authority. Not only can it be understood by any believer. It also tells us all we need to know – to live for God, love God and love like God.

Jesus is the answer
A Pentecostal minister I knew who counselled drug addicts had this statement on the wall behind his desk, in the direct eye line of the person being counselled:

Jesus is the answer – now what is your question?

Is this true? Look at the following texts:

> Praise be to the God and Father of our Lord Jesus Christ, who has blessed us in the heavenly realms with **every spiritual blessing in Christ** (Eph. 1:3).

Every spiritual blessing is found in Christ, not in a meeting, or a conference or through another individual. All spiritual blessings are found in Christ.

> My purpose is that they may be encouraged in heart and united in love, so that they may have the full riches of complete understanding, in order that they may know the mystery of God, namely, Christ, in whom are hidden all the treasures of wisdom and knowledge (Col. 2:2-3).

Notice the 'mystery of God'. What would people pay to find that out? Imagine the take-up in a university or adult education centre if the answer was guaranteed? Yet in Christ we have it all. In Christ all the treasures of wisdom and knowledge are known.

> …you have been given fullness in Christ, who is the Head over every power and authority (Col. 2:10).

Everything we need

There's a line in the film *Jerry Maguire* where Tom Cruise says to his girl, 'You complete me'. A bit sentimental perhaps. But look at Jesus. He does make us complete. He gives us fullness through His suffering, death and resurrection.

> Grace and peace be yours in abundance through the knowledge of God and of Jesus our Lord. His divine power has given us everything we need for life and godliness through our knowledge of him who called us by his own glory and goodness (2 Pet. 1:2-3).

Jesus gives everything we need to live a godly life. But I've failed before? His reply is – in me is everything you need. But you don't know where I live? His reply is – in me is everything you need. But others have written me off? His reply is – in me is everything you need.

Whatever your excuse for not being godly, His reply is always the same:

> His divine power has given us everything we need for life and godliness through our knowledge of him who called us by his own glory and goodness (2 Pet. 1:3).

Learn about Jesus. This is the reason God has spoken clearly about Him.

The Bible makes a difference
⊳ **The Bible equips us for every good work because it's God's book about Jesus**
(2 Tim. 3:16-17)

⊳ **The Bible's truth about Jesus helps us to live a life separate from the world**
(2 Pet. 1:2-4)

⊳ **The truth about Jesus makes us contented, happy and free**
(Luke 11:28 and James 1:25)

The Bible builds the perfect church
Not new ideas, changing the way things are done or even freshening up the services (Eph. 4:11-26). The Bible not only applies to our individual lives but to our church life. People say, 'You'll never find the perfect church.' But I'm going to it one day and I want my church on earth to reflect it. The Bible tells us how we can make the church attain to the full measure of Christ.

Written for the situation we're in

If you are accused by your conscience, the Bible says He is your Advocate.

If you don't understand life, the Bible says he is your Prophet.

If you are guilty of sin, the Bible says he is your High Priest.

If you feel hated and out of control, the Bible says he is your King, the King of Kings.

If you are confused about the purpose of your life, the Bible says he is the Way.

If you feel unsatisfied, the Bible says he is your bread and water.

It doesn't matter what mess we are in, there is a promise in the Bible about Jesus that will help. In fact the Bible will turn me into a person who will love God and love like God. Read how men have had faith in Christ and found this to be true. Be warned by men who have rejected Him and see the consequences.

Does He understand me? Sometimes I can hardly understand myself, yet I know that He knows all about me. After all isn't He God?

The Puritan, Thomas Brooks once wrote:

Christ has come from the eternal heart of his Father to a region of sorrow and death;

> *that God should be manifested in the flesh, the Creator made a creature;*
> *that he that was clothed with glory should be wrapped with rags of flesh;*
> *he that filled heaven and earth with his glory should be cradled in a manger;*
> *that the God of the law should be subject to the law;*
> *the God of the circumcision circumcised;*
> *the God that made the heavens working as a carpenter for Joseph;*
> *that he that binds the devils in chains should be tempted;*
> *that he, who owns the world and everything in it should hunger and thirst;*
> *that the God of strength should be weary;*

the Judge of all flesh should be condemned;
the God of life put to death;
that he that is one with the Father should cry out of misery, 'My God, My
God why have you forsaken me?';
that he that had the keys of death and hell should lie in another man's
tomb;
that his head, before whom the angels cast their crowns, should be
crowned with thorns;
that his eyes, purer than the sun, should be shut by the darkness of death;
those ears, which heard nothing but the hallelujahs of angels and saints,
should hear the blasphemies of the crowd;
that mouth and tongue, that spoke as never any man spoke, should be
accused of blasphemy;
those hands, that held the sceptre of heaven itself, should be nailed to the
cross for human sin;
his every sense irritated,
with the spear and the nails,
the smell of death,
the taste of vinegar and gall,
the sound of curses,
the sight of his mother and disciples mourning for him;
his soul was without comfort and forsaken...[1]

He understands you and me.

He has taken such huge steps to get rid of our sin. Now He commands and empowers us to love God and love like God.

Each time we read the Bible we must ask, how does understanding Jesus teach me to love God and love like God?

Only when we understand this, have we really understood properly.

(ENDNOTES)
[1] Thomas Brooks, Volume 1, pages 17-18.

1:5
Why is it so difficult to read the Bible?

The problems we all face

My response to the Bible must be whole-hearted, so why is it sometimes so hard to read? The same can be true when we listen to sermons, as God's Word is proclaimed.

As a young Christian it did not take long after I was converted for the excitement of the Bible to slowly disappear. I found myself in sermons counting organ pipes and daydreaming of playing football matches. When it came to reading the Bible, newspapers, TV and even homework became more important. Why is this?

It is not the Bible's fault, or even the preacher's. (God still speaks and changes lives in some of the very dullest sermons.)

All the evidence we need to see that God's Word is God's Word is in God's Word. No amount of external evidence or additional entertainment improves the text itself. Such things actually take our attention away.

It is a bit like a toddler going to the Mona Lisa with a felt-tip because he feels a moustache would make her more attractive!

The devil

The devil will always whisper in our ears distracting thoughts. He always says, 'Did God really say?' This is his constant line of attack. He loves to take the seed of the Word away (Luke 8:12).

The answer is not to simply resist the devil. Anyone who tries this finds it far too hard. We must submit to God and *then* resist the devil (James 4:7-8). We must draw near to God and He will draw near to us. We must submit to God with whole-hearted commitment, recognizing that listening to Satan is unfaithfulness to God.

Our heart
We read God's Word but we simply do not want to be changed by it.

> Anyone who listens to the word but does not do what it says is like a man who looks at his face in a mirror and, after looking at himself, goes away and immediately forgets what he looks like (James 1:23-24).

We must do more than simply resolve to stop sinning. As William Gurnall says:

> *Do not challenge sin to a duel with your own resolve. You are not strong enough or smart enough to win. God can give you more grace than you have sin, more humility than you have pride.*[1]

We must be as passionate about Christ as we are about sin. No one puts this more beautifully than Charles Haddon Spurgeon:

> *You ought to be just as eager after holiness as you were after sin. Brethren, be just as hot to honour Christ as you once were to dishonour him. The devil says, 'Drink, drink; drink yourselves blind' and they do it as eagerly as if it were for their good. They are martyrs for Satan. Never did a soldier fling himself upon death for his king so recklessly as these servants of Satan yield themselves for his service. They will do anything; they will destroy their health and, what is worst of all, destroy their souls for ever for the sake of sin's brief delights. They know that there is a hell, they know that the wrath of God abides for ever on guilty men, but they risk all and lose all for sin. In that same way should we serve our Lord. Be willing to lose character for him; be willing to lose health for him; be willing to lose life for him; be willing to lose all, if by any means you may glorify him whose servant you have become.*
>
> *Oh, who will be my Master's servant? Here he comes! Do you not see him? He wears upon his head no diadem but the crown of*

> *thorns; down his cheeks you see the spittle flowing, his feet are still rubied with their wounds, and his hands are still bejewelled with the marks of the nails. This is your Master and these are the insignia of his love for you.*[2]

We should have a passion for Christ that drives out all other passions.

Conclusions

Someone came out with this line recently, 'The Bible is not about you, it is about God.' But the Bible doesn't speak in those terms. The Bible is about Jesus and therefore about you.

Because the Psalmist understands the Bible is about Jesus he says the following:

> I delight in your decrees; I will not neglect your word (Ps. 119:16).

> My soul is weary with sorrow; strengthen me according to your word (Ps. 119:28).

> The law from your mouth is more precious to me than thousands of pieces of silver and gold (Ps. 119:72).

> Because I love your commands more than gold, more than pure gold (Ps. 119:127).

> Your compassion is great, O Lord; preserve my life according to your laws (Ps. 119:156).

The Bible tells all we need to know about Jesus – therefore all we need to know!

That is why we are supposed to see it as something delicious. All of it!

(ENDNOTES)

[1] William Gurnall, *The Christian in Complete Armour*, Volume 1, page 212

[2] C H Spurgeon, *Metropolitan Tabernacle*, Volume 25 (1879) page 383

Part Two
Creation to new creation

2:1
God creates

The film was the sad but true, *The Elephant Man*. Our living room was filled. The lights were off. Every emotion had been touched and we were drawing up to the tragic but triumphant climax. Then suddenly the smell of cattle dung mingled with chips entered the room – which could only mean my brother, a farm labourer, was home.

Suddenly the lights were on and this 6 feet 3 in. frame was stepping over bodies offering everybody a chip. Everyone except Dave could sense the atmosphere had now become distinctly tense but we were all Christians, so we just glared at him.

Oblivious to the chaos he was causing, he threw himself down on the chair:

'So what's it about then?'
'Get out. Go on get out. You can't come in halfway through. Out!'

The Bible is a book with a clear beginning and end. It starts with creation. It ends with the renewal of the old creation and the beginning of a new order:

Then I saw a new heaven and a new earth, for the first heaven and the first earth had passed away…'the old order of things has passed away' (Rev. 21:1, 4).

The whole of the Bible is working towards this great climax. Unless you see this you can be in real danger of breaking in halfway through and missing the point.

This leaves us with a number of questions. If Jesus is the great theme of the Bible, how does He fit into this? How does God create? Why does He create? What ruined the old creation? How does God create a new one?

God creates

I knew a minister who believed that to be a true pastor you had to try to see people in their workplace. It was only there you could understand how they work and who they are. Could this be why the Bible starts by showing us how God works? As we observe this, so simply explained at the beginning of the Bible, we will be able to see how He works throughout.

From the beginning we need to be careful not to assume we know what is going on before we listen to the text. Notice even though the Bible is clear God is one, Genesis chapter 1 shows all is not as it first seems:

Then God said, 'Let us make …' (Gen. 1:26).

Notice the plural 'us'. In the beginning was God – the Father, the Son and the Spirit. This is how the creation starts. And they create.

God the Father creates

'You are worthy, our Lord and God, to receive glory and honour and power, for you created all things, and by your will they were created and have their being' (Rev. 4:11).

God the Spirit creates

Now the earth was formless and empty, darkness was over the surface of the deep, and the Spirit of God was hovering over the waters (Gen. 1:2).

When you send your Spirit, they are created, and you renew the face of the earth (Ps. 104:30).

There is one member of the Trinity who is not involved yet. And before He is involved the creation is without hope. The same language is used later in the Bible about people's lives before Jesus enters:

> 'My people are fools;
> they do not know me.
> They are senseless children;
> they have no understanding.
> They are skilled in doing evil;
> they know not how to do good.'
> I looked at the earth,
> and it was formless and empty;
> and at the heavens,
> and their light was gone (Jer. 4:22-23).

Without Christ is without hope.

But then God the Son – the Word – creates and makes the Father known

> And God said, 'Let there be light,' and there was light (Gen. 1:3).

> In the beginning was the Word, and the Word was with God, and the Word was God. He was with God in the beginning. Through him all things were made; without him nothing was made that has been made (John 1:1-3).

> No-one has ever seen God, but God the One and Only, who is at the Father's side, has made him known (John 1:18).

It is Jesus and only Jesus who makes sense of the work of God. In Genesis we see the way the triune God always works:

> 'For through him (Jesus) we both have access to the Father by one Spirit' (Eph. 2:18).

The Father through the Son by the Spirit – a pattern we will see again in the new creation.

God creates everything

Not only do we see how God creates, but something else of great significance.

God creates everything – everything you know, everything you see. When you look in the mirror you are staring at God's creation.

There is an enormous consequence to this. People think that theologians (people who study God) are strange. Many lecturers and authors go out of their way to encourage this idea! But the way you look at the world reflects your understanding of, or lack of understanding, of God. Nothing makes sense without Him.

Cut yourself off from the source of everything, from the one who keeps everything going, from the one who will bring everything to an end and you will be in trouble. Without Christ is without hope – any hope!

Every problem in life is really a theological problem. That is, every problem ought to be understood in the light of our knowledge of Christ in the Bible.

What's the point of creation?

We've seen how the world was made but we are left with the why. Children are always asking the question, 'Why?' And parents, uncles and aunts usually end up replying, 'That's just the way it is.' But is it?

I knew a student whose mother did everything for him. When he went away to college he found himself confused by the simplest of tasks. One day he decided to make himself egg on toast, 'Surely that's what toasters are for?' He laid the toaster on its side, cracked the egg on the bread and slid them, slowly and carefully into the toaster. The toaster was ruined and he was fortunate not to cause a huge fire.

He didn't understand what the toaster was for.

What is the world for? Once we know that, everything else should make sense. If I get this wrong, however, there will be serious consequences. The Bible's answer is loud and clear.

He is the image of the invisible God, the first-born over all creation. For by him all things were created: things in heaven and on earth, visible and invisible, whether thrones or powers or rulers or authorities; **all things were created by him and for him**. He is before all things, and in him all things hold together (Col. 1:15-17).

Everything is made through Jesus. Everything is made for Jesus – absolutely everything. Outside of Him there is only void and emptiness. Without Christ is without purpose. Without Christ is without hope.

2:2
What about us?

Who are we?

As a small boy one question irritated me more than any other: 'What are you going to be when you grow up?' How do you answer such a question? I had no idea.

Even at such a young age I knew it scratched at a bigger question which I'm not sure I could have put into words but gnawed away at me nonetheless.

How can I know what I'm going to be when I'm not sure who I am?

God created man and woman differently to everything else in creation. They are capable of being something a tree and an animal simply cannot be.

> So God created man in his own image, in the image of God he created him; male and female he created them (Gen. 1:27).

We are capable of reflecting God. In each individual is the potential to reflect God, to be holy as He is holy, to love because He is love. All creation is for Jesus but nothing can reflect Him, look like Him and show what He is like, quite like us. We are made to show off the glory of God.

So what do men do? (I pause here for women to insert their own comments and then we can get back to the point!)

> Then God said, 'Let us make man in our image, in our likeness,
> and **let them rule** over the fish of the sea and the birds of the air,
> over the livestock, over all the earth, and over all the creatures
> that move along the ground' (Gen. 1:26).

Man is to rule over creation. But with power comes responsibility.
If man falls, creation falls with him.

So how will this pinnacle of creation come to life?

> The Lord God formed the man from the dust of the ground
> and breathed into his nostrils the breath of life, and the man
> became a living being (Gen. 2:7).

Jesus forms and moulds him but it is the breath of God that
brings new life. 'Breath' can also be read as 'Spirit'. In the new
creation we are also born by the Spirit (John 3).

God creates a home for man

God creates a home for man with everything he could want, a
place where he can rest and know blessing.

> And God blessed the seventh day and made it holy, because
> on it he rested from all the work of creating that he had done
> (Gen. 2:3).

He creates a home where everything he needs can be found.
In truth the passage in Genesis 2 almost sounds like an estate
agent's advert for the perfect place to live. Their home has a
variety of beautiful trees producing sumptuous food and a
tranquil river runs through it. Everything they could want is
here. And unlike a home described by an estate agent, when
they arrive – it's good!

There is a condition on them staying:

> And the Lord God commanded the man, 'You are free to eat
> from any tree in the garden; but you must not eat from the tree
> of the knowledge of good and evil, for when you eat of it you
> will surely die'(Gen. 2:16-17).

The condition for them enjoying everything they could desire is to obey the Word of God. They don't have to do a long list of things. They simply have to avoid doing one thing. It seems so easy.

Making a house a home

'Sel, where do you think of as home?'

Selwyn Morgan had been a minister of a growing city church in Reading. He loved to preach in India and went for a month each year. Now in semi-retirement pastoring a church in Barry, South Wales, his answer came without him taking a breath, 'Where Jan is!'

Jan his wife could make the most difficult teenagers I brought to his house feel at home, with a word, a coffee and a few homemade biscuits. She would clean up the vomit of a twelve-year-old after he had thrown up during a meeting I was running. The gang, as many as thirty some Saturday nights, was as rough as any I had known – especially the girls! But when Jan wasn't there they demanded to know why. She shouted at them, listened to them, sat with them but most of all she loved them. Sometimes I think they endured my preaching because they knew it was home to be where Jan was, and the other ladies who helped.

Jan knew how to make a home, and she changed lives.

God gave Adam a wife (Gen. 2:18-25). Our Lord entered the garden and walked with them in the cool of the day (Gen. 3:8). Surely this beautiful garden would now feel like home.

2:3
What's gone wrong with the first creation?

As I walked into the doctor's surgery I noticed him staring in that 'you've still got toothpaste on the side of your mouth' kind of way.

'You don't wear a wedding ring. Are you married?' he asked.

'I am married but my wedding ring doesn't fit any more.'

'Mmm…interesting. Do you have trouble finding shoes to fit?'

'Yes I do actually. They never seem wide enough any more.'

I was a little bemused. I had only come because I had an in-growing toenail!

'Have you noticed a change in your facial appearance?'

'People who knew me years ago comment on how different I look now. And I've put on five stone in the last seven years.'

Most people would have enlarged on things at this point but I tend to get tongue-tied whenever I go to the doctors (or when overcharged by a mechanic).

'Do you sweat a lot?'

'Yes and thanks for asking.'

Silence. Probably best to keep a lid on the sarcasm.

'Struggle to sleep?'

'Yes.'

'I'm pretty confident you have a condition called acromegaly – which is caused by a small growth on the pituitary gland at the front of the brain. Not too much to worry about. I want to arrange a blood test and an appointment with an endocrinologist. Take a wedding photograph with you.'

Badly-fitting shoes, a wedding ring that didn't fit, sweating, five stone in weight and rugged features. (I liked the sound of that one, having grown up with a 'pretty face' as one aunt put it.)

The symptoms seemed unrelated but as it turned out they all had the same cause.

Why isn't life simple? Why doesn't God speak and we listen? Why do we struggle to obey? Where does sickness come from? Why are there wars and arguments? Why do we feel so lost? And most importantly – why has my relationship with God broken down?

The answer is all found in one chapter of the Bible.

Why did it all go wrong?

Satan's line of attack is to undermine God's Word, 'Did God really say?' Their failure was to ignore God's Word and follow their own sinful desires:

> When the woman saw that the fruit of the tree was good for food and pleasing to the eye, and also desirable for gaining wisdom, she took some and ate it. She also gave some to her husband, who was with her, and he ate it (Gen. 3:6).

The sinful desire of the flesh – she saw that the tree was 'good' for 'food'.

The sinful desire of the eyes – it was 'pleasing to the eye'.

The pride of life – it was 'desirable for gaining wisdom'.

These are the desires we are now born with and cannot control:

> For just **as through the disobedience of the one man the many were made sinners** (Rom. 5:19).

Many people try to avoid this truth. But who, looking at their heart, can deny they are sinful?

We often call this first and original sin 'the fall', because it was a long fall down from the wonderful life of the Garden of Eden. We 'fell' into disease, despair, decay and death. Most of all we fell short of the glory of God.

But look who comes to help.

When our Lord comes looking for them, they hide and cover themselves in fig leaves. It would be comical if the consequences were not so tragic. It would be comical if we hadn't made such fools of ourselves when Jesus came looking for us. This is a tragedy for the world, but more specifically, this is a tragedy for you and me at this moment. The tragedy of my life and the world I live in is unfolding before my very eyes in the Bible. I need to sit up and take notice.

Sin seems such a small word

They have the first marital row in Genesis 3, then they have a family row (Gen. 4) which leads to the death of one of their sons and then to all the arguments and wars in history. Because of the first sin in Genesis 3, death entered the world with all the untold pain and anguish that brings. But even worse – God's anger is now on them. This is seen in a series of curses, leading to them being removed from the home God built for them.

> So the Lord God banished him from the Garden of Eden to work the ground from which he had been taken. After he drove the man out, he placed on the east side of the Garden of Eden cherubim and a flaming sword flashing back and forth to guard the way to the tree of life (Gen. 3:23-24).

Wherever they are from now on they are lost. How they must have felt at the pain caused by their sin!

Have you ever seen a married couple arguing? It can seem funny for those looking on but it is soul-destroying for the couple.

Think of the horror of standing at their son Abel's grave, and seeing him buried. How Adam and Eve must have felt their hearts being torn out.

Is there anyone who has not stood at the grave of a loved one and felt that indescribable pain? Is there anyone who has not watched the news with horror when seeing the destruction of people on an enormous scale? Is there anyone when watching nations warring against nations who has not wondered where it all will end? But here is where it all began.

Sin seems such a small word to describe such indescribable anguish. Sometimes I wonder whether that is why the word is not used here in Genesis 3. This disobedience has many terrible consequences which are around us now; every death, every tear, every war, every earthquake, every flood.

Worst of all, the God who is love and can help is so often unknown and blasphemed.

Only the blood of God can solve this

A theme is introduced which now will dominate time and the rest of eternity (Rev. 12:11). God's provision for covering up their shame is the shedding of blood (Gen. 3:21) for without it there is no forgiveness of sin (Heb. 9:22). Without this blood sacrifice there is no escape from certain death, destruction and despair.

All the Christian has, Jesus has bought with his blood (Heb. 9:12). It is our redemption (Eph. 1:7). It is how we are made clean (Heb. 13:12). It is how we can be reconciled with God and make sense of life (Col. 1:20).

It is little wonder that everything God does in the Bible for the saving of His people starts with the shedding of blood. This is how serious the sin of the Garden of Eden is. Only 'the blood of God' (Acts 20:28) can destroy its effects.

Who will come and shed his blood to cover their sins and destroy the evil of this world?

'And I will put enmity between you and the woman, and between your offspring and hers; **he will crush your head**, and you will strike his heel' (Gen. 3:15).

We haven't changed

What follows the exile from the Garden of Eden makes for pretty grim reading.

Family troubles occur. Cain will only bring the works of his hands and not the blood sacrifice that God requires (Gen. 4:3, Heb. 11:4). Jealous that God accepts his brother's faith, he kills him. The world boasts of its evil before God and has to be judged for its rejection of Christ. Noah and his family are saved by trusting Christ through building the ark (1 Pet. 3:18-22). Mankind tries to build a society that does not need God but cannot solve any of the problems caused by the fall. God judges their foolish schemes by bringing division between nations, causing there to be many languages, and a deep-rooted wall of hostility.

We often think that humanity has progressed from those days. Certainly technology has improved. But the Bible says '…evil men and impostors will go from bad to worse, deceiving and being deceived' (2 Tim. 3:13).

The Bible's emphasis is that we haven't changed. The book of Romans states clearly the condition of humanity in the Old Testament is the condition of humanity in the New (Rom. 3:10-18). And if anything it is worse.

There will be terrible times in the last days (2 Tim. 3:1b).

Look at the history of the twentieth century and even the beginning of the twenty-first, and any serious analysis will reveal that we are worse than we were before.

2:4
Noah and the covenants

Big questions now need to be answered – questions which not only help us understand Scripture but ourselves.

How can a sinful man walk with God when He is so holy?
How can he meet with God without God casting him out?
What is the basis for this relationship?
How can God continue to walk with him, when he regularly fails?
How can a man face God daily without feeling overwhelmed by shame?
How does a man walk with God when his heart feels hard to God?
How can his heart become soft so he can have a real and not superficial relationship with God and others?
What happens when he fails (as the Bible emphasizes he will) and not just fails but falls into sins which would make any of us blush to be seen walking with him, let alone God who knows everything?
How can he ever conquer specific sins in his own life?
How does he know his relationship with God will last a lifetime?
How close can God and man become?

Enoch walked with God. So did Noah and Abraham. It is possible for every Christian.

I look at myself and think I can't be the Christian I should be. I can't defeat my sin. I can't be the witness I should be. I can't go on for another year like this. I can't go on for another week. I can't face another day or even an hour seems too much. God must barely tolerate me. I know I am going to heaven but what kind of relationship do I have with God on earth and how do I know it will be okay through and after death?

Enoch, Noah and Abraham didn't look at themselves! That is a good start because there are no answers there.

So what made Enoch wake up every morning and follow God instead of hiding from Him? He walked with God for 300 years, which is 15,600 weeks, 109,575 days, or 2,629,800 hours. Every day he said I can follow God and die to self. How did he do it? What is the basis for this relationship?

A covenant which God established with Noah.

Not the covenant of works
In the Garden of Eden God made a promise – an agreement or covenant (Hosea 6:7). He loved Adam. Adam had to love Him with all his heart, mind, soul and strength. That was the kind of obedience God wanted.

If Adam was obedient to God He promised he would enjoy eternal life, he would be His friend and enjoy His blessings. He would even come and walk with him. God so loved Adam that if Adam was obedient he would have eternal life.

Because of this promise, if anything bad happened to him he could say to God, 'But you said.' Adam knew God could not and would not fail him.

Covenant of works – cause and effect
I have a friend who is a doctor and one day I told her that whenever I twist my arm into a certain position it really hurts. This was her reply:

'Don't twist your arm that way then.'

For her the answer was a simple matter of cause and effect. If you're stupid enough to twist your arm back to front, then you will cause yourself pain. Arms aren't made to be twisted in certain directions and if you do it will hurt.

Before the fall, Adam lived a life of perfect obedient love and was able to walk with God and enjoy life. Once he broke God's command he could no longer avoid death and punishment. Under the covenant of works there was no way back. He was condemned. There was and is no way back for the disobedient.

There is not a great deal in Genesis to explain how high the standard is to earn a relationship with God (Rom. 5:12-14). But because everyone dies we can be sure that everyone failed.

So what is the standard?

In the law God spells out through Moses exactly what His standard is. But as we will see everybody breaks this covenant as well. Even though there are sacrifices that can be made, we all know that we cannot be pure enough to keep the law. Who can be clean enough to approach the living God?

> Who may ascend the hill of the Lord?
> Who may stand in his holy place?
> He who has clean hands and a pure heart,
> who does not lift up his soul to an idol
> or swear by what is false (Ps. 24:3-4).

If we had to fulfil the law for ourselves, we would be left feeling hopeless. Read the Ten Commandments. Who can keep them? Who can escape the punishment (death) for breaking them?

> 'but you must not eat from the tree of the knowledge of good and evil, for when you eat of it you will surely die' (Gen. 2:17).

> For the wages of sin is death (Rom. 6:23).

> 'For every living soul belongs to me, the father as well as the son – both alike belong to me. The soul who sins is the one who will die' (Ezek. 18:4).

61

The Bible tells us the soul that sins will die. Everyone who follows Adam has sinned, therefore everyone should die. That is the old covenant. The law of Moses establishes it beyond doubt.

The reason we feel such failures even though we are Christians, is that we still live as if we are under this old covenant with God. So either we are trying do things to please Him and feeling 'rubbish' because of our puny efforts, feeling like Christians that God barely tolerates. Or we behave as the worst of Christians with hard hearts and feel we are better then everyone else.

Living as if we are under the covenant of works simply doesn't work.

The new covenant

Last summer we were told Swansea City Football Club would be playing their final season at the famous old Vetch ground. I told my son I would take him before the Swans moved to their new stadium. Several months later he asked when we were going. 'Soon,' I replied. A couple of months later the question came again. 'When are we going?'

Suddenly I realized there were only two games of the season left and the last game had sold out months ago. I wasn't sure I could get a ticket as I was going away. I tried my best to explain how I had forgotten.

Calmly he replied, 'But you said.'

His words made me realize there was more at stake than tickets to a football game. As far as he was concerned we had made an agreement – a promise, a covenant. And if I broke it, my reputation as a dad who does what he says, was going to be broken. If I didn't get the tickets I wasn't the dad he thought I was or the dad I said I was.

I phoned my father and he bought the tickets. He kept the promise – the agreement, the covenant, for me even though I hadn't and couldn't do a thing.

We read in Genesis 5:24 that Enoch, a sinful man (Rom. 5:12) not only walks with God just like Adam before he sinned, but he doesn't even see death (Heb. 11:5).

Enoch walked with Christ, listened to Christ, preached Christ, and ascended with Christ. We are even told that Enoch preached the second coming of Christ:

> Enoch, the seventh from Adam, prophesied about these men: 'See, the Lord is coming with thousands upon thousands of his holy ones to judge everyone, and to convict all the ungodly of all the ungodly acts they have done in the ungodly way, and of all the harsh words ungodly sinners have spoken against him' (Jude 14-15).

So what's going on? The covenant with Adam is clear – the wages of sin is death. Adam failed to obey God. Adam dies. How then can God be fair and let the sinner Enoch enjoy the privileges that only sinless Adam could enjoy?

There must be a new promise at work. There must be another covenant, a deeper covenant that cannot be broken by human sin, a covenant that will never become old and broken.

What has Enoch got that Adam lost?

Enoch knew of another covenant, a new promise, a guarantee not based on obedience, but on God's kindness – kindness we don't deserve (or grace).

> 'For God so loved the world that he gave his one and only Son, that whoever believes in him shall not perish but have eternal life' (John 3:16).

Enoch believed in God's one and only Son (Heb. 11:5-6) and received eternal life. We need to be careful that we are not arrogant enough to believe that we know more of God or salvation than the godly men and women who have gone before us. In fact, the Bible constantly reminds us to look to these great saints who walked with God so long ago.

How much did Enoch know? We only have nine verses in the Bible that mention him by name. But they are an amazing nine verses! I don't know quite what he knew, but if he walked with God for at least three hundred years I imagine he knew a lot.

They knew what went before

One of the dangers when studying the Bible is to treat it as if it were a series of disconnected, separate stories, as if nobody knew about anything that went before.

Genesis goes out of its way to point out that Adam lived at the same time as Noah's father, and that Noah, living in the line of the godly, would have known the truth taught to Adam. Interestingly enough, what is often forgotten is that Noah would have known Abraham's father. The reason the lists of ages are recorded is to show us that the gospel truth was passed on from Adam to Noah to Abraham. Truth carefully treasured and reverently handed on to the church in each generation (Gen. 5).

Think of it this way. In Genesis 3:15, the Lord God preached the gospel sermon of the promised Seed. This promise of the Seed was the most precious and wonderful gospel truth for the church for hundreds of years. From Adam right down to Abraham the church must have clung to and repeated the promise over and again. Then, in Genesis 12 the Lord appeared to Abraham and declared another promise about the Seed. How utterly thrilling it must have been! After hundreds and hundreds of years the great promise of the divine Messiah was renewed to His church.

The covenant with Noah

When the word covenant is introduced in the life of Noah, the background of Genesis has cleared up what the word means. Our Lord, who would destroy Satan's work, is preached to Adam. Abel offered sacrifices that pointed to the great sacrifice and was declared righteous. Seth knew life because he called on the name of the Lord. Enoch knew life because he knew Christ.

Noah's father, Lamech, knew Adam for many years. He also knew Seth and Enoch. He would have passed on to his son the stories of the fall, of the many who called on the name of the Lord that first time, of Enoch's walk with the Lord and his ascension. These great characters were Noah's relatives.

When Noah arrives on the scene he walks with God (Gen. 6:8) just as Enoch did 17 verses earlier. His conversion is again because of God's grace to him.

A covenant with God Himself

Then we read the most extraordinary phrase. God says, 'I will establish my covenant with you' (Gen. 6:18). What is this promise that makes it possible for sinful men, who deserve death and punishment, to walk with a pure and holy God? What is this promise that makes it possible for sinful Noah to escape the judgment of God?

God now establishes the promise with Noah. The gospel covenant that lies at the heart of the whole Bible is preached to Noah when he needs it most.

From eternity, God the Father made an agreement with God the Son and God the Holy Spirit (John 3:34). Put simply, this was a 'covenant' where the Son would live the life Adam (and we) should have lived by the power of the Holy Spirit.

He would be called the Christ (anointed one) from birth (Luke 2:11). He would be anointed by the Holy Spirit to do the work the Father had given Him to do (Acts 10:38, Luke 4:18-19).

Jesus the Christ would do exactly what the Father required of Him, 'Not my will but yours be done'.

> 'The one who sent me is with me; he has not left me alone, for I always do what pleases him' (John 8:29).

He would suffer the punishment we should have suffered. He would conquer sin and prove it by rising from the dead.

Before He ascends, He has absolute confidence that those who trust Him are as united to God as He is and He wants them all to know it is true.

'Go instead to my brothers and tell them, "I am returning to my Father and your Father, to my God and your God"' (John 20:17b).

An eternal guarantee

The question that remains is, does the guarantee stand? The Old Testament shows it set in eternity. Look at Jesus' welcome in heaven. After all He is the only one with 'clean hands' and a 'pure heart' who does not 'lift his soul to an idol or swear by what is false'. He ascended the hill of the Lord and suffered at Calvary. Listen to His welcome:

Lift up your heads, O you gates;
be lifted up, you ancient doors,
that the King of glory may come in.
Who is this King of glory?
The LORD strong and mighty,
the LORD mighty in battle.
Lift up your heads, O you gates;
lift them up, you ancient doors,
that the King of glory may come in.
Who is he, this King of glory?
The LORD Almighty –
he is the King of glory. (Ps. 24:7-10).

Hebrews reminds us the guarantee is set in eternity. Listen as the Father says to Jesus in heaven:

'Your throne, O God, will last for ever and ever,
and righteousness will be the sceptre of your kingdom.
You have loved righteousness and hated wickedness;
therefore God, your God, has set you above your companions
by anointing you with the oil of joy.'

He also says,
'In the beginning, O Lord, you laid the foundations of the
earth, and the heavens are the work of your hands.
They will perish, but you remain;
they will all wear out like a garment.
You will roll them up like a robe;
like a garment they will be changed.
But you remain the same, and your years will never end.'

To which of the angels did God ever say,
'Sit at my right hand until I make your enemies a footstool
for your feet'?
(Heb. 1:8b-13).

Jesus speaks and even sings of the guarantee that sinners can
be made holy because of the covenant between the Father and
the Son.

Both the one who makes men holy and those who are made
holy are of the same family. So Jesus is not ashamed to call
them brothers. He says,

'I will declare your name to my brothers; in the presence of the
congregation I will sing your praises.'

And again, 'I will put my trust in him.'

And again he says, 'Here am I, and the children God has given
me.' (Heb. 2:11-13).

There can be no question (as these quotes are taken from the
Old Testament) that this arrangement was understood by the
Old Testament believer.

That is why the covenants between God and man in the Old
Testament involve blood sacrifice because they look forward
to the blood that equips the sinner to do good (Heb. 13:20).
The covenant they knew in the Old Testament is the eternal
covenant – it is from eternity to eternity.

This eternal covenant, the eternal gospel (Rev. 14:6) between
the Father and the Son is the way that we are saved. All who

put their faith in the Son receive the benefits of His perfect life, His atoning death, His mighty resurrection and glorious ascension.

Nobody in this new, everlasting covenant can be condemned any more. Their life is hid in Christ and they can live out that life of Christ in obedience to the living God.

In this new covenant Jesus is everything:

'to Jesus the mediator of a new covenant' (Heb. 12:24).

This is the most important teaching of the Old Testament.

> For what I received I passed on to you as of first importance: that Christ died for our sins **according to the Scriptures**, that he was buried, that he was raised on the third day **according to the Scriptures** (1 Cor. 15:3-4).

No condemnation

Because of this promise, Noah could not be separated from the love of God. He could say, 'But you said. Remember Jesus. He suffered and died in my place'. God would be a liar if he did not accept him. And so it is for all who put their trust in Jesus:

> Who is he that condemns? Christ Jesus, who died – more than that, who was raised to life – is at the right hand of God and is also interceding for us. Who shall separate us from the love of Christ? (Rom. 8:34-35 see also Rom. 8:38-39).

2:5
Noah enjoying the covenant

God has one thing he wants to say to the believer: 'I will be your God and you shall be my people' (See Gen. 12:7, Exod. 6:7, Ezek. 36:28, 2 Cor. 6:16-18, Rev. 21:2-3).

God invented marriage to reveal the intimacy he wants with His people through the covenant. Imagine the happiest marriage you know. A couple who belong together and love each other's company – a marriage where the home is a place of peace and happiness. This is how the Bible describes the relationship between God and His people. The Lord is the believer's husband (Jer. 3:14). The marriage is a covenant of peace (Ezek. 36:26, Hosea 14:4).

We should never think that God merely tolerates us. Because He has made an agreement, if we believe on Jesus, He delights in us and sets His affection on us (Deut. 10:15). And we in turn are to delight in our God (Isa. 58:2, 14).

Noah walked with God – a close and intimate walk.

This covenant helps us to live in a sinful world
Noah was able to walk with God because his sin and condemnation had been replaced by righteousness.

> By faith Noah, when warned about things not yet seen, in holy fear built an ark to save his family. By his faith he condemned the world and became **heir of the righteousness that comes by faith** (Heb. 11:7).

This is what makes him righteous (Gen. 6:9).

And he was enabled to trust God in a sinful changing world.

He built a boat, of enormous size to contain every living bird and animal. He had to believe it was going to rain for forty days and nights. Hard enough to believe if you live in Swansea – and remember nobody had ever seen rain before (Gen. 2:5-6). He had to preach judgment – never a popular message. He had to endure people mocking him for one hundred and twenty years.

He lived at a time when the church was compromised – (Gen. 6:1-6), when the wickedness of man was relentless (Gen. 6:1:5). He lived at a time where people were carrying on with the business of weddings, entertainment and fun (Matt. 24:37-38) ignorant of the God who one day they would have to give an account to.

In the face of such trials he knew this world was passing. He knew the covenant was everlasting (2 Sam. 23:5) and he knew his sin was taken away by the 'Lamb that was slain from the creation of the world' (Rev. 13:8).

He knew Jesus would come and die and rise and confirm his promise:

> For I tell you that Christ has become a servant of the Jews on behalf of God's truth, to confirm the promises made to the patriarchs (Rom. 15:8).

And he knew that his position in Christ was secure:

> 'I give them eternal life, and they shall never perish; no one can snatch them out of my hand. My Father, who has given them to me, is greater than all; no one can snatch them out of my Father's hand' (John 10:28-29).

Jesus, who mediates this covenant, could keep Noah when everything around him said 'give up'.

One last question – how?

How did Noah enjoy the privileges of the new covenant? Hebrews 11 gives the answer – saving faith.

The eternal covenant states that if anyone calls on the name of the Lord they will be saved (Gen. 4:26, Joel 2:32, Acts 2:31, Rom. 10:13) and enjoy life with God. It makes no difference whether anyone calls on His name in the Old or the New Testament (Rom. 10:12).

And it is simple faith in the triune God that gives us life.

> But these are written that you may believe that **Jesus** is **the Christ**, the **Son of God**, and that by believing you may have life in his name (John 20:31).

A life where we can walk with God in confidence knowing the life of his Spirit. This is the promise of the covenant (Isa. 59:21).

At one time, when I read John's gospel I thought if this is about me having life in His name why is it all about Jesus' relationship to the Father? Now I can see that it is this relationship which is the source of my life as the Father and Son pour out the Holy Spirit on me.

How do you get saving faith?

Faith has to have an object – someone or something to believe in. Anyone can believe (and it can be argued that everyone has faith in something or someone) but the only faith that saves is faith in Christ. Only Jesus can cause a man to walk with God. Only He can rescue someone from judgment to come.

The object of saving faith is Jesus Christ and His death and resurrection. We have to understand that He is not just a Saviour, but He is our Saviour. We have to stop trusting or putting our faith in other things and put our faith completely in Him.

> Jesus Christ is the same yesterday and today and forever (Heb. 13:8).

Noah's Saviour can be ours. To use his illustration we have to step off the dry ground this world provides and step onto the boat.

I had a friend who once took me to the river Thames and as he was stepping onto a boat, suddenly panicked. He didn't believe in the boat any more and he had gone too far to believe in the land. His faith was placed in his legs stretching an infinite distance! It soon proved to be false faith and he ended up in the water!

Saving faith requires total commitment to Christ. Noah stepped off this world and trusted the ark. He didn't trust his swimming abilities, his house, or somebody else's house. He certainly didn't put his trust in faith. He put his trust in the ark. It is not how much you believe, it is what you believe in that counts. As one man put it, 'God does not look for great faith. He looks for small faith in a great Saviour'.

Only one person is holy and all holiness comes through trusting Him.

Only one person has life and all life comes through trusting Him.

Only one person has peace and all peace comes through trusting Him.

Only one person is love and all love comes through trusting Him.

We must trust solely in the person and work of the Lord Jesus Christ. That means dying to self, not thinking for one moment in life or death that there is anything I can do myself. I must trust Him and rely on Him in every situation.

> I have been crucified with Christ and I no longer live, but Christ lives in me. The life I live in the body, I live by faith in the Son of God, who loved me and gave himself for me (Gal. 2:20).

Noah did. Do you?

Ups and down in the life of Noah

Noah's life was hidden in Christ. The moment he believed he died to his old way of life and was meant to look for things above. His life was hidden in Christ even when at the end of his life he lived like a wicked man and set his eyes on earthly things. He might have lost the joy of his salvation but he was safe from judgment.

We know he is in glory now because God established an unbreakable covenant with him. That is why this covenant is called the 'new' covenant. It is actually older than the covenant of works, but it can never be broken and can never pass away. It is always brand new; unbreakable and unchanging.

Nowhere is the Christian life with its many ups and downs summed up better in the Bible than in Colossians:

> Since, then, you have been raised with Christ, set your hearts on things above, where Christ is seated at the right hand of God. Set your minds on things above, not on earthly things. For you died, and your life is now hidden with Christ in God. When Christ, who is your life, appears, then you also will appear with him in glory (Col. 3:1-4).

This is what we see in the life of Noah. This is what we will see in the life of Abraham and this is what we will see in our lives, if we have trusted Jesus.

2:6
A new creation

The second Adam

Before the exile from Eden there is a great promise. From Eve will come a child who will destroy the works of the evil one and regain all that Adam lost – a second Adam.

> And I will put enmity between you and the woman, and between your offspring and hers; he will crush your head, and you will strike his heel (Gen. 3:15).

In all of the despair that occurs after the fall, this Seed is mentioned through the terrible incidents (Gen. 5, 9:18-28, 11:10-32) to remind us that Jesus is coming in human flesh: 'the son of Adam, the son of God' (Luke 3:38).

He will destroy the consequences of the fall, creating a new humanity: 'For as in Adam all die, so in Christ all will be made alive' (1 Cor. 15:22 see also 1 Cor. 15 and Rom. 5:12-21). But it will cost the blood of God (Acts 20:28). And this new humanity, the church, will overcome Satan.

> The God of peace will soon crush Satan under your feet. The grace of our Lord Jesus be with you (Rom. 16:20).

Charles Wesley sums it all up in his great hymn:

> *Hail, the heaven-born Prince of Peace!*
> *Hail, the Sun of Righteousness!*

Light and life to all he brings,
Risen with healing in his wings.
Mild he lays his glory by.
Born that man no more may die.
Born to raise the sons of earth,
Born to give them second birth.

> *Hark! the herald angels sing*
> *Glory to the new born King*

Come desire of nations, come
Fix in us thy humble home;
Rise, the woman's conquering Seed,
Bruise in us the serpent's head,
Now display thy saving power,
Ruined nature now restore;
Now in mystic union join
Thine to ours and ours to thine!

God creating a new creation

My sister felt it would be funny to teach my children a line that her own kids persecuted her with. So while driving through France, while crossing the Channel on the ferry, while driving through England, while crossing the Severn bridge into Wales, all we heard from the back of the car was, 'Are we nearly home yet?' Was I glad to get home!

That same cry, 'Are we nearly home?' goes up relentlessly throughout the Bible. And from this point on we hear of God building a new home for his people – a new Eden.

▶It is the great promise of the exodus redemption

'So I have come down to rescue them from the hand of the Egyptians and to bring them up out of that land into a good and spacious land, a land flowing with milk and honey' (from Exod. 3:8, see also Deut. 8:7-9).

▶It is the great hope of the exile in the latter prophets

The Lord will surely comfort Zion
and will look with compassion on all her ruins;
he will make her deserts like Eden,
her wastelands like the garden of the Lord
(from Isa. 51:3, see also Isa. 65:17-19ff).

▶It's what Jesus preached the kingdom would be like

'Blessed are the poor in spirit, for theirs is the kingdom of heaven' (Matt. 5:3).

'Blessed are the meek, for they will inherit the earth' (Matt. 5:5).

'Do not let your hearts be troubled. Trust in God; trust also in me. In my father's house are many rooms; if it were not so, I would have told you. I am going there to prepare a place for you. And if I go and prepare a place for you, I will come back and take you to be with me that you also may be where I am' (John 14:1-3).

▶It is the great hope of the church

Neither circumcision nor uncircumcision means anything; what counts is a new creation (Gal. 6:15).

Therefore, if anyone is in Christ, he is a new creation; the old has gone the new has come! (2 Cor. 5:17).

But in keeping with his promise we are looking forward to a new heaven and a new earth, the home of righteousness (2 Pet. 3:13).

A home where Jesus lives

What makes this place a better home is that Jesus is there.

For to me, to live is Christ and to die is gain (Phil. 1:21).

I desire to depart and be with Christ, which is better by far (Phil. 1:23b).

The place Jesus will take the Christian when he returns is a place where all traces of the curse, of sin and its consequences, are removed.

> Then I saw a new heaven and a new earth, for the first heaven and the first earth had passed away... 'Now the dwelling of God is with men, and he will live with them. They will be his people, and God himself will be with them and be their God. He will wipe every tear from their eyes. There will be no more death or mourning or crying or pain, for the old order of things has passed away' (from Rev. 21:1-5).

> No longer will there be any curse...They will see his face...There will be no more night. They will not need the light of a lamp or the light of the sun for the Lord God will give them light. And they will reign for ever and ever (from Rev. 22:3-5).

In this place there will be no anger of God and all the consequences that brings, because there will be no more sin.

As a boy when a Christian died I was told, 'He's been called home to be with the Lord.' I thought it was just something people said to cheer up grieving families. Little did I realize how profound that statement is. And little did I know of the real comfort it brings.

Are we nearly home yet?

Looking forward

How does the chaos of the fall and Babel end in a new creation? Is it just for individuals like Noah and Abel or is there something greater? Out of the chaos of Babel come these words: 'The Lord said' (Gen. 12:1). With these words come hope.

Part Three
Father Abraham

3:1
The significance of Abraham's faith

I remember when my daughter was born. For nine months my wife had been carrying her and planning and decorating the nursery. 'How do you feel about becoming a father?' people would ask.

'Your life will never be the same again you know.'

The tone always felt distinctly patronizing to me. I would shrug my shoulders and say, 'It hasn't sunk in yet.' I am a bit of an 'out of sight, out of mind' kind of person. But I remember when this tiny bundle of life was passed to me by the midwife. 'I think I'll leave you alone now,' she said and was gone.

The labour seemed almost surreal and like a strange dream – well for me at least! But as I sat on the floor staring at this beautiful child, terrified of moving in case I did anything wrong, I thought in fear and joy of the responsibilities of the rest of my life. From now on my life really would never be the same again. As long as I lived I would always be a dad. The consequences of that moment really weren't going away.

What really frightened me was that I was this poor child's father! It was me she would look to for her understanding of at least a large part of her world. She might never see it but my impact on her life for good or bad would be huge all the same.

The father of all who believe – Abraham
The good news about the Lord Jesus Christ had been preached and believed on by Abel, Enoch and Noah. But as we read the

life of Abraham, and to a lesser extent the patriarchs, we see the gospel changing everything else that follows in history. The Bible makes that very clear.

Genesis 3-11 makes for such sad reading as the fall in Eden spills out into every part of life. But Genesis 12 starts not with another curse but with God's blessing – this is good news.

God speaks out of the chaos of Babel to Abraham, just as he spoke out of the chaos in the beginning to create the world. What is said is of enormous significance in our understanding of the rest of the Bible: 'God...preached...the gospel unto Abraham' (Gal. 3:8, KJV). The world will never be the same again. He is to become 'the father of all who believe' (Rom. 4:11).

The consequences

▷ Because of the gospel preached to Abraham the exodus occurs (Exod. 2:24)

▷ Because of the gospel preached to Abraham the land is taken (Exod. 33:1, see also Deut. 34:4)

▷ Because of the gospel preached to Abraham, David and the other godly kings have great hope in prayer (1 Chron. 29:18, see also 2 Kings 13:23 and 2 Chron. 30:6)

▷ Because of the gospel preached to Abraham the latter prophets have great hope (Micah 7:19-20, see also Isa. 51:1-2)

▷ The New Testament traces the line of Jesus back to Abraham (Matt. 1:1)

▷ Mary and Zechariah understand Jesus' birth in the light of the gospel preached to Abraham (from Luke 1:54-55, see also Luke 1:72-73)

▷ Acts sees the gospel going out to the nations as a fulfilment of the gospel preached to Abraham (Acts 3:25-26)

▷ The great-grandchildren of Abraham symbolize the foundation of heaven (Rev. 7:4-8)

Our understanding of Abraham will change our understanding of the Bible. From now on everything is to be understood in the light of the promise given to him.

If we understand his faith we can understand our own.

3:2
The message

Who gives it?

The Lord comes and confirms the gospel promise in person:

> **The Lord appeared** to Abraham near the great trees of Mamre while he was sitting at the entrance to his tent in the heat of the day (Gen. 18:1).

There is only one way God can appear and that is through Jesus: 'He is the image of the invisible God' (Col. 1:15). It would be easy to brush over the significance of these verses, but they are astonishing – the Lord appears to a sinful man. It is only Jesus who reveals the will of God to men and women.

> 'All things have been committed to me by my Father. No-one knows the Son except the Father, and no-one knows the Father except the Son and those to whom the Son chooses to reveal him' (Matt. 11:27).

The angel of the Lord

Sometimes in these passages he appears as 'the angel of the Lord'.

People get confused with the word 'angel'. Angels are creatures and appear throughout the Bible but the 'angel of the Lord' is obviously God.

So why does God uses a word like 'angel' as one of his titles?[1]

The word simply means 'sent one'. We know that one of the ways Jesus loves to describe Himself in John's Gospel is 'the one sent from the Father'. The glory of the Son is that He is always sent to do the will of His Father.

> 'For the very work that the Father has given me to finish, and which I am doing, testifies that **the Father has sent me**' (John 5:36).

> 'For **the one whom God has sent** speaks the words of God, for God gives the Spirit without limit' (John 3:34).

In the Gospel of John alone Jesus refers to Himself as 'sent from the Father' on 46 occasions.

If we remember this, we can understand why God the Son is so often described as 'the angel of the Lord'. Look carefully at the passages that speak about 'the angel of the Lord' and you will see that those who meet Him knew that they had met God Himself.

Note that this is not just **an** angel – but 'the angel of the Lord'. This is not an angelic creature – this is the Lord Himself. We do find created angels throughout the Bible, but these must never be confused with this divine 'sent one', sent from the heart of the Father.

Look at Hagar's response when she meets him:

> She gave this name to the Lord who spoke to her: 'You are the God who sees me,' for she said, 'I have now seen the One who sees me' (Gen. 16:13).

Look at the way in which the angel of the Lord Himself gives us a mini-overview of the Bible:

> The angel of the Lord went up from Gilgal to Bokim and said, 'I brought you up out of Egypt and led you into the land that I swore to give to your forefathers' (Judg. 2:1).

He takes responsibility for all the works of God up to this point. He delivered them from Egypt, promised the land and made His covenant with them. In disobeying Him, they disobey God.

Look at Samson's parents:

> Manoah realized that it was the angel of the Lord. 'We are doomed to die!' he said to his wife. 'We have seen God!' (Judg. 13:21b-22).

Manoah knows he has seen God – Jesus the 'sent one from the Father' – the 'angel of the Lord'.

The message he has to believe

> The Lord had said to Abram, 'Leave your country, your people and your father's household and go to the land I will show you. I will make you into a great nation and I will bless you; I will make your name great, and you will be a blessing. I will bless those who bless you, and whoever curses you I will curse; and all peoples on earth will be blessed through you' (Gen. 12:1-3).

Genesis 17 repeats and elaborates on the covenant. The promise includes a seed, and as many descendants as sand on the seashore, a land which has God's blessing like the Garden of Eden and a blessing to all nations of the earth.

A seed – and as many descendants as sand on the seashore

> The promises were spoken to Abraham and to his seed. The Scripture does not say, 'seeds', meaning many people, but 'and to your seed', meaning one person, who is Christ (Gal. 3:16).

Abraham receives the promise that his seed, Christ, will be the hope for the world. He also is promised that his children, 'the children of Abraham' who believe on Christ will be the church, the hope for the world.

There is no contradiction in this. Just as when Jesus says, 'I am the light of the world' (John 8:12) and 'You are the light of the world' (Matt. 5:14). Our privilege as Christians is that we are 'in Christ Jesus'. What is true of Him first is true of us second.

So who are Abraham's children?

'Abraham is our father,' they answered. 'If you were Abraham's children,' said Jesus, 'then you would do the things Abraham did. As it is, you are determined to kill me, a man who has told you the truth that I heard from God. Abraham did not do such things. You are doing the things your own father does.' 'We are not illegitimate children,' they protested. 'The only Father we have is God himself' (John 8:39-41).

'You belong to your father, the devil, and you want to carry out your father's desire. He was a murderer from the beginning, not holding to the truth, for there is no truth in him. When he lies, he speaks his native language, for he is a liar and the father of all lies' (John 8:44).

The Pharisees were adamant Abraham was their father. Jesus' answer is as shocking as it is clear: 'You belong to your father, the devil'. Being able to trace your family tree back to Abraham is not good enough. You may be able to do that and yet still end up in hell.

So who are Abraham's children?

Jesus said to him, 'Today salvation has come to this house, because this man, too is a son of Abraham. For the Son of Man came to seek and to save what was lost' (Luke 19:9-10).

Understand, then, that those who believe are children of Abraham (Gal. 3:7, see also Rom. 4:11-16).

Those who listen to the gospel of Jesus Christ, how He came to seek and save the lost – the gospel preached to Abraham – and believe on Jesus, are Abraham's true children.

A land – which has God's blessing like the Garden of Eden

'The whole land of Canaan, where you are now an alien, I will give as an everlasting possession to you and your descendants after you; and I will be their God' (Gen. 17:8).

> By faith Abraham, when called to go to a place he would later receive as his inheritance, obeyed and went, even though he did not know where he was going. By faith he made his home in the promised land like a stranger in a foreign country; he lived in tents, as did Isaac and Jacob, who were heirs with him of the same promise. For he was looking forward to the city with foundations, whose architect and builder is God (Heb. 11:8-10).

Abraham never owned the land in Canaan, so did God's promise fail? Of course not. He was looking for the 'city with foundations, whose architect is God'. The land in Canaan would picture the new creation – and certainly it is of great importance for this reason – but its reality is eternal.

Blessing to all nations of the earth

> 'And you are heirs of the prophets and of the covenant God made with your fathers. He said to Abraham, "Through your offspring all peoples on earth will be blessed." When God raised up his servant, he sent him first to you to bless you by turning each of you from your wicked ways' (Acts 3:25-26).

> The Scripture foresaw that God would justify the Gentiles by faith, and announced the gospel in advance to Abraham: 'All nations will be blessed through you' (Gal. 3:8).

This is the gospel believed on by Isaac, Jacob, Moses, Joshua, David. And the vast majority of these Old Testament saints are able to trace their family tree back to Abraham.

There are some outside the nation of Israel who believe – Joseph's Pharaoh, Rahab, Naaman, Ruth and Nebuchadnezzar to name a few. But this blessing to the Gentiles will be revealed fully in the New Testament.

We who are Christians now will enjoy heaven with the patriarchs.

> 'I say to you that many will come from the east and the west, and will take their places at the feast with Abraham, Isaac and Jacob in the kingdom of heaven' (Matt. 8:11).

Additional note:

Circumcision was the outward sign that you belonged to God's people, showing that an inward work of God had taken place (Gen. 17) in Jesus. See Deuteronomy 10:14-16 and Jeremiah 4:4.[2]

(ENDNOTES)

[1] In many ways the same problem would apply to titles like 'the Son of Man' or 'the suffering Servant'. However, people seem to especially struggle with the title 'the angel of the Lord'.

[2] In the 'Questions' section at the back of the book there is more explanation on this – see question 10.

3:3
Just like me

Abraham's faith and ours

When we come to this promise to Abraham, we have to come to it understanding that it was a promise with consequences, lasting consequences; a promise that affects our understanding of the entire Old Testament.

Jesus makes clear that the promises to Abraham were not temporal and did not die with him. He is enjoying the promises right now (Luke 16:22) and will enjoy them forever. He says this three times in the gospels:

> 'Have you not read in the book of Moses, in the account of the bush, how God said to him, "I am the God of Abraham, the God of Isaac, and the God of Jacob"? He is not the God of the dead, but of the living. You are badly mistaken!' (Mark 12:26-27, see also Matt. 22:32 and Luke 20:37).

Abraham, because of his faith in Jesus Christ, is enjoying the 'land' promised to him right now. Get this wrong and you are, to use Jesus' words, 'badly mistaken'. But it is a common mistake (John 8:53, 58).

But did he enjoy God's presence in a different way to us?

Again Jesus says:

> 'Your father Abraham rejoiced at the thought of seeing my day; **he saw it** and was glad' (John 8:56).

The theme of Romans is that righteousness comes from God:

> 'through faith in Jesus Christ to all who believe. **There is no difference**' (Rom. 3:22).

Abraham, and all Old Testament believers, found righteousness by putting faith in Christ alone.

> It was not through law that Abraham and his offspring received the promise that he would be heir of the world, but through the righteousness that comes by faith (Rom. 4:13).

He also turned from his sin:

> 'Long ago your forefathers…lived beyond the River and worshipped other gods. But I took your father Abraham from the land beyond the River and led him' (Josh. 24:2b-3).

> They tell how you turned to God from idols to serve the living and true God (1 Thess. 1:9b).

Just like you and me Abraham was not born a believer. He worshipped created things not the Creator. If you are not sure whether you were an idolater before you were a Christian, ask yourself what did you think about most of the time? What was your motivation for living? Was it created things? Just like you and me (if you are a Christian) he turned from these idols to serve the living God.

Was Abraham a good man?

Just like us – no. Genesis goes out of its way to show that Abraham wasn't saved by works and points out his sinfulness even after he believed.

He lies immediately after the giving of the promise, first to Pharaoh (ch. 12) and then to Abimelech (ch. 20). He causes havoc by getting Hagar pregnant. The boy lives with him for twelve years as a visible daily reminder of his sin. Even at the end of his life as he is about to die we are told he has concubines that he really shouldn't have had (Gen. 25:6).

If this was my biography, it would have been a very uncomfortable read. I am sure I would have begged for many incidents to be left out. It is hardly the life story you would imagine being written of the 'father of all who believe'.

But in all of this he doesn't lose his salvation – it rests on what God will do.

> The Lord had said to Abram, 'Leave your country, your people and your father's household and go to the land **I will** show you. **I will** make you into a great nation and **I will** bless you; **I will** make your name great, and you will be a blessing. **I will** bless those who bless you, and whoever curses you **I will** curse; and all peoples on earth will be blessed through you' (Gen. 12:1-3).

Note all the 'I wills'. If you're looking for something special about Abraham you'll be disappointed – but that's the whole point. Our contribution to our salvation is our sin. Salvation is about what God has done in Christ. It is what God does and Abraham's faith in what God does that makes Abraham right.

> Abram believed the Lord, and he credited it to him as righteousness (Gen. 15:6).

> For it is by grace you have been saved, through faith – and this not from yourselves, it is the gift of God (Eph. 2:8).

His faith in Jesus is the reason he is in heaven. It is all God's kindness in Jesus which he most definitely did not deserve.

But it's not just that he's forgiven – there's more.

3:4
The friend of God

Abraham, the friend of God

There is nothing worse than someone saying, 'I forgive you', but then reminding you constantly of what you said or did. Being in their company is painful and you constantly feel in their debt. The friendship is shattered because of your failure.

Abraham's salvation – and ours – is nothing like that.

> And the scripture was fulfilled that says, 'Abraham...was called God's friend' (James 2:23).

> 'I no longer call you servants, because a servant does not know his master's business. Instead, I have called you friends, for everything that I learned from my Father I have made known to you' (John 15:15).

This adulterous, lying, failing, frightened man is a friend of God. I am a sinner who fails constantly. And yet as I read the life of Abraham, and the other believers in the Old Testament who fail so badly, I see that I can be God's friend – if I believe in the Lord Jesus Christ, whoever I am, whatever I've done.

Listen to these quotes from C.H. Spurgeon:

> Unbelief will destroy the best of us; faith will save the worst of us. He that believes on the Lord Jesus (has) eternal life. [1]

> If the bridge of grace will carry the elephant, it will certainly carry the mouse. If the mercy of God could bear with the hugest sinner, it can have patience with you.[2]

Abraham, David, Manasseh, Peter and Paul are 'giant' sinners giving us confidence to trust in Christ. Paul sums it up:

> But where sin increased, grace increased all the more, so that, just as sin reigned in death, so also grace might reign through righteousness to bring eternal life through Jesus Christ our Lord (Rom. 5:20b-21).

Even though Abraham fails God. God never fails him. His failure leads to misery and disappointment but never to a place where there is total death and hopelessness. From the moment he puts his faith in Christ, the covenant God becomes his shield and very great reward. That is why he is told not to be afraid (Gen. 15:1-2).

The hymn 'Amazing Grace' has a great line, 'It's grace that brought me safe this far and grace will lead me home'. It was grace that brought Abraham out of Ur of the Chaldeans and it is grace that got him to heaven.

And those who followed …

Isaac

The promise is repeated to Isaac (Gen. 26) and he goes on to commit exactly the same sin as his father – which emphasizes this gospel is for sinners. Again Isaac is a weak man but a weak man who trusts God.

Jacob

We then come to Jacob, Isaac's son. Jacob is given the promise and not his older and better brother Esau. This promise is not based on natural descent but on God's grace. As if to really drive home the point, Jacob comes across as a sinful man with no redeeming qualities. He tries to con his brother, his father and his father-in-law – he even tries to con God. He even sends his wives and children into danger to protect himself. Then Jesus meets him – and beats him (Gen. 32:24-32).

This is the crisis event of his life. Remarkably he is named Israel – the name for the people of God (the name 'Israel' is mentioned 2,303 times in the Bible). He goes on to have twelve sons – who become the twelve tribes of Israel.

Joseph

Genesis ends with God still on the throne. Believers and unbelievers continue to sin, the creation has fallen but God's purposes cannot and will not fail. We see this most clearly in the life of Joseph.

His brothers do everything they can to destroy him but God uses their sin to bring about their salvation. Again we see that for people to know salvation they must first see their sin.

> But Joseph said to them, 'Don't be afraid. Am I in the place of God? You intended to harm me, but God intended it for good to accomplish what is now being done, the saving of many lives' (Gen. 50:19-20).

Joseph shines as a type (picture) of Christ. He saves the people of God by suffering first himself. He also introduces the idea of the Exodus – it is coming soon as God had planned.

> By faith Joseph, when his end was near, spoke about the exodus of the Israelites from Egypt and gave instructions about his bones (Heb. 11:22).

However as with all types of Christ he points away from himself to the Saviour. He by himself can do nothing (Gen. 41:16).

The end of the story

Right at the end of the story of the patriarchs, Israel (Jacob) summarizes his own, his father's and his grandfather's faith – and the faith of all who are to follow:

Then he blessed Joseph and said, 'May the God before whom my fathers Abraham and Isaac walked, the God who has been my shepherd all my life to this day, **the Angel who has delivered me from all harm** – may he bless these boys. May they be called by my name and the names of my fathers Abraham and Isaac, and may they increase greatly upon the earth' (Gen. 48:15-16).

He trusts in the 'sent One' of God.

'For God so loved the world that he gave his one and only Son, that whoever believes in him shall not perish but have eternal life. For God did not send his Son into the world to condemn the world, but to save the world through him' (John 3:16-17).

This is the God of Abraham, Isaac and Jacob.

The patriarchs were sinful men who are enjoying heaven now because they believed in Jesus, looking forward to the new creation, the true promised land.. They show how life is lived when trusting the gospel. They are our examples of faith. Revelation 21:10-14 even describes them as part of the 'gates' in the new heaven and earth.

Note:
A type is a picture, shadow, or sign of what is to come. God only saves through Jesus (Acts 4:12) and every type points to Him. The shadow often shows how God saves, pointing to the fulfilment in Jesus.

Never entering but seeing the land
Abraham never entered the land promised to him on earth. But he knew his descendants would see it. In a deep dream the Lord tells him about the Exodus that will take place:

Abram fell into a deep sleep, and a thick and dreadful darkness came over him. Then the Lord said to him, 'Know for certain that your descendants will be strangers in a country not their own, and they will be enslaved and ill-treated four hundred years. But I will punish the nation they serve as slaves, and afterwards they will come out with great possessions' (Gen. 15:12b-14).

And he saw its eternal reality.

(ENDNOTES)

[1] Metropolitan Tabernacle Pulpit, vol. 62, p.33
[2] Metropolitan Tabernacle Pulpit, vol. 59, p.390

Part Four
Redemption

4:1
A deliverer who redeems

Exodus can be a very frustrating book! It leaves so many unanswered questions in its early chapters.

How did such a small number of Israelites produce enough children to threaten the world's only superpower in such a small period of time? What is the name of the Pharaoh Moses faced? What happened to the two midwives who showed such courage and whose names were recorded? Why do we hear nothing of Moses' upbringing in Egypt? From birth to forty is 'one day after Moses had grown up'. Why did God make someone with a speech problem the greatest prophet in the Old Testament?

Actually the Bible does answer that one – but as for the other mysteries while it is obvious they would all make great stories, God has a far greater story to tell.

Because there is just one main point he is trying to drive home.

Slavery is a frightening thing
As boys we would often visit our aunt who lived in a house chiselled out of a mountain in the valley town of New Tredegar.

We would climb to the top of a nearby mountain and then the challenge would go out, 'Who can get to the bottom fastest?' At first it felt like we were Olympic sprinters; taking huge strides, in the excitement shouting abuse, striving to run as fast as gravity could take us down the slope. But it wasn't long before there was silence as we realized our legs had gained a life of their own and were running faster than the rest of our bodies.

First we were in charge of our legs then they were in charge of us. I remember quietly praying to myself, 'Please stop, please stop, pleeeease.'

It was a terrifying experience to be hurtling down a hill while under the control of another force and it was sheer relief to crash into a tree or rock. I was a slave of gravity. Not once did we hit the barbed wire fence at the bottom but there were times we got very close.

That feeling of being driven where I didn't want to go still causes me to sweat. The only time I've known it since is when driving down the motorway and hitting black ice. You are no longer the master of the car – the car is master over you.

Slavery is a frightening thing. When you're in its grip all you want is for someone to step in and redeem you whatever the price. The great picture of the redemption all mankind needs is revealed in this one book.

The people have been gathered by God because of the gospel promise to Abraham. Abraham now has many descendants (Exod. 1:1-7) but how can they enjoy the land when they are slaves of Pharaoh? And if God's judgment comes how will they escape (Ezek. 20:7-8)? God has made a promise to redeem them (Gen. 15:12-21) but how does He work out the promise?

God raises a deliverer to show what Jesus is like

'He will speak to the people for you, and it will be as if he were your mouth and **as if you were God to him**' (Exod. 4:16).

Then the Lord said to Moses, 'See, **I have made you like God** to Pharaoh, and your brother Aaron will be your prophet' (Exod. 7:1).

God calls Moses to show his people and Pharaoh what Jesus is like. Moses is miraculously saved at birth – his name means 'saved'. He will speak God's Word, redeem the people from slavery and lead them. As they look at Moses they will see something of Jesus.

Moses tells the people that although he is like Jesus, Jesus is the one they must follow:

> 'The Lord your God will raise up **for you** a prophet like me from among your own brothers. **You must listen to him**' (Deut. 18:15).

Moses' life is a living powerful sermon that points to Jesus – a sermon well understood in the New Testament. The disciples know exactly who Jesus is because of him.

> 'We have found the one Moses wrote about in the law, and about whom the prophets also wrote – Jesus…' (John 1:45b).

> 'And that he may send the Christ, who has been appointed for you – even Jesus…For Moses said, "The Lord your God will raise up for you a prophet like me from among your people; you must listen to everything he tells you"' (Acts 3:20, 22).

Moses trusted Christ

> From the fullness of his grace we have all received one blessing after another. For the law was given by Moses; grace and truth came through Jesus Christ. No-one has ever seen God, but God the One and Only, who is at the father's side has made him known (John 1:16-18).

Moses points to Jesus in the law, but any grace and truth he received, and the Israelites received, came through Jesus Christ. Only in Jesus, can the truth about the Father be known. Moses knew this and it changed his life.

> He regarded disgrace for the sake of Christ as of greater value than the treasures of Egypt (Heb. 11: 26a).

As we read Moses let's make sure we fix our thoughts on Jesus:

'If you believed Moses, you would believe me, for he wrote about me. But since you do not believe what he wrote, how are you going to believe what I say?' (John 5:46-47).

The same point is made in a different way in Hebrews:

Therefore, holy brothers, who share in the heavenly calling, fix your thoughts on Jesus...Jesus has been found worthy of greater honour than Moses...Moses was faithful as a servant in all God's house, testifying to what would be said in the future. But Christ is faithful as a son over God's house. And we are his house, if we hold on to our courage and the hope of which we boast (Heb. 3:1-6).

Moses was a servant in God's house. Jesus built it.

The redemption

Pharaoh appears to run the world and God's people suffer. But as we read Exodus we see that in fact Pharaoh is under the judgment of God for his sin and his refusal to obey the gospel. Meanwhile the world revolves around God's people.

Warnings always come before judgment (Rev. 9). So not only does he hear the gospel preached, the heavens declare it to him too. This is what the plagues are about. They are warnings to flee from the wrath to come until the worst plague comes – the Lord visiting every home and punishing sin by taking the life of each first-born boy.

But how can God's people escape the judgment of a holy God? It is clear from the way they reject Moses that they deserve to be punished for their sins (Ezek. 20:6-8).

Then Moses summoned all the elders of Israel and said to them, 'Go at once and select the animals for your families and slaughter the Passover lamb. Take a bunch of hyssop, dip it into the blood in the basin and put some blood on the top and on both sides of the door-frame. Not one of you shall go out of the door of his house until the morning. When the Lord goes through the land to strike down the Egyptians, he will

> see the blood on the top and sides of the door-frame and will
> pass over that doorway, and he will not permit the destroyer to
> enter your houses and strike you down' (Exod. 12:21-23).

The answer is clear. When the Lord comes to judge, he will see
that judgment has already come to some houses – when he sees
the blood of the slaughtered lamb which points to His death.

John the Baptist made sure people knew who He was:

> ...John saw Jesus coming towards him and said, 'Look, the Lamb
> of God, who takes away the sin of the world!' (John 1:29).

The crowds in heaven praise Jesus precisely because He is the
Passover lamb:

> In a loud voice they sang: 'Worthy is the lamb, who was slain,
> to receive power and wealth and wisdom and strength and
> honour and glory and praise!' (Rev. 5:12).

He is the Judge and the one who has been judged in our place.

In Egypt, on the morning after the Passover, they would
have run into their first-born's bedroom and realized that the
judgment of God had passed over their house, because of the
lamb's blood. We too can know our sins are forgiven. We too
can know life is worth living because Jesus lives:

> And he is the head of the body, the church; he is the beginning
> and the firstborn from among the dead, so that in everything
> he might have the supremacy (Col. 1:18).

Redemption through blood
The exodus is such a vivid picture of our salvation. It is essential
we understand it properly.

We are redeemed from darkness and brought into the
kingdom of light (Col. 1:13-14). We are redeemed from sin and
the wrath of God and able to be called God's friends and enjoy
kindness we don't deserve (Eph. 1:7). Our redemption was not
paid for by anything the world could offer – such as animal

blood (after all an animal would hardly be dying voluntarily) or silver or gold (1 Pet. 1:18-19). It would be sickening in the eyes of God to think His anger with our sin could be bought off that cheaply.

Nothing but the blood of Jesus could take away our sin.

Beyond redemption?

'There is many a slip from cup to lip' is the true if quaint saying. It is one thing for these people to be redeemed but when we see their nature, what hope is there of them making it to Sinai – let alone any further – to enjoy what God has done for them and to enjoy the presence of God Himself?

> 'See, I am sending an angel ahead of you to guard you along the way and to bring you to the place I have prepared. Pay attention to him and listen to what he says. Do not rebel against him; he will not forgive your rebellion, since my Name is in him. If you listen carefully to what he says and do all that I say, I will be an enemy to your enemies and will oppose those who oppose you. My angel will go ahead of you and bring you into the land' (Exod. 23:20-23, see also 14:19 and 13:21-22).

> Now I want to remind you, although you once fully knew it, that Jesus, who saved a people out of Egypt, afterwards destroyed those who did not believe (Jude 5, ESV).

Jesus leads and protects them on their journey. He is the one who rules over them and has all authority. He will never leave them or forsake them.

Their redemption (and their remembering it) dominates everything from now on. God makes a covenant because He has redeemed them (Exod. 19:4-5). He lives with them because he has redeemed them (Lev. 11:44-45).

The Passover meal has one purpose – to remind them of their redemption (Exod. 12:24-28) and the covenant it brings.

4:2
A covenant

Salvation is not just negative

The first thing God does after he redeems his people is gather them to Mount Sinai – and speak to them (ch. 19).

> Then Moses went up to God, and the Lord called to him from the mountain and said, 'This is what you are to say to the house of Jacob and what you are to tell the people of Israel: "You yourselves have seen what I did to Egypt, and how I carried you on eagles' wings and brought you to myself. Now if you obey me fully and keep my covenant, then out of all nations you will be my treasured possession. Although the whole earth is mine, you will be for me a kingdom of priests and a holy nation." These are the words you are to speak to the Israelites' (Exod. 19:3-6).

God's purpose in redemption is to bring a people to Himself. The purpose of the covenant is to make His people a treasured possession, a kingdom of priests and a holy nation.

Salvation is not just negative. It is not just about forgiveness of sins and being saved from the wrath of God. It is that – and we thank God it is that – but we mustn't stop there.

He has saved them for Himself. He has huge purposes for them. He wants to treasure them and use them to show off His glory.

The covenant summed up

This covenant is summed up in the Ten Commandments:

> 'I am the Lord your God, who brought you out of Egypt, out of the land of slavery' (Exod. 20:2).

This covenant is for all God's people (Exod. 21-24). Once saved, they must love God and love all those who have been redeemed and gathered by God. And yet before long it is evident that they just can't keep their end of the bargain.

> 'Come, make us gods who will go before us. As for this fellow Moses who brought us up out of Egypt, we don't know what has happened to him' (Exod. 32:1b).

The covenant is broken, a new one is needed and we haven't even left Sinai yet!

The law in the Old Testament

I had a Mini once and I hadn't a clue how to look after it. I only had to travel two or three miles and it would overheat. It needed water constantly. In fact I always made sure there were a couple of bottles of water in the car before I went anywhere.

One weekend I was due to travel home to Swansea (I lived over 200 miles away in England at the time). I calculated I would need over a hundred bottles of water – and a trailer to carry them! So I dropped the car with a mechanic and said I would call back in the afternoon. When I returned he shook his head.

'Can you fix it?'

'Nope. It's finished. You've melted a piston.'

He opened the bonnet and showed me the molten engine. Even I could see I wasn't going anywhere in this.

I had a car. It looked okay. I had tax and the MOT. But what was the point if it couldn't take me anywhere.

Why did God give the law if it couldn't save us?

The law not only describes the righteous life that God demands but also the remedy for our sin.

All the laws concerning sacrifices and the priesthood, were given by God to lead us to the great high priest, the spotless lamb of God who alone can take away the sin of the world.

The old King James version of the Bible puts Galatians 3:24 so well – 'the law was our schoolmaster to bring us unto Christ, that we might be justified by faith.'

A prophetic picture

The law is a prophetic picture of the life, death, resurrection, ascension and return of Jesus Christ.

Jesus in His life keeps the Ten Commandments perfectly. In His death He offers the perfect sacrifice. In His resurrection He provides the new birth that circumcision points to (Col. 2:11). In His ascension He provides a way into the Most Holy Place. In His return He will establish true justice and cleansing for the whole world.

If we believe we can be saved by fulfilling the law ourselves, either we haven't read it properly or we don't know our own hearts.

He keeps the law for us

God makes this covenant with Christ who keeps the law for us. We have to put our faith in Him.

In Deuteronomy Moses explains the law to Israel. Fulfilling the law is not their job. The central message of the law is trust in Christ who can. It is Christ who will renew the hearts of His people. It is Christ who will do the work of the law. They just can't do it themselves.

'The Lord your God will circumcise your hearts and the hearts of your descendants, so that you may love him with all your heart and with all your soul, and live... Now what I am commanding you today is not too difficult for you or beyond your reach' (Deut. 30:6, 11).

The apostle Paul goes back to Moses' words when he wants to explain how the law preached Christ.

Christ is the end of the law so that there may be righteousness for everyone who believes. Moses describes in this way the righteousness that is by the law: 'The man who does these things will live by them.' But the righteousness that is by faith says: 'Do not say in your heart, "Who will ascend into heaven?"' (that is, to bring Christ down) 'or "Who will descend into the deep?"' (that is, to bring Christ up from the dead). But what does it say? 'The word is near you; it is in your mouth and in your heart,' that is, the word of faith we are proclaiming (Rom. 10:4-8).

Without Christ the law makes us feel terrible. David can sing, 'O how I love your law!', because with Christ the law brings victory for all who believe. When we read it we see its beauty. It is all the more beautiful because we have a Saviour who has kept it for us.

Why read the law?

The Old Testament believer could see that the law was temporary. We see several examples of this – most famously David. When he was hungry (1 Sam. 21:6), he entered the house of God and ate the consecrated bread. It was only lawful for the priests to eat this and yet the Bible says that he was blameless. Why? Because he knew the law was just a picture pointing him to Christ.

Jeremiah 3:16 shows that the Old Testament believers knew the temporary nature of even the ark of the covenant. The symbols that pointed to Christ had to be obeyed, and there were serious consequences for disobeying for this very reason. But they were only symbols.

God hates people simply going through the motions of keeping the law, as if that could save anyone. Do you think 'hate' is too strong a word – listen to Isaiah:

'The multitude of your sacrifices –
what are they to me?' says the Lord.
'I have more than enough of burnt offerings,
of rams and the fat of fattened animals;
I have no pleasure
in the blood of bulls and lambs and goats.
When you come to appear before me,
who has asked this of you,
this trampling of my courts?
Stop bringing meaningless offerings!
Your incense is detestable to me.
New Moons, Sabbaths and convocations –
I cannot bear your evil assemblies.
Your New Moon festivals and your appointed feasts
my soul hates.
They have become a burden to me;
I am weary of bearing them.
… Though your sins are like scarlet,
they shall be as white as snow;
though they are red as crimson,
they shall be like wool' (Isa. 1:11-18).

But He loves it when His people remember Jesus and His perfect sacrifice. David knew when his heart was right, God would be pleased with him.

You do not delight in sacrifice, or I would bring it;
you do not take pleasure in burnt offerings.
The sacrifices of God are a broken spirit;
a broken and contrite heart,
O God, you will not despise.
In your good pleasure make Zion prosper;
build up the walls of Jerusalem.
Then there will be righteous sacrifices,
whole burnt offerings to delight you;
then bulls will be offered on your altar (Ps. 51:16-19).

Listen to Jesus explaining this in Matthew.

He answered, 'Haven't you read what David did when he and his companions were hungry? He entered the house of God, and he and his companions ate the consecrated bread – which was not lawful for them to do, but only for the priests. Or haven't you read in the Law that on the Sabbath the priests in the temple desecrate the day and yet are innocent? I tell you that one greater than the temple is here. If you had known what these words mean, "I desire mercy, not sacrifice," you would not have condemned the innocent. For the Son of Man is Lord of the Sabbath' (Matt. 12:3-8).

Jesus the Son of Man is Lord of the Sabbath. He makes sense of the law. He keeps the law. He makes it possible for those who desecrate the law to be innocent. Only in His suffering, death and resurrection does the law make sense.

No-one can keep the law but everyone who calls on the name of the Lord shall be saved – because He has kept it for us.

A copy of the heavenly reality

When I grew up in church, baptism seemed such a strange and out-of-place event. The communion service seemed even more strange, as small bits of bread and tiny cups of wine were passed around – and I was not even allowed to take part. The whole occasion appeared quite irresistible and exciting.

After I became a Christian I took communion and it was a great disappointment. The bread was slightly stale and there wasn't enough wine to quench the thirst of a gnat. It was only years later that I found communion could be spiritually and emotionally the most moving part of the service – *when I saw what the symbols pointed to.*

It is clear to us and them that this covenant and the sacrifices that follow it are pictures, copies and symbols of heavenly realities:

It was necessary, then, for the copies of the heavenly things to be purified with these sacrifices, but the heavenly things themselves with better sacrifices than these (Heb. 9:23).

> 'This is the covenant I will make with the house of Israel after that time, declares the Lord. I will put my laws in their minds and write them on their hearts. I will be their God, and they will be my people' (Heb. 8:10).

In the Sermon on the Mount Jesus gets right to the heart of the law and explains its real meaning. He takes the outward picture and reveals the inward truth:

> 'You have heard that it was said to the people long ago, "Do not murder, and anyone who murders will be subject to judgment." But I tell you that anyone who is angry with his brother will be subject to judgment' (Matt. 5:21-22a).

William Gurnall puts it like this:

> Most of us would never commit murder, but how often have we taken a neighbour into some dark alley of our thoughts and there torn him limb from limb with a desire for revenge over some petty quarrel[1].

How can we pretend God doesn't see our hearts? The outward is a symbol of the inward, the real.

The Ten Commandments point to a far greater reality. They are like wedding vows between God and His people. Marriage vows outside the service seem very negative. It even seems a little macabre to say, 'In sickness and in health…for richer or poorer…till death do us part.' But in the context of a marriage they take a completely different meaning.

DL Moody described them this way:

1. Love to God will admit no other gods.
2. Love resents everything that debases its object by representing it by an image.
3. Love to God never will dishonour His name.
4. Love to God will reverence His day.
5. Love of parents makes one honour them.
6. Hate, not love, is a murderer.
7. Lust, not love, commits adultery.
8. Love will give, but never steal.

9. Love will not slander or lie.

10. Love's eye is not covetous.[2]

How can he see them like this? Because God is infinitely lovable and He starts by saying, 'I am the Lord your God. Have no other gods before me.'

The people also are copies and pictures of what God really wants (Exod. 19:3-6). In coming to God at Sinai and serving Him, they show us what salvation is all about.

> But you are a chosen people, a royal priesthood, a holy nation, a people belonging to God, that you may declare the praises of him who called you out of darkness into his wonderful light. Once you were not a people, but now you are the people of God; once you had not received mercy, but now you have received mercy (1 Peter 2:9-10).

We have been redeemed to God, through our deliverer Christ, who has committed Himself to us. From slavery to promise, He's made 'wretches' His 'treasure'.

Do we need to read the law today?

If the law points to heavenly realities, and it is all fulfilled in Christ, do we need to read it anymore?

First of all the full heavenly reality is yet to be revealed. Secondly even though we see that Christ has fulfilled the law, we still need to study it to understand more fully who He is and why He came.

Many parts of the law still stand for us today, for example in Ephesians we read:

> Children, obey your parents in the Lord, for this is right. 'Honour your father and mother' – which is the first command-ment with a promise – 'that it may go well with you and that you may enjoy long life on the earth' (Eph. 6:1-3).

It would be a tragedy to no longer enjoy the delights of the Sabbath day while waiting to enter the full reality of the eternal Sabbath rest.

Even though we have to see that Christ has fulfilled all the sacrifices, we still need to study the law to understand who He is and why He came. Even the food laws that Jesus brings to an end, we need to study to have a full understanding of the uncleanness of the human heart, as we are so corrupt in deceiving ourselves about it. These laws provide such a profound and detailed analysis of the human problem.

We must read the law and see what the Old Testament believer would have seen. We must join with him spontaneously bursting into song going up to the temple, seeing with him what the pictures and copies of the law point to and enjoy that same blessing!

(ENDNOTES)

[1] The Christian in Complete Armour, vol. 1, p.197
[2] Notes from my Bible, DL Moody

4:3
When God moves in

Kings have thrones, Judges have the bench, Prime Ministers have the front bench of parliament, and fathers often have a special armchair. These are all visible symbols of authority and rule. Nobody else is allowed to sit in this seat.

God has redeemed His people and made a covenant with them, but who is in charge? Will they have a king on the throne like the other nations? Will they have a democracy? Where is the throne for their king? Where is his symbol of authority?

> 'There, above the cover between the two cherubim that are over the ark of the Testimony, I will meet with you and give you all my commands for the Israelites' (Exod. 25:22).

This is what the ark is all about. It is made to contain the Ten Commandments and it is where Jesus sits. He is their king and He rules from His throne – the ark of the covenant.[1]

Over and again in the Old Testament he speaks with authority between the cherubim.

What does God's house tell us about God's plan?

When I was a boy someone gave me a plastic aircraft carrier model kit. It had about five hundred pieces but as far as I was concerned it might as well have been five million. On a rainy day soon after Christmas I decided to put it together – in an afternoon.

The instructions looked complicated so I decided to start with the little airplanes that rested on the deck. It took a good ten minutes to get the cap off the glue, and it broke in the process.

After making three very sticky planes I decided it was time for a well-deserved break – there were only another twenty planes to be made. I placed them on the box and waited for them to dry. When I came back, there were no planes as such to be seen. It just looked as if someone had sneezed on the box.

I put the model kit at the back of the cupboard, in the 'I should have a go, but probably never will box' and came to the conclusion that only certain types of boys liked these kits and I wasn't one of them.

I came to the same conclusion reading about the tabernacle in the Bible. Any attempt to understand it seemed futile. I would hear even preachers laugh at people who thought the 'pots' and 'pans' had meaning. The tabernacle was for the 'geeks' in the Christian church. Of course my theology of the clarity of Scripture would never allow me to say it out loud. But in practice I skim-read these kinds of passages.

And yet the Bible places great importance on the tabernacle. It is constantly referred to in the life of Jesus. The letters tell us it is the key to understanding the church. And it is the backdrop for our understanding of the new heavens and new earth.

It is replaced by the temple which has an identical purpose (but is made of different materials and emphasizes different aspects of the same truth). The temple not only dominates the former prophets, it is a main theme in many of the latter prophets, even when it is destroyed.

Far from being like the passage for 'geeks' it is more like a passage for a child learning to read.

The tabernacle and temple are huge pictures to help them (and us) understand the gospel and make sense of the world multi-media gospel visual aids.

So what is this enormous visual aid saying?

The ark, the table and the lampstand

The tabernacle represents heaven and earth – the whole creation. But before it is made God makes sure the Israelites make three pieces of furniture – three pieces 'older' than heaven and earth.

The dominant piece of furniture is the ark of the covenant. Through the Bible the ark is referred to as a throne. On the top of the ark are two cherubim and between them is the throne where the king who rules his people sits.

> 'There, above the cover between the two cherubim that are over the ark of the Testimony, I will meet with you and give you all my commands for the Israelites' (Exod. 25:22).

When Daniel in the Old Testament and John in the New are given visions of heaven, the first thing they see is a throne on which the Father is seated:

> At once I was in the Spirit, and there before me was a throne in heaven with someone sitting on it (Rev. 4:2).

The table of presence displays the bread of 'Presence' all the time. In Exodus the angel of the Lord is described as the 'Presence' (Exod. 33:14-15). In the New Testament, Jesus speaks of Himself as 'the bread of life' (John 6:35).

The lampstand brings light to all that is in front of it (Exod. 25:37). Zechariah had a vision of it and an angel told him what it meant:

> He asked me, 'What do you see?' I answered, 'I see a solid gold lampstand with a bowl at the top and seven lights on it, with seven channels to the lights. Also there are two olive trees by it, one on the right of the bowl and the other on its left.' I asked the angel who talked with me, 'What are these, my lord?' He answered, 'Do you not know what these are?' 'No, my lord,' I replied. So he said to me, 'This is the word of the Lord to Zerubbabel: **"Not by might nor by power, but by my Spirit,"** says the Lord Almighty' (Zech. 4:1b-6).

The lesson is clear. The gospel grows not by power, not by might, but by 'my Spirit'.

The pictures are clear. The triune God existed before the world was made. The ark represents the Father's throne in heaven. The table represents the Son. The lampstand represents the Spirit.

Three pictures of the triune God.

The altar of incense

After the tabernacle room is built and the furniture placed, after the dividing curtain has been hung and the altar of atonement built outside the tent —one more piece of furniture was placed in the tent – the altar of incense.

But how can there be room for anything else after the Trinity? John explains this in Revelation:

> Each one had a harp and they were holding golden bowls full of incense, which are the prayers of the saints (Rev. 5:8b).

David understands this truth when he asks that his prayer might come before the Lord 'like incense' (Ps. 141:2).

The prayers of believers come before the triune God. The church, and her prayers, takes its place in the middle of the Trinity, at the boundary of heaven and earth.

What a wonderful privilege! We are not left outside, but fixed in the very heart of reality, in the middle of the Trinity, caught up into their glorious fellowship.

A home with a throne

The tabernacle is first described as a single room. Many of us know that the tabernacle/temple is divided into two: the Most Holy Place and the Holy Place. However, it is divided only by a curtain. The tabernacle itself is first of all a single room – see Exodus 25:1-30.

When God created all things through Christ, there was no division between heaven and earth. We need to keep that in mind. At the end of the all things heaven and earth will be reunited (see Rev. 21:1-4).

Once we have understood this, **then** the Lord introduces the next part of the tabernacle (Exod. 26:31-27:9).

The curtain

The curtain is built to divide the tabernacle and make the king unseen. It has cherubim worked into it (Exod. 26:31) to remind us that since Adam fell the world is not perfect. Because of the curtain the one who rules cannot be seen or known.

The two 'rooms' of the tabernacle represent the heavens and the earth (Heb. 9:23-25)

Glorious vandalism

The sacrificial system is set up to destroy the curtain. The priests (who represent the people) cannot come as they are. They are given special clothes to cover their unrighteousness (Exod. 28-29). All of this points to the cross.

When Jesus dies the curtain is torn from top to bottom and access to the Father is now possible (Matt. 27:51).

> For he himself is our peace, who has made the two one and has destroyed the barrier, the dividing wall of hostility, by abolishing in his flesh the law with its commandments and regulations. His purpose was to create in himself one new man out of the two, thus making peace, and in this one body to reconcile both of them to God through the cross, by which he put to death their hostility. He came and preached peace to you who were far away and peace to those who were near. For through him we both have access to the Father by one Spirit (Eph. 2:14-18).

All the pieces together

Let's put all the pieces together as God commands in Exodus 40.

The heavens and the earth are set up and they are perfect. The triune God – Father, Son and Holy Spirit make their home in the heavens and earth. We are to enjoy friendship with God and speak to Him and He to us without anything breaking that relationship.

But sin has entered and ruined our world. It is still good but not perfect. Nobody can see the one who rules it and there is so much we need to know that is left unseen.

People can live in this world but what we need is a sacrifice that can destroy the dividing curtain. Jesus our priest and sacrifice does just that.

Believe on the Lord Jesus Christ and be saved

But why the detail?

In our house the floors are wooden – my wife doesn't like carpets. There is an oil painting over the fireplace from Italy, left to me by my aunt. Everything is immaculate (apart from the children's pictures on the kitchen wall).

There is one room, however, which looks like nothing else. There are piles of books and papers on the floor and a chaos that only one person can understand. That room is my study. And there is a purpose behind every detail.

The prayer stuck on the wall written by 'Marie Phillips aged 6' means nothing to anyone else but to me it reminds me of all the children and all the people of Birchgrove whom we prayed for and gave up everything for during six exciting years when planting a church. I can hardly read it without a lump in my throat. I hope it tells a great deal about me and a crucial part of my life.

So it is with God's home. Each item of furniture, as in all our houses, has a story to tell about the character of the one who lives there.

It is dull to the stranger – but a delight to the one who loves God.

God wants to live with His people

When I was a milkman and collecting money one morning, a

man called me into his garage, 'Come and see this. It's my pride and joy.'

Inside was a very expensive sports car. He told me how much it was worth, how much it would be worth in ten years' time, how fast it could go and how he maintained it himself. There was less than 50 miles on the clock. I was a bit perplexed and asked, 'How is it so low?'

Out came the story in great detail of how the car was delivered on the back of a truck to the house.

'Don't you ever drive it?'

'Oh no. I might damage it. I've got another car for that.'

An expensive sports car and he had never driven it! He had never known what it felt like on the open road. His pride and joy – but he had never enjoyed it.

God does not look at His treasured possessions like that.

He has redeemed His people, made a covenant with them, built a throne in the middle of them and now wants to move in and be part of their everyday life.

The triune God moving and living among His people – is there anything more extraordinary than this? God is not a distant God. We even see how He wants a tent to live in among His people's tents. The triune God wants intimacy.

The triune God meets Moses
Centred between the tabernacle's plan (Exod. 25-31) and manufacture (Exod. 35-40) we see its purpose.

▷ Jesus meets Moses
The Lord would speak to Moses face to face, as a man speaks with his friend (Exod. 33:11).
▷ The Father meets Moses through Jesus

> 'But,' he said, 'you cannot see my face, for no-one may see me and live.' Then the Lord said, 'There is a place near me where you may stand on a rock. When my glory passes by, I will put you in a cleft in the rock and cover you with my hand until

I have passed by. Then I will remove my hand and you will see my back; but my face must not be seen' (Exod. 33:20-23).

and that rock was Christ (1 Corinthians 10:4).[2]

⊳The work of the Spirit

'See, the Lord has chosen Bezalel son of Uri…and he has filled him with the Spirit of God, with skill, ability and knowledge in all kinds of crafts' (Exod. 35:30 – 36:1).

The Israelites had done all the work just as the Lord had commanded Moses. Moses inspected the work and saw that they had done it just as the Lord had commanded. So Moses blessed them (Exod. 39:42-43).

The Spirit empowers and lives in the people so that they can build a home for God and obey His Word.

The king moves in

Jesus (the angel travelling in a pillar of cloud by day and night) leads them to a place where they can live with God. And after the work on the tabernacle is complete, He moves in.

Then the cloud covered the Tent of Meeting, and the glory of the Lord filled the tabernacle. Moses could not enter the Tent of Meeting because the cloud had settled upon it, and **the glory of the Lord filled the tabernacle**. In all the travels of the Israelites, whenever the cloud lifted from above the tabernacle, they would set out; but if the cloud did not lift, they did not set out – until the day it lifted. So the cloud of the Lord was over the tabernacle by day, and fire was in the cloud by night, in the sight of all the house of Israel during all their travels (Exod. 40:34-38).

⊳Jesus moves in – in the Gospels

The Word became flesh and made his dwelling among us. We have seen his glory, the glory of the One and Only, who came from the Father, full of grace and truth (John 1:14).

(Note in the original, 'dwelling' is translated 'tabernacled'.)

▶God moves into His church

And in him you too are being built together to become a dwelling in which God lives by his Spirit (Eph. 2:22).

▶He will live with His people for ever in heaven

And I heard a loud voice from the throne saying, 'Now the dwelling of God is with men, and he will live with them. They will be his people, and God himself will be with them and be their God' (Rev. 21:3).

God is not a distant God, a million miles from His people, but a God who wants real intimacy.

Putting this into practice is where the problems begin.

(ENDNOTES)

[1] It is fascinating to think about the way that the earthly picture mirrors the heavenly reality. On the earth, the angel of the Lord sat in the Most Holy Place, representing the way that the Father in heaven sits on the throne. In the heavenly reality, God the Son is the priest and sacrifice ministering before his Father, but in the earthly tabernacle it was the human Levitical priests and the animal sacrifices which represent the future work of the Son.

[2] Deuteronomy 32:4, 15, 18 etc. The book of Psalms picks up on this title for God the Son – e.g. 62:2, 7; 71:3; 89:26; 92:15 etc.

4:4
Living with God

To this day I'm unsure why the lecturer started to confess the details of her early married life.

'I loved my husband, but after being married for six months I left him, and went home to my mother...'

'He always puts salt on his food before tasting it mum. It doesn't matter what I cook, it's always the same.'

'Is that it you silly girl?'

'The problem was he was so perfect. He wouldn't lose his temper or be mean to me – it drove me mad. He was so frustrating to live with.'

Sadly, my wife has never had this problem in our marriage – well apart from the fact that I'm frustrating!

Living with someone – sharing money, living space, bodies and time – can be quite a shock. All of this needs working through if a relationship is to survive. Most of all, as my lecturer learned when she went back to her husband; it involves learning to accept when you are wrong.

Living with someone brings all kinds of frustrations and difficulties, especially if the one you are living with is the sinless triune God. It really is one thing for God to move in next door. How is it possible for us to live with Him and be like Him?

'Speak to the entire assembly of Israel and say to them: 'Be holy because I, the Lord, your God, am holy' (Lev. 11:44-45, 19:2, 20:7).

But just as he who called you is holy, so be holy in all you do;
for it is written: 'Be holy, because I am holy' (1 Pet. 1:15-16).

'Be perfect, therefore, as your heavenly Father is perfect'
(Matt. 5:48).

God hasn't changed and we haven't changed. So as we read
the book of Leviticus, the question remains – how do these
earthy pictures reflect the heavenly reality? How can we live
with God?

Holiness in God's eyes is not the 'spooky' feeling of walking into
an old church, it has to do with every 'nitty-gritty' detail of life:

Sacrifice to cover sin
There were many and varied sacrifices that could be offered.
They covered every occasion in life so that all kinds of sin
could be dealt with. The greatest of all the sacrifices was the
Day of Atonement (Lev. 16-17). Everybody knew exactly how
their sin could be covered as they were given long and detailed
instructions.

▷ **The heavenly reality**
  **We have been made holy through the sacrifice of the body of
  Jesus Christ once for all.** Day after day every priest stands and
  performs his religious duties; again and again he offers the
  same sacrifices, which can never take away sins. But when this
  priest had offered for all time one sacrifice for sins, he sat down
  at the right hand of God (Heb. 10:10-12).

Priests to bring sacrifices to God
Detailed instructions are given for the priest to be a mediator
between the people and God – so that they could come to
God in their time of need. The problem was – the priests were
sinners too!

▷ **The heavenly reality**
  Therefore, **since we have a great high priest** who has gone
  through the heavens, Jesus the Son of God, let us hold

firmly to the faith we profess. For we do not have a high priest who is unable to sympathise with our weaknesses, but we have one who has been tempted in every way, just as we are – yet was without sin. Let us then approach the throne of grace with confidence, so that we may receive mercy and find grace to help us in our time of need (Heb. 4:14-16).

We are all able to walk into God's presence: 'and **has made us to be a kingdom and priests** to serve his God and Father' (Rev. 1:6).

Being clean
Uncleanness meant removal from God's people and therefore removal from God's presence. The earthly shadow points to all kinds of things that make us unclean.

> ### ▸ The heavenly reality
> 'Are you so dull?' he asked. 'Don't you see that nothing that enters a man from the outside can make him "unclean"? For it doesn't go unto his heart but into his stomach and then out of his body.' (In saying this, Jesus declared all foods 'clean'.) He went on: 'What comes out of a man is what makes him "unclean". For from within, out of men's hearts, come evil thoughts, sexual immorality, theft, murder, adultery, greed, malice, deceit, lewdness, envy, slander, arrogance and folly. All these evils come from inside and make a man "unclean"' (Mark 7:18-23).

Jesus makes us clean by suffering 'outside the camp' – in the very place the unclean went: 'And so Jesus also suffered outside the city gate to make the people holy through his own blood (Heb. 13:12).

Being holy
God wants to be with them in every part of their lives – nothing is left out. They are to be separate in everything.

▷ **The heavenly reality**

So I tell you this, and insist on it in the Lord, that you must no longer live as the Gentiles do, in the futility of their thinking. They are darkened in their understanding and separated from the life of God because of the ignorance that is in them due to the hardening of their hearts. Having lost all sensitivity, they have given themselves over to sensuality so as to indulge in every kind of impurity, with a continual lust for more. You, however, did not come to know Christ that way. Surely you heard of him and were taught in him in accordance with the truth that is in Jesus. You were taught, with regard to your former way of life, to put off your old self, which is being corrupted by its deceitful desires (from Eph. 4:17-22).

Eternal symbols

As you looked at the camp, you could see that the tabernacle, the sacrifices and the dressed-up priests were part of their 'religion' – but what about the other details? What jobs did they have? What did they eat? What kind of social life did they enjoy?

Recently I've known what it is to grieve for a friend. What happens is that you realize how unreal and how unimportant these things are. They can all disappear in a moment. That is why in the Pentateuch there is so little on the Israelites' lives, but so much on all that points to reality.

This world and everything in it is passing away but the symbols point to something that is real and eternal – a covenant relationship with the eternal God.

They are the reality.

If only we could remember this how much happier we would be. If only we spent time thinking about the details reflecting reality, instead of worrying what others think of us or how much is in the bank, how much boredom, emptiness and pointlessness would disappear from our lives.

Living with God means living with others

There is a great deal in these books about the poor, the widow and the fatherless, and how God wants Israel to help those among His people who are in need. Their mistreatment of those in need is a reflection of how their relationship with God has broken down.

Years ago, I was sitting in a church on Christmas Day with a 12-year-old boy who had come to Christ. He was being beaten for his faith but was determined to be with God's people that Christmas morning.

All the children were encouraged to show off what they had been given. He had very little. A collection was taken for bikes to be sent off to children in other countries. He had no bike.

There was a huge gap between him and God's people – a division and loneliness between them and him and he was made to feel like an outsider.

How could anyone looking on say the gospel was true if they had seen this? Sadly I have seen this kind of thing many times in church.

The Bible shows how God hates it – and so must we. We must help those in financial need who come into our churches. There are over 2,000 verses in the Bible on helping the poor in our congregations.

The Bible's emphasis is not that we campaign for the needs of the poor in the world, but that we secretly put our hands in our pockets and give to those who are in need in our own churches.

God hates divisive snobbery and patronizing help.

Look around on Sunday – who can you help?

Part Five
Promised land

5:1
The church – the covenant community

As a Christian, one of the great shocks is the discovery that someone who is a member of a church, and to all intents and purposes belongs, doesn't believe at all.

The church up to the end of Genesis was made up of believers. Then suddenly at the beginning of Exodus there is a huge increase in the numbers of those who belong to the church (Exod. 1:6-7).

Even though all these people were Abraham's children outwardly (and looking on you would say they were part of the church) it is clear they were not real believers. They were not all Abraham's true children.

They have so much (see Rom. 9:4-5). They truly are a special people. But one of the problems of privilege is that it brings responsibility and so many of the Israelites refused to believe the message preached to them.

Read about the church in Numbers. The vast majority are lost and only a remnant is saved. Again in Joshua and Judges the church is not always what it should be.

Saying that you are a Christian doesn't make you a Christian. It is not outward circumcision God wants but circumcision of the heart.

The Bible says 'not all' Israel are 'Israel', and anyone who knows the Old Testament knows this is true (Rom. 3:28-29, 9:6).

However the true church always remains. Why? As long as there is a remnant of believers the whole church still enjoys God's protection and the blessing of the gospel. There is still repentance available for all. But *having* the gospel and *believing* the gospel are two very different things.

What we see in the church is a group of people who have the enormous privilege of hearing and enjoying the gospel but within that group is a division – those who have believed and those who have not. They all make up the church but only those who have believed will be saved on judgment day.

Look how Jesus, that great and final expositor of the Bible, explains this in the New Testament.

> Jesus told them another parable: 'The kingdom of heaven is like a man who sowed good seed in his field. But while everyone was sleeping, his enemy came and sowed weeds among the wheat, and went away. When the wheat sprouted and formed ears, then the weeds also appeared. The owner's servants came to him and said, "Sir, didn't you sow good seed in your field? Where then did the weeds come from?" "An enemy did this," he replied. The servants asked him, "Do you want us to go and pull them up?" "No," he answered, "because while you are pulling the weeds, you may root up the wheat with them. Let both grow together until the harvest. At that time I will tell the harvesters: First collect the weeds and tie them in bundles to be burned; then gather the wheat and bring it into my barn."' (Matt. 13:24-30).

So we see the church in the Old Testament was mixed. Sometimes unbelievers influenced the church and made it look like the world. Sometimes believers led the church and behaved as a people who were different to the world.

But as long as there is a remnant of believers who hold to the truth there is hope.

5:2
Moving on

A famous preacher once told of a strange phenomenon that occurred in the American Civil War. After the liberation of slaves in the south, stories circulated that some of the slaves carried on living and behaving as if they were still slaves, even though they were free men. Although there was a declaration stating they were free they struggled to believe it was true for them. To move on they needed to understand the meaning of their freedom.

The people have camped at Mount Sinai for eleven months, from Exodus 19:2-3 to Numbers 10:11. When will they ever move on and why is it so important they wait?

Only when they understand the true freedom that has been bought in their redemption can they begin to move forward.

When can they move on?
The first ten chapters of Numbers make sure that the Word of God given in Exodus and Leviticus is put into practice. True freedom is found in believing and living for the truth found in Jesus.

> Jesus said, 'If you hold to my teaching, you are really my disciples. Then you will know the truth, and the truth will set you free' (John 8:31b-32).

> 'So if the Son sets you free, you will be free indeed' (John 8:36).

Holding on to Jesus' teaching does not mean just skim-reading but reading, understanding and putting it into practice.

The people are numbered to find those who are active for war (Num. 1:3) and those inside the camp, so that the law of separation can be put into practice (Num. 5:1-31). The Levites are consecrated for their work as priests and the Passover is celebrated to remind them of their redemption (Num. 9). They recall their need of God's presence (Num. 9:15-23). They are then gathered by the sound of the silver trumpets. Then and only then are they are led to move on from Mount Sinai (Num. 10:12-13).

God is determined to prepare us by His Word before we can go anywhere. This failure to enjoy their freedom is not due to bad teaching.

Getting to the land – but not getting there

Numbers is a desperately sad book. Such hope and yet a whole generation of souls is lost.

The people are provided with all they need for the journey. They are under the cloud of God's presence (Num. 9:15-23). They are baptized into that presence (Num. 33:8, see also Exod. 14:19-21). They all eat the same supernatural food (Num. 11:4ff). They drink from the supernatural rock that follows them (Num. 20:2-13). But they constantly rebel.

One verse sums them up: 'for you are a stiff-necked people' (Deut. 9:6b).

A warning

What does the book mean?

> For I do not want you to be ignorant of the fact, brothers, that our forefathers were all under the cloud and that they all passed through the sea. They were all baptized into Moses in the cloud and in the sea. They all ate the same spiritual food and drank the same spiritual drink; for they drank from the spiritual rock that accompanied them, and that rock was Christ (1 Cor. 10:1-4).

Everything needed for their life and godliness is provided for them in Jesus (2 Pet. 1:2-3) as it is for us. Balaam, looking on under the inspiration of God, sees, 'The Lord their God is with them, the shout of the King is among them' (Num. 23:21).

Their King is greater than other kings. His kingdom will be greater than other kingdoms (Num. 24:7). But they do not see it. What happens to them is a warning – to us all.

> Now these things occurred as examples to keep us from setting our hearts on evil things as they did… These things happened to them as examples and were written down as warnings for us on whom the fulfilment of the ages has come. So, if you think you are standing firm, be careful that you don't fall! No temptation has seized you except what is common to man. And God is faithful; he will not let you be tempted beyond what you can bear. But when you are tempted, he will also provide a way out so that you can stand up under it. Therefore, my dear friends, flee from idolatry (1 Cor. 10:6-14).

We are to read Numbers and be warned to follow God. We are to read and realize the temptations we go through are common to everyone and He has provided a way out – of them all.

But why do they face these temptations – and why do we?

Trials and temptations show us what is really in our hearts. Life is full of trouble. We can feel that if only life was different or better, we ourselves would be different and better. But this kind of thinking simply proves that we have failed God's test.

God is in control of everything in this world. He orders everything for our good. The question to ask when going through trials is, 'Can I trust Him? Can I live by faith in His gospel?' Every trial tells us a great deal about ourselves.

Job said, 'Though he slay me, yet will I trust him.' The people in Numbers said, 'If he doesn't give us what we want, we won't.'

Job had eternal life. They did not.

Have you?

They heard the gospel preached – as we do

They failed to make it to the promised land because of their unwillingness to believe the gospel, the same gospel that is preached to us.

> Who were they who heard and rebelled? Were they not all those Moses led out of Egypt? And with whom was he angry for forty years? Was it not with those who sinned, whose bodies fell in the desert? And to whom did God swear that they would never enter his rest if not to those who disobeyed? So we see that they were not able to enter, because of their unbelief.
>
> Therefore, since the promise of entering his rest still stands, let us be careful that none of you be found to have fallen short of it. **For we also have had the gospel preached to us, just as they did;** but the message they heard was of no value to them, because those who heard did not combine it with faith (Heb. 3:16-4:2).

The result of their unbelief in the gospel is catastrophic – not one or two people but a whole generation is lost.

Has the promise failed if this is the result? Clearly, no. It is just that many of them failed to believe.

> 'God is not a man, that he should lie, nor a son of man, that he should change his mind. Does he speak and then not act? Does he promise and not fulfil?' (Num. 23:19).

> It is not as though God's word had failed. For not all who are descended from Israel are Israel. Nor because they are his descendants are they all Abraham's children...In other words, it is not the natural children who are God's children, but it is the children of the promise who are regarded as Abraham's offspring (Rom. 9:6-8).

Again we see that the true child of Abraham is the believer in Jesus.

Jesus is described in John's Gospel as the one who is greater than Moses (6:14), the Good Shepherd (10:1-18), the life-giving serpent (3:14), the Passover Lamb (19:36), the water giver (4:10-15), the manna from heaven (6:26-58) and the glory of the Shekinah (1:14-18).

He is all we need. The question is what will we do with Him?

> 'Whoever believes in the Son has eternal life, but whoever rejects the Son will not see life, for God's wrath remains on him' (John 3:36).

This verse sums up the stark contrast that is worked out through the book of Numbers. We, like the hymn writer, need to rely on Jesus and believe in Him to have eternal life.

> Guide me, O my great redeemer
> Pilgrim through this barren land;
> I am weak, but you are mighty,
> Hold me with your powerful hand:
> Bread of heaven, Bread of heaven,
> Feed me now and evermore.
>
> Open now the crystal fountain
> Where the healing waters flow;
> Let the fiery, cloudy pillar
> Lead me all my journey through:
> Strong deliverer, strong deliverer,
> Ever be my strength and shield.
>
> When I tread the verge of Jordan
> Bid my anxious fears subside;
> Death of death, and hell's destruction,
> Land me safe on Canaan's side:
> Songs of praises, songs of praises,
> I will ever sing to you.
> William Williams

5:3
Preparing for life in the land

A completely new generation grows up and it is they who are to take the land.

> 'See, I have given you this land. Go in and take possession of the land that the Lord swore he would give to your fathers – to Abraham, Isaac and Jacob – and to their descendants after them' (Deut. 1:8).

The people are sinful and deserve to be cast off but because of the promises back in Genesis to Abraham, Isaac and Jacob, God will bring them into the land.

Deuteronomy is a book repeating and explaining the covenant and its consequences once again to a new generation: 'Moses began to expound this law saying…' (Deut. 1:5b).

When God gathers His people together he always speaks to them. The book is made up of three sermons (1:6-4:40, 4:44-28 and 29–30), then Moses' final address and an account of his death. The sermons have four themes in common:

A *covenant*
God has not forgotten His promises to Abraham and the patriarchs (Deut. 7:13-14). The people may have given up on God but God cannot give up on them. The people may fail but God cannot.

They are to live lives that reflect these great truths.

> 'So if you faithfully obey the commands I am giving you today
> – to love the Lord your God and to serve him with all your
> heart and with all your soul' (Deut. 11:13).

The land they are about to enter looks back to a new Garden of
Eden and looks forward to a new Jerusalem:

> 'Look down from heaven, your holy dwelling-place, and
> bless your people Israel and the land you have given us as you
> promised on oath to our forefathers, a land flowing with milk
> and honey' (Deut. 26:15).

The past shapes the present

Their past redemption shapes their present. The first three
chapters of the book are a review of what has happened in the
past. It is because they have been set free they are able to live.

> 'Remember that you were slaves in Egypt, and follow carefully
> these decrees' (Deut. 16:12, see also 7:18, 8:14, 10:19, 13:5,
> 15:15, 20:1, 24:18, 22ff).

Throughout the book nothing is done without reference to their
redemption in Egypt. Nothing can be explained or enjoyed
until this is grasped. Their past dominates the present and the
future.

The good life of obeying Christ

There is not an area of life that is untouched by this covenant.

> This day I call heaven and earth as witnesses against you that
> I have set before you life and death, blessings and curses.
> Now choose life, so that you and your children may live
> (Deut. 30:19).

These sermons are to lead them to choose life – to choose life
is to choose Jesus.

> Simon Peter answered him, 'Lord, to whom shall we go? You
> have the words of eternal life' (John 6:68).

They have the opportunity to live with God in a new Garden of Eden. They have the opportunity to live a different kind of life to the nations – obedience is not the path to blessing it is the blessing itself.

The exile as a warning

'In furious anger and in great wrath the Lord uprooted them from their land and thrust them into another land, as it is now' (Deut. 29:28, also 28:64-68).

It is clear they will be removed from the land if they break the covenant, just as Adam and Eve were removed from the Garden of Eden. And sadly this is exactly what happens. The Lord offers no hope that the Israelites can ever fulfil this covenant themselves because of their sin.

And the Lord said to Moses: 'You are going to rest with your fathers, and these people will soon prostitute themselves to the foreign gods of the land they are entering. They will forsake me and break the covenant I made with them' (Deut. 31:16, also 31:29).

But does Moses see the promise himself? He dies before entering the land, so has he failed? A thousand times no. No more than Abraham, Isaac and Jacob failed.

They are all in the promised land now – the land Canaan could only picture. Moses enters the promised rest with his fathers (Deut. 31:16) – the real promised land.

Instead, they were longing for a better country – a heavenly one. Therefore God is not ashamed to be called their God, for he has prepared a city for them (Heb. 11:16).

He dies but one greater than Moses will come who will not only give the Pentateuch but grace and truth by fulfilling it.

The Bible is a book that contains history. Even though all the historical facts in the Bible are true it would be wrong to approach the Bible as a history book. That is clearly not its purpose. Many facts historians would find important it deliberately leaves out, for example, which Pharaoh was around at the time of the Exodus. The history we are told is selected to tell us about Jesus and how God can be known through Him. The Pentateuch is a good example of this.

5:4
Living in Christ

Can you beat the heavyweight boxing champion of the world in a fight? It seems unlikely but the answer is yes – if you are in a tank!

At the end of his three sermons Moses summarizes the requirements of the covenant and then says – you won't be able to keep them:

> 'For I know that after my death you are sure to become utterly corrupt and to turn from the way I have commanded you. In days to come, disaster will fall upon you because you will do evil in the sight of the Lord and provoke him to anger by what your hands have made' (Deut. 31:29).

How can anyone keep the law with a sinful nature? Moses certainly thinks there is no hope of them beating the impossible odds that face them. How can they take the land and live enjoying the freedom God gives? Listen to this:

> 'Now what I am commanding you today is **not too difficult for you or beyond your reach**. It is not up in heaven, so that you have to ask, "Who will ascend into heaven to get it and proclaim it to us so that we may obey it?" Nor is it beyond the sea, so that you have to ask, "Who will cross the sea to get it and proclaim it to us so that we may obey it?" No, the word is very near you; it is in your mouth and in your heart so that you may obey it. See, I set before you today life and prosperity, death and destruction' (Deut. 30:11-15).

Is he contradicting himself? In chapter 31, he says they haven't got a chance of knowing peace and prosperity or of taking the land because of their sinful hearts. In chapter 30, he says it is not too difficult for them or beyond their reach – it is very near them.

Absolutely not – he is preaching Christ to them. You can't win on your own – but you can if you're in Christ.

They can only live the obedient life – in Christ

> Then Jesus was led by the Spirit into the desert to be tempted by the devil (Matt. 4:1).

Jesus comes in the gospels and is tempted in the wilderness in every point but with one significant difference – he is without sin. How does He do it – by quoting and fulfilling the book of Deuteronomy.

Where Israel failed in the desert, Jesus succeeds. Jesus keeps the law for us. In fact the law is incomplete without Him.

> **Christ is the end of the law** so that there may be righteousness for everyone who believes. Moses describes in this way the righteousness that is by the law: 'The man who does these things will live by them.' But the righteousness that is by faith says: 'Do not say in your heart, "Who will ascend into heaven?"'(that is, to bring Christ down) or '"Who will descend into the deep?"' (that is, to bring Christ up from the dead). But what does it say? 'The word is near you; it is in your mouth and in your heart,' that is, the word of faith we are proclaiming: That if you confess with your mouth, 'Jesus is Lord,' and believe in your heart that God raised him from the dead, you will be saved (Rom. 10:4-9).

The only one who can give us 'the righteousness by the law' is the one who makes sense of the law, who makes the law complete – the one whom the law points to. We must read it trusting Christ and calling on Him.

We can live the obedient life but only in Christ – in Christ alone.

The Pentateuch ends with Deuteronomy. It is the foundation of the rest of the Old Testament and the Bible. Deuteronomy 34:10 shows us that the Old Testament prophets were not innovators but expositors of Moses.[1] Our understanding of the Pentateuch will affect the way we read the rest of the Bible. The Former Prophets start in Joshua – with entry into the land – and end in 2 Kings with the Exile. Things are no better at the end of this section than they are at the beginning. However, as with the Pentateuch, the Former Prophets write about Jesus – this is what we must see.

They can only take the land – in Christ

'Be strong and very courageous. Be careful to obey all the law my servant Moses gave you; do not turn from it to the right or to the left, that you may be successful wherever you go. **Do not let this Book of the Law depart from your mouth; meditate on it day and night**, so that you may be careful to do everything written in it. **Then you will be prosperous and successful.** Have I not commanded you? Be strong and courageous. Do not be terrified; do not be discouraged, for the Lord your God will be with you wherever you go' (Josh. 1:7-9).

In the book of Joshua the land will be taken (Joshua means 'Jesus' in Hebrew). It is essential we see it is Jesus who is the King and he rules through His Word, which is to be meditated on day and night. It is through Him strength and victory come. The purpose of the book of Joshua is summarized at the end:

So the Lord gave Israel all the land he had sworn to give their forefathers, and they took possession of it and settled there. The Lord gave them rest on every side, just as he had sworn to their forefathers...**Not one of all the Lord's good promises to the house of Israel failed**; every one was fulfilled (Josh. 21:43-45).

They will take the land because it is a picture of the gospel preached to Abraham. There will be major obstacles in the way and they will have to see great and seemingly impossible enemies defeated. So how can this happen?

Look who Joshua meets

> Now when Joshua was near Jericho, he looked up and saw a man standing in front of him with a drawn sword in his hand. Joshua went up to him and asked, 'Are you for us or for our enemies?' 'Neither,' he replied, 'but as commander of the army of the Lord I have now come.' Then Joshua fell face down to the ground in reverence, and asked him, 'What message does my Lord have for his servant?' The commander of the Lord's army replied, 'Take off your sandals, for the place where you are standing is holy.' And Joshua did so (Josh. 5:13-15).

Joshua meets Jesus. It is by faith in Jesus that they overcome impossible odds. It is Jesus who is the ruler. It is because of Jesus they take the land. In fact in the first and famous battle of Jericho, as the walls crumble and they remain unscathed, it really is as if they are in a tank!

> By faith the walls of Jericho fell, after the people had marched around them for seven days (Heb. 11:30).

> Finally, be strong in the Lord and in his mighty power. Put on the full armour of God so that you can take your stand against the devil's schemes. For our struggle is not against flesh and blood, but against the rulers, against the authorities, against the powers of this dark world and against the spiritual forces of evil in the heavenly realms (Eph. 6:10-12).

In our fight against the devil – who seems such an impossible enemy – our only hope of victory is being strong in the Lord. But what a hope! This is what the book of Joshua is about.

> For if Joshua had given them rest, God would not have spoken later about another day. There remains, then, a Sabbath-rest for the people of God; for anyone who enters God's rest also rests from his own work, just as God did from his. Let us, therefore,

make every effort to enter that rest, so that no-one will fall by following their example of disobedience (Heb. 4:8-11).

Jesus brings the inheritance – which Joshua only points to

Praise be to the God and Father of our Lord Jesus Christ! In his great mercy he has given us new birth into a living hope through the resurrection of Jesus Christ from the dead, into an inheritance that can never perish, spoil or fade – kept in heaven for you, who through faith are shielded by God's power until the coming of the salvation that is ready to be revealed in the last time (1 Pet. 1:3-5).

Jesus gives the true inheritance that never perishes, spoils or fades. Jesus gives us a renewed creation where heaven and earth are reunited.

Wandering away from the true king – Judges

The angel of the Lord went up from Gilgal to Bokim and said, 'I brought you up out of Egypt and led you into the land that I swore to give to your forefathers. I said, 'I will never break my covenant with you, and you shall not make a covenant with the people of this land, but you shall break down their altars.' Yet you have disobeyed me. Why have you done this? Now therefore I tell you that I will not drive them out before you; they will be thorns in your sides and their gods will be a snare to you.' When the angel of the Lord had spoken these things to all the Israelites, the people wept aloud (Judg. 2:1-4).

The people receive their physical inheritance but the book of Judges shows us that something is still missing. Jesus, the angel of the Lord, is their King. He gives them all they need but they keep wandering away from Him.

There is a very simple if tragic pattern to the book and each time the spiral deepens. They rebel, they are judged, they cry out to the Lord for help. God has mercy and raises up a deliverer. They rebel again – and things get worse. The end of the book

143

makes painful reading – we see what sin can do to a nation with so much missed potential.

The deliverers are examples of how God saves and how we should live (Heb. 11:32-33) but again they are clearly examples and not the reality. There is only one solution for Israel to break the cycle. And by the end, the book cries out over and again for that solution.

> At that time the Israelites left that place and went home to their tribes and clans, each to his own inheritance. In those days Israel had no king; everyone did as he saw fit (Judg. 21:24-25, also 17:6, 18:1, 19:1 and 21:25).

Their despair, sin and sense of lost hope is caused by their rejection of Jesus, the angel of the Lord – the King.

(ENDNOTES)
[1] Alec Motyer in a Letter to Steve Levy from Summer 2007

Part Six
Kings to exile

6:1
Moving the signpost

I was preaching in a small country town in mid Wales. There's really only one way to get there from Swansea – on the 'heads of the valley' road. But once I got through Merthyr I realized the road was closed. No big deal – just a case of following the diversion signs.

It wasn't long before I was travelling through winding, narrow country lanes. I was a bit late but no need to panic – as long as I kept following the signs I'd get there. I came out in Tredegar – miles from where I needed to be. On my third circuit of the town I realized something was seriously wrong. And I was now very late!

I found out some teenagers had moved the diversion signs the night before. (At which point I became in favour of hanging again or at least public flogging!)

Who moved the signpost?

True believers see the Lord as King. Balaam back in Numbers sees, 'The Lord their God is with them, the shout of the King is among them'. Everyone should know their King is enthroned among the cherubim.

Hannah, in the temple courts near the ark, sees where the signpost is pointing: 'He will give strength to his king and exalt the horn of his anointed' (1 Sam. 2:10). She trusts in the real king – Jesus – long before Saul or David or any of the kings have even come on the scene. She sees that only the Christ, the Lord's anointed, is king.

The great symbol of Jesus' kingship is the ark – from where he gives his commands between the cherubim.

But as I found to my cost, the problem with symbols and signposts is they can be moved and become more of a hindrance than a help.

The beginning of the book of Samuel is dominated with the ark of the covenant – the symbol and signpost pointing to where the King is enthroned. Good news you would think. But no. The Israelites cannot see that unlike the nations around them and their idols, they must bow before the true King and not the ark.

A signpost becomes an end in itself. It is pushed around by foolish men who think they can push God around.

We will do anything, however foolish, to make sure we are in charge and we don't have to change. But it ends in disaster.

Disaster!

The ark ends up in captivity with the Philistines and when returned it is left on the fringes of the life of the people of God (1 Sam. 7:1).

We now see the last of the Judges, Samuel (1 Sam. 7:15-17). And he too fails (1 Sam. 8:1-3). The people have tried the pushing-the-ark route of leading themselves. They have seen they cannot control the Judges. And with the symbol of God's kingship almost abandoned by His people, they now make a breathtaking request.

> 'Now appoint a king to lead us, **such as all the other nations have**' (1 Sam. 8:5b).

Their request is so full of sin. Firstly they are not saved to be like the world and the other nations – they are saved to be different. Secondly, in wanting this they are rejecting Jesus as King. Listen to God's reply:

> And the Lord told him: 'they have rejected me as their king'
> (1 Sam. 8:7b).

They already have a King. He sits between the cherubim of the ark they've been pushing around. They have had a King since the day of redemption. Look at the next verse:

> They have rejected me as their king. As they have done
> from the day I brought them up out of Egypt until this day,
> forsaking me and serving other gods, so they are doing to you
> (1 Sam. 8:7b-8).

The people have always had a King – an anointed King – a 'Sent One' from the Father. He has told them how to live so that it will be well with them all the days of their life. But they have rejected Him. They have rejected the Christ, the Christ Hannah rejoiced in at the beginning of the book. This, as the rest of chapter 8 goes on to say, is a disaster!

Is God surprised?

So is God caught by surprise with this request? Of course not; listen to Moses:

> When you enter the land the Lord your God is giving you and
> have taken possession of it and settled in it, and you say, 'Let us
> set a king over us like all the nations around us' (Deut. 17:14).

God is never caught by surprise, not even by the wickedness of people's hearts. Back in the law he makes provision for a king because he knows exactly what their sinful hearts will want. He is also the God who is able to turn what is clearly meant for evil into something which points back to Jesus.

What kind of king does God allow?

The king has to be chosen by God (Deut. 17:15-20). He is not allowed horses, lots of wives or large amounts of gold and silver. His first job is to write down a copy of the law to remind him of who really is in charge. He is to do what God tells him and be careful he is obedient in everything God says. He is to realize he is no better than anyone else.

In other words they can have a king, as long as he doesn't rule! They can have a king, but don't let him be the King. Why? Jesus says – you've already got a king – me!

How different their new king will be to the prophet who is coming:

> The Lord your God will raise up for you a prophet like me from among your own brothers. You must listen to him (Deut. 18:15).

> I will raise up for them a prophet like you from among their brothers; I will put my words in his mouth, and he will tell them everything I command him. If anyone does not listen to my words that the prophet speaks in my name, I myself will call him to account (Deut. 18:18-19).

How different their new king will be to Jesus the Prophet and King:

> And that he may send the Christ, who has been appointed for you – even Jesus…For Moses said, 'The Lord your God will raise up for you a prophet like me from among your own people; you must listen to everything he tells you' (Acts 3:20 and 22).

> 'but the Lamb will overcome them because he is Lord of lords and King of kings' (Rev. 17:14b).

Prophets always trump kings.

Wrong king

The king is chosen. His name is Saul and he is the kind of king all the nations would be proud of – a king after the people's heart.

> 'Now here is the king you have chosen, the one you asked for; see, the Lord has set a king over you' (1 Sam. 12:13).

God anoints and empowers him but still he fails miserably (1 Sam. 15) because he thinks he is king not Jesus. He has no interest in the ark of the covenant. He feels he has the right to command God's people, when he clearly has been told he has no such right. He chooses not to obey the Lord. His crime is high treason against Jesus, a serious sin by anyone's standards.

> But Samuel replied: 'Does the Lord delight in burnt offerings and sacrifices as much as in obeying the voice of the Lord? To obey is better than sacrifice, and to heed is better than the fat of rams' (1 Sam. 15:22).

Saul is the wrong king because he was chosen as the type of king the people wanted. The next king will be different.

> 'But now your kingdom will not endure; **the Lord has sought out a man after his own heart** and appointed him leader of his people, because you have not kept the Lord's command' (1 Sam. 13:14).

This king will submit to the Christ. This king will call Jesus his Lord. And this king will be a signpost pointing to Jesus.

I'm sure this is why God removes great Christian leaders and stops them living into their hundreds. We would just bow down and worship the signpost; forgetting it is of limited use. Moses had to die. Joshua had to die. All the Judges had to die. Eventually Samuel dies but there is one King who always remains.

6:2
Pointing to the real King

Young boys will do everything they can to look like their football heroes. They spend hours watching them play and devour every piece of information on them they can find. They dress like them, have their hair cut like them, even spit like them – hoping upon hope that when people see them, they'll see something of their hero. And it's not just children.

When I grew up in Wales, nearly every preacher dressed in a dark pinstriped suit, wore glasses in an odd way (halfway down their nose) and preached in deep, nasal tones.

If you closed your eyes, it sounded as if Dr Martyn Lloyd-Jones (the greatest preacher Wales produced in the twentieth century) was preaching – with one difference – if you closed your eyes for too long, you drifted off (unlike when listening to the man himself)!

If you worship someone and speak about them all the time it won't be long before you look a bit like them. You will never be the same as them but after a time people will see something of the other person in you.

David never thought he was the answer to Israel's problems. He knew that right from the start of his life.

> David said to the Philistine, 'You come against me with sword and spear and javelin, **but I come against you in the name of the Lord Almighty,** the God of the armies of Israel whom you have defied' (1 Sam. 17:45).

It is important to see that however much he points to Jesus, he had to trust in Jesus himself. Over and again in the book of Psalms he shows his trust is not in himself, but in his and our Saviour. And his desire is to teach others this truth.

> Then I will teach transgressors your ways, and sinners will turn back to you (Ps. 51:13).

We must read his life and trust in Christ alone. David loves Jesus so much he longs to reflect His glory. As you look at him it is obvious you will see something of the One he loves. But as great as this makes David, he must not be the focus of our attention; that is always reserved for our Lord.

What kind of king?

God chooses another king from the tribe of Judah as he had said (Gen. 49:10). He is not a king after the people's heart. He is the youngest and smallest of Jesse's sons. Not even Jesse thought he would make the shortlist (1 Sam. 16:10-12). He is anointed, and when anointed the Spirit of the Lord comes upon him in power.

> So Samuel took the horn of oil and anointed him in the presence of his brothers and from that day on the Spirit of the Lord came upon David in power (1 Sam. 16:13).

'The Christ' (Greek) and 'the Messiah' (Hebrew) both mean 'the Anointed one' (See the NIV footnote for John 1:20).

David's victory

Because of his anointing he defeats Goliath. Because of his anointing the people know victory and enjoy the spoils of victory (1 Sam. 17:51-54).

> But to each one of us grace has been given as Christ apportioned it. This is why it says: 'When he ascended on high, he led captives in his train and gave gifts to men'...It was he who

gave some to be apostles, some to be prophets, some to be evangelists, and some to be pastors and teachers, to prepare God's people for works of service, so that the body of Christ may be built up (Eph. 4:7-12).

Jesus defeats sin, death, hell, and Satan. He knows the victory and showers gifts on the church.

David suffers

Instead of enjoying increasing popularity, David has to live in the knowledge that the people do not know he is the Lord's anointed. He endures suspicion (1 Sam. 18:11-12), secret opposition (1 Sam. 19:11) and open hostility (1 Sam. 19:9-10). He narrowly escapes death (1 Sam. 19:10-26:25). Then everyone forsakes him (1 Sam. 30:1-6). He suffers as Jesus suffered.

'Did not the Christ have to suffer these things and then enter his glory?' (Luke 24:26).

David gathers

David left Gath and escaped to the cave of Adullam. When his brothers and his father's household heard about it, they went down to him there. All those who were in distress or in debt or discontented gathered around him, and he became their leader. About four hundred men were with him (1 Sam. 22:1-2).

He gathers a group of men around him who are in debt, distressed and discontented. The change in their lives is dramatic. One 'stood his ground and struck down the Philistines till his hand grew tired and froze to the sword'. Another one 'took his stand in the middle of the field. He defended it and struck the Philistines down, and the Lord brought about a great victory' (2 Sam. 23:8-12).

There are other great victories for David's 'mighty men'. Those who were once rebels are now able to do great things through him.

The final conquest

Saul dies and David now represents the Lord's anointed king. The jewel in the physical land, Jerusalem, is taken against impossible odds. It is David who finally brings the conquest of the land.

> The king and his men marched to Jerusalem to attack the Jebusites, who lived there. The Jebusites said to David, 'You will not get in here; even the blind and the lame can ward you off.' They thought, 'David cannot get in here.' Nevertheless, David captured the fortress of Zion, the City of David (2 Sam. 5:6-7).

David's son

> David's first desire is to bring the symbol of God's kingship, the presence of God, to the heart of the people. So he brings the ark to Jerusalem. He wants to build a home for God in amongst the homes of the people but God denies his request. Someone else is coming to do just this:
>
> 'When your days are over and you rest with your fathers, I will raise up your offspring to succeed you, who will come from your own body, **and I will establish his kingdom. He is the one who will build a house for my Name, and I will establish the throne of his kingdom for ever.** I will be his father, and he shall be my son…Your house and your kingdom shall endure for ever before me; your throne shall be established for ever' (2 Sam. 7:12-16).

David is not the true Lord's Anointed – he is only a picture and he knows it (see the Psalms – e.g. Ps. 2 or Ps. 110). David's *Son* is the Lord's Anointed (2 Sam. 7). David's 'offspring' will bring a kingdom, a new Garden of Eden that will last forever.

> 'You will be with child and give birth to a son, and you are to give him the name Jesus. He will be great and will be called the Son of the Most High. **The Lord God will give him the throne of his father David,** and he will reign over the house of Jacob

for ever; his kingdom will never end' (Luke 1:31-33, see also Rev. 22:16 and 2 Tim. 2:8).

Jesus succeeds where David failed, 'completing the work' the Father gave Him to do (John 17:4). It is because of this truth that when in need of mercy there is only one to help:

> As Jesus approached Jericho, a blind man was sitting by the roadside begging. When he heard the crowd going by, he asked what was happening. They told him, 'Jesus of Nazareth is passing by.' He called out, **'Jesus, Son of David, have mercy on me!'** Those who led the way rebuked him and told him to be quiet, but he shouted all the more, 'Son of David, have mercy on me!' Jesus stopped and ordered the man to be brought to him. When he came near, Jesus asked him, 'What do you want me to do for you?' 'Lord I want to see,' he replied. Jesus said to him, 'Receive your sight; your faith has healed you.' Immediately he received his sight and followed Jesus, praising God. When all the people saw it, they also praised God (Luke 18:35-43).

Jesus, the Son of David!

The rest of the book of 2 Samuel shows how David is not the Lord's anointed but a sinner who needs a Saviour. He commits adultery, murders, loses control of his family and destroys huge numbers of his people – because he forgets that Jesus is the king.

David knows he is a sinner. He is an example of saving faith (Rom. 4:6). He is a Christian who confesses Jesus as Lord.

> 'David said about him: "**I saw the Lord always before me.** Because he is at my right hand, I will not be shaken"' (Acts 2:25).

> Seeing what was ahead, **he spoke of the resurrection of the Christ,** that he was not abandoned to the grave, nor did his body see decay (Acts 2:31).

> While the Pharisees were gathered together, Jesus asked them, 'What do you think about the Christ? Whose son is he?' 'The son of David,' they replied. He said to them, 'How is it then

that David, speaking by the Spirit, calls him "Lord"? For he says, "'The Lord said to my Lord: "Sit at my right hand until I put your enemies under your feet."' If then **David calls him "Lord"**, how can he be his son?' (Matt. 22:41-45).

He too had to cry, 'Son of David, have mercy on me!'

He is held up as the example king to all who follow because he trusted the real King and called him 'Lord'.

6:3
The Lord's throne

My two-year-old son has taken to impersonating church services. He starts by shouting, 'Good morning. Sing songs.' He puts his hands in the air, closes his eyes and mumbles toddler gibberish for the prayer, finishing with, 'Amen.' However, when it comes to the sermon, he simply says, 'Follow Jesus. Shall we pray?' Surely the best summary of preaching ever! If only Solomon had continued by saying, 'Follow Jesus' and 'Shall we pray?'

Solomon shows great wisdom
Solomon asks the Lord for wisdom (1 Kings 3:7-9) and God gives it to him:

> When all Israel heard the verdict the king had given, they held the king in awe, because they **saw that he had wisdom from God** to administer justice (1 Kings 3:28).

Solomon finds his wisdom in the only place where true wisdom is found – Jesus, the wisdom of God.

> It is because of him that you are in Christ Jesus, **who has become for us wisdom from God** – that is, our righteousness, holiness and redemption (1 Cor 1:30).

In the wisdom Jesus gives, everything we need is found – righteousness, holiness and redemption.

If you have Jesus you have all you need.

Solomon builds a temple for God

The temple is built as a replacement for the tabernacle. In the wilderness the people lived in tents with a God who lived in a tent. Now the people live in houses, Solomon wants a house for God.

In many ways even though this is a spectacular structure, it is a slightly simpler visual aid. The main furniture in the tabernacle is brought along (1 Kings 8:3) but the emphasis is on the ark (1 Kings 8:8-21).

> 'I have built the temple for the Name of the Lord, the God of Israel. I have provided a place there for the ark, in which is the covenant of the Lord that he made with our fathers when he brought them out of Egypt' (1 Kings 8:20b-21).

The temple is the tabernacle – but twice as big. It is a permanent structure rather than a portable tent. All the truths and symbols of the tabernacle are found there. The temple illustrates the heavens and earth. The ark illustrates the throne and rule of God. The cherubim illustrate the division caused by sin. The sacrificial system illustrates the great sacrifice of Jesus.

One greater than the temple

And Jesus moves into the temple, as he did in the tabernacle:

> the cloud filled the temple of the Lord. And the priests could not perform their service because of the cloud, for **the glory of the Lord filled his temple** (1 Kings 8:10b-11).

And Solomon knows it is a picture of something far greater:

> '**But will God really dwell on earth?** The heavens, even the highest heaven, cannot contain you. How much less this temple I have built!' (1 Kings 8:27-30).

The temple is the place to go to meet with God in all circumstances (1 Kings 8:31-53), the place to go to live with God. Jesus then comes in the gospels and says something quite remarkable:

> 'I tell you that **one greater than the temple is here**' (Matt. 12:6).

The temple, old and new

▷Jesus in his death fulfils the meaning of the old temple

> And the curtain of the temple was torn in two (Luke 23:45b).

He even prophesies its destruction.

> 'Do you see all these great buildings?' replied Jesus. 'Not one stone here will be left on another; every one will be thrown down.' (Mark 13:2).

▷Jesus in his death and resurrection fulfils the heavenly reality that the temple only pointed towards

> Jesus answered them, 'Destroy this temple, and I will raise it again in three days.' The Jews replied, 'It has taken forty-six years to build this temple, and you are going to raise it in three days?' But **the temple he had spoken of was his body** (John 2:19-21).

> For God was pleased to have all his fullness dwell in him (Col. 1:19).

The fullness of God could not live in a temple as Solomon well knew.

▷The real temple

> ...built on the foundation of the apostles and prophets, with Christ Jesus himself as the chief cornerstone. **In him the whole building is joined together and rises to become a holy temple** in the Lord (Eph. 2:20-21).

> For **we are the temple of the living God.** As God has said: 'I will live with them and walk among them, and I will be their God, and they will be my people' (2 Cor. 6:16).

Now Jesus is ascended on high, we can meet with God as we meet with His church which Jesus bought with His blood.

▷No need for a temple any more

> I did not see a temple in the city, because the Lord God Almighty and the Lamb are its temple (Rev. 21:22).

There is a time coming when there will be no need for the visible representation of His presence any more.

The nations praise because of Solomon

Men of all nations, sent by all the kings of the world, come to listen to Solomon (1 Kings 4:34). The Queen of Sheba sums up their attitude perhaps best of all.

> She said to the king, 'The report I heard in my own country about your achievements and your wisdom is true. **But I did not believe these things until I came and saw with my own eyes.** Indeed, not even half was told me; in wisdom and wealth you have far exceeded the report I heard. How happy your men must be! **How happy your officials, who continually stand before you and hear your wisdom!** Praise be to the Lord your God, who has delighted in you and placed you on the throne of Israel. Because of the Lord's eternal love for Israel, he has made you king, to maintain justice and righteousness' (1 Kings 10:6-9).

She sees the 'Wisdom of God' in the person of Jesus that has been given to Solomon, and she is overwhelmed with happiness. Jesus is better than Solomon because he is the source of Solomon's wisdom.

> 'The Queen of the South will rise at the judgment with this generation and condemn it; for she came from the ends of the earth to listen to Solomon's wisdom, and now **one greater than Solomon is here**' (Matt. 12:42).

Solomon is not the Lord's Anointed because he sins terribly by turning away from God at the end of his life. He is less like the Lord's Anointed than his father David.

As Solomon grew old, his wives turned his heart after other gods, and his heart was not fully devoted to the Lord his God, as the heart of David his father had been (1 Kings 11:4).

His rejection of Jesus as King is the beginning of the end.

Road to exile

The people still long to be like the nations who are unclean. More importantly they turn away from the living God to idols (1 Kings 1:26, 2 Kings 17:12, 21:11, 23:24) just as the Israelites did after the Exodus (1 Kings 12:28 and Exod. 32).

The land is divided in the reign of Solomon's son. As soon as the division occurs it brings the beginning of the end.

The kings as a whole fail. At the end of their lives it is what happens in the 'eyes of the Lord' that counts, for he is the Judge. These men, some of whom played God with people's lives, were always under the eyes of the great God and Judge.

The standard is David (2 Kings 14:3 and 16:2). Some kings are like him, notably Josiah, but even he is incapable of turning away God's anger.

> Neither before nor after Josiah was there a king like him who turned to the Lord as he did – with all his heart and with all his soul and with all his strength, in accordance with all the Law of Moses. **Nevertheless, the Lord did not turn away from the heat of his fierce anger,** which burned against Judah (2 Kings 23:25-26).

Josiah, the signpost, can't turn away the anger of God on sinners but Jesus Christ, crowned with thorns on the cross, does.

Prophets

It is important to notice the role of the prophets who dominate 1 and 2 Kings. Two of them take up huge sections of the books – Elijah (1 Kings 17:1 – 2 Kings 2:12) and Elisha (1 Kings 19:16 – 2 Kings 13:21).

They bring God's word to the people. Through them the nation is led. They are also the ones who (through God) state Israel's destiny. The kings are taught to tremble before the prophets.

Why? Because the prophets speak on behalf of the real King – Jesus.

It becomes increasingly obvious that the kings are out of control of events. They can't stop famine, wars or exile. It is not the kings who rule. If you want to see where the real power lies, listen to the prophets.

Notice King David trembles before Nathan (2 Sam. 11), King Solomon trembles before Ahijah (1 Kings 11) as does King Jeroboam (1 Kings 14). King Baasha trembles before Jehu (1 Kings 16) and King Ahab before Elijah (1 Kings 18).

The word of the Lord rules.

It is important also to notice how they are mistreated. The hearts of men are desperately wicked and the prophets are imprisoned, threatened and killed. But in all of this the Word of the Lord reigns.

The one thing I know is that I don't know myself. When I reject Jesus' authority over my life and He reminds me that He is Lord, I will do anything – and I mean anything, to silence Him.

'Woe to you, teachers of the law and Pharisees, you hypocrites! You build tombs for the prophets and decorate the graves of the righteous. And you say, "If we had lived in the days of our forefathers, we would not have taken part with them in shedding the blood of the prophets." So you testify against yourselves that **you are the descendants of those who murdered the prophets**' (Matt. 23:29-31).

Of course I would have 'murdered the prophets' before I became a Christian as I too violently objected to his rule.

In the past God spoke to our forefathers through the prophets at many times and in various ways, **but in these last days he has spoken to us by his Son** (Heb. 1:1-2b).

Jesus is clearly better than the prophets as the prophets speak on His behalf. The prophets spoke of the radiance of God's glory – Jesus is God's glory. The prophets spoke of the purification of sin – Jesus brings it. How much better to see Him.

Where is he?

There is no one quite like David in his trust in Jesus. But not one of David's sons is able to bring the Kingdom of God. Israel, the northern kingdom falls (2 Kings 17) and is exiled to Assyria. Judah falls to Babylon (2 Kings 24-25). Is there any hope left now the land has gone?

The book of 2 Kings ends with a son of David sitting on the throne. But he has to submit to the authority of Babylon, the enemy of God.

Where is the Son of David who will bring a kingdom that will never end? Where is the Son of David who will establish the throne of His kingdom for ever? Where is the Son of David who will bring the presence of God to the heart of the people? The question remains, where is the Christ?

But in the decline of Israel and Judah, Jesus still reigns.

Part Seven
Latter prophets

7:1
Men on a mission

Years ago I visited some young men who had often attended my church but were now in prison. When I arrived I was greeted by a godly (and very posh!) Anglican priest and after I spoke with the boys he invited me to preach in the prison chapel at a later date.

I was quite excited but when the morning arrived over 70 young men streamed into the room (with only three prison officers) looking like I did when I was forced into church as a boy. I heard a loud thud and as I looked around I saw a boy being punched in the back.

The service started, and as choruses were sung, those who were Christians raised their hands. Abuse and threats followed but their hands stayed up. I raised mine – something I don't normally do but identifying with others was definitely the call of the hour – and boy did I pray!

It was announced that I was from Swansea. The Swansea boys cheered but the Cardiff boys were cursing and the temperature was rising in the room. Then it was announced the reading would be given. I looked around and a small old lady with a huge hat was doddering to the front. The comments made by some of the boys were typical of young men separated from women but were painful none the less.

She calmly opened up the Bible and read. She read as if their lives depended on it and not as if hers did. She read as if it was God's word to them. Then she closed the Bible. There was silence and I jumped in and preached for 30 minutes – again to total silence. I preached humbled by an old lady who reminded me that this is the God who rules the world. He's speaking and all must listen.

The prophets stand in front of their kings, their religious leaders and their neighbours. They stand in front of the surrounding nations, and even the mighty all-conquering Babylon. They stand and demand that they all turn around (repent). They explain that if they do not, they are careering towards destruction. If they do they may not be saved from exile but they will be saved for God and His kingdom. This is a message preached long after the exile has finished and the people have returned. It is a message for today.

They have little care for their reputations. They are determined, even blunt, to make sure the truth is stated in the clearest way. They are men on a mission, fearless against seemingly impossible odds, often stating the total destruction of all that appears secure.

They speak of enormous hope to the hopeless in spite of what can be seen before them. If it is brave to speak of judgment in the good times, how much more in the bad. But is it bravery or have they realized that there is someone else who must be feared above the fear of man.

These men don't make personal judgments. They speak with an authority that cannot come from within themselves. So who gives it to them?

Sent by Jesus

Listen to Isaiah the first and longest of all the prophets, whose calling has all the hallmarks of the other prophets.

He 'sees Jesus' glory' (John 12:41) and it changes the way he looks at everything. It happens when Uzziah, the most secure of earthly kings, passes away, and it is clear there is only one King on the throne of the world.

> ...I saw the Lord seated on a throne, high and exalted, and the train of his robe filled the temple...
>
> 'Holy, holy, holy is the Lord Almighty;
>
> the whole earth is full of his glory'(Isa. 6:1-3).

He cries out, 'I am ruined!...my eyes have seen the King, the Lord Almighty.' And when he hears the voice of the Lord saying, 'Whom shall I send? And who will go for us?' replies, 'Here am I. Send me!'

Other kings die but there is one on the throne who tells him what to say. After being sent by Jesus everyone else seems pretty insignificant. All that matters is that the real King is heard. Ezekiel and Jeremiah have similar experiences. The other prophets are also to speak God's words.

They are not just the 'prophets'. God says they are 'My servants the prophets'. Only when we see this, can we make sense of their extraordinary behaviour. In fact when we understand this they do not seem that extraordinary at all. The only strange behaviour is the behaviour of those who refuse to repent and believe!

They see and speak with and meet the King and they hear from Him what the real state of His people is and what is happening in His world. They see their place in His scheme when all around them appears to be chaos and they are repeatedly told to trust Him.

We too through the Word of God can see the real state of the church and the world. When all around us appears to be chaos, there is a King in heaven who will work out His purposes. We must put our trust in Him.

These men know Jesus and see Him for who He is. If you struggle with their writings, you need to see Jesus for who He really is once again.[1]

Some common questions

▷Did they understand their own writings?

This seems a strange question to ask, but so often it is assumed they were ignorant of the gospel. We've seen how Jesus commissioned them. Peter clearly tells us they 'spoke of the grace that was to come to you' and 'the *Spirit of Christ* in them was pointing when he predicted the sufferings of Christ and the glories that would follow' (1 Pet. 1:10-11). So yes, they did understand their own writings.

▷Did they know the purpose of their books and who they were writing for?

Again a strange question. '*It was revealed to them* that they were not serving themselves but you, when they spoke of the things that have now been told you by those who have preached the gospel to you by the Holy Spirit sent from heaven' (1 Pet. 1:12a). So yes. They knew who they were writing for.

▷Are they exciting reading?

'Even angels long to look into these things' (1 Pet. 1:12b). If that doesn't answer the question what does!

Still on the throne

It is important to realize God's covenant did not fail because of what happened to Israel in their sin and exile. The prophets explain this in the clearest terms. They were pointing to salvation in Christ – the only salvation that matters.

Emrys Davies, one of my predecessors, was preaching in a conference just before he died. As an aside he mentioned that the town council of Aberystwyth (where the conference was being held) had asked him thirty years previously to lead a series of open-airs on the promenade.

'They wouldn't do it today you know.'

Everyone laughed. What a ridiculous thought – a council asking a fearless gospel preacher to hold a series of open-airs. Realizing the reaction he boomed out almost in a rage,

'He's still on the throne you know!'

And so He is, and as we read the latter prophets we see that in days when the world seems to be winning, He is still on the throne asserting His authority and proclaiming the gospel.

(ENDNOTES)

[1] The Word of the Lord who came to Abraham in Genesis 15:1-4, comes to the prophets also. For example, see Jonah 1:1. Their calling is not as spectacular in the text as Isaiah (Isa. 6) or Ezekiel (Ezek. 1) or even Jeremiah (Jer. 1), but it is no less significant, because the Word who became flesh came to them.

7:2
When did they preach?

All of these books are dominated by the exile – the time of promised judgment for God's people's rebellion against Him. It was a time which looked back to the removal from the Garden of Eden, a time warning of hell and a time when the wrath of God was being revealed from heaven (Rom. 1:18) as it is today.

The latter prophets are all based around the exile – some before (pre-exilic), some during the exile (exilic), and some afterwards (post-exilic).

The exile consisted of two parts – the ten tribes of Israel were exiled to Assyria, and the two tribes of Judah to Babylon. The Babylon exile is the most significant. Babylon defeated Assyria – in fact they seemed to defeat everyone.

There is a huge battle between David's city – Zion – and Babylon. Great significance is put on this in the end of 2 Kings. As you read on in the Bible the entire world is represented in these two cities – Babylon the great, and Zion the city of God.

So how do we understand a world dominated by Babylon? What hope is there for God's city that can appear so weak? (The world hasn't changed!) And where does each book fit in?

Breakdown of the books
Pre-exilic prophets to Israel – Amos, Hosea, Jonah, Nahum, Obadiah

Pre-exilic prophets to Judah – Joel, Isaiah, Micah, Zephaniah, Jeremiah, Habakkuk

Exilic prophet – Ezekiel

Post-exilic prophets – Haggai, Zechariah, Malachi

The latter prophets also provide a commentary on the former prophets. The exile is described as a return to 'Egypt' (Hosea 11:1-5 and Isa. 52:4) so that we get the link with the Exodus. Notice how they speak of the meanings of King David and the temple. They also explain the law.

The timing and significance of the exile is important because of what it points to in the gospel.

The reason the exile occurred
Contempt for the name of God caused the exile. But the people just couldn't see it.

> 'But you ask, "How have we shown contempt for your name?"'(Mal. 1:6b).

Even though they had Zion, they had forgotten the Saviour who gave it to them, and the purpose of it pointing them to heaven. In a word they had become 'complacent' (Amos 6:1).

They had turned the temple from a place of rejoicing in the Saviour's presence to a place where they pretended sin didn't exist. It had become their 'lucky place' that would protect them in times of trouble (Jer. 7:3-15).

The priests had forgotten they were to point to the great High Priest and were concerned only with increasing their own numbers – which simply ended in an increase of sin (Hosea 4:7-9).

They had turned the sacrifices and feasts to enjoy God into an excuse for enjoying themselves – God was left out (Hosea 8:13-14). They had become something so awful even God hated them (Amos and Isa. 1).

They prayed and fasted but even that was twisted to avoid Jesus being Lord over every part of their lives (Isa. 1:15, Jer. 14:11-12 and Zech. 7:4-11).

They could even hear and enjoy the preaching of God's Word – but never putting it into practice they turned it into a form of entertainment (Ezek. 33:30-33).

They had started to worship what God had created and rejected Christ the Creator (Rom. 1:25). The land, and all the blessings that were in it, pointed them to the Saviour, but they had turned them into obstacles.

The exile, as painful as it was, was necessary to bring them back to Christ. And after many warnings it happens.

The land in ruins, the temple destroyed, the priests removed, nowhere to sacrifice or feast, even a famine of God's Word (Amos 8:11-12). But still God does not destroy the world.

The reason for the exile is their rejection of Christ and the misuse of all God had given them through Him. Just as Adam and Eve are exiled, so the Israelites are exiled.

But His purpose is to bring them back to Himself when they will look only to Him and live.

'Do I take any pleasure in the death of the wicked?' declares the sovereign Lord. Rather, am I not pleased when they turn from their ways and live? (Ezek. 18:23).

Over and again in Ezekiel when Israel and the nations are judged the reason is clearly given, 'Then they will know that I am the Lord.' (Ezekiel uses this phrase twenty times).

Not all bad news!

Still trusting

However in this time where all the signs are removed, there remain prophets and others who keep on trusting the Saviour whom all the signs are pointing to.

But how can they when all around them has collapsed?

> Though the fig-tree does not bud
>> and there are no grapes on the vines,
>> though the olive crop fails
>> and the fields produce no food,
>> though there are no sheep in the pen
>> and no cattle in the stalls, yet I will rejoice in the Lord,
>> I will be joyful in God my Saviour.
>
> The Sovereign Lord is my strength (Hab. 3:17-19a).

How is it possible to live like this?

Romans, that great Bible study aid on the Old Testament, quotes the key verse in Habakkuk (2:4) and explains how we can live for God.

> I am not ashamed of the gospel, because it is the power of God for the salvation of everyone who believes: first for the Jew, then for the Gentile. For in the gospel a righteousness from God is revealed, a righteousness that is by faith from first to last, just as it is written: *'The righteous will live by faith.'* (Rom. 1:16-17).

The answer is found in the gospel of Jesus Christ. Even if all the signs that point to Him – the land, Zion, priests and sacrifices – are twisted and destroyed, he does not and cannot leave those who look to Him. They are saved!

Listen again to Romans

> Who shall separate us from the love of Christ? Shall trouble or hardship or persecution or famine or nakedness or danger or sword? As it is written: 'For your sake we face death all day long; we are considered as sheep to be slaughtered.' No, in all these things we are more than conquerors through him who loved us. For I am convinced that neither death nor life, neither angels nor demons, neither the present nor the future, nor any powers, neither height nor depth, nor anything else in all creation, will be able to separate us from the love of God that is found in Christ Jesus our Lord (Rom. 8:35-39).

7:3
The message: the judgment of God

We once ran a meeting for gangs who hung around on the streets, who spent their time drinking, smoking, stealing and fighting. I had asked David Davies ,who was in his late eighties at the time, to preach.

'I know he's old but he preached in the huge Congo revival in the 1950s,' I confidently announced to the other leaders.

'That's the 1950s. They'll kill him.'

'Trust me on this one.'

Well he came. And the first five minutes were awful. The boys, in spite of my many and varied threats, were mucking about. I was sweating at the thought of what I was about to put this dear old man through. I also felt a bit of a fool for what I thought was my misplaced confidence. But he too had noticed they weren't listening.

'One man who was saved was a tribal chief. He told me that once you've eaten human flesh all other meat is bland.'

He went on to describe how they would eat a man while he was still alive. Then he spoke of how God changed many in the tribe and how He could change them too.

He didn't understand drugs, drink, or the music they listened to, but he knew sinners of the jungle were no different to sinners in Swansea. They had the same problem – unbelief – and the same solution – Jesus.

So it was in the days of the latter prophets. What mattered was that people heard about their need of a Saviour.

Preparing for mercy

When you read the latter prophets, sin is described as an 'open wound' and a 'sore'. There is lot of talk of God as judge and a lot of talk about how His anger is being poured out.

But why do they want us to understand God's wrath? Why is there so much detail of His wrath? Why is much of it so graphic and relentless in chapter after chapter of description?

Paul shows us in Romans that this is the *beginning* of the good news.

> For in the gospel a righteousness from God is revealed, a righteousness that is by faith from first to last…The wrath of God is being revealed from heaven against all the godlessness and wickedness of men who suppress the truth by their wickedness (Rom. 1:17-18).

Two things are worth noting here. The wrath of God is the beginning of the good news. And to live a righteous life by faith you must understand how the wrath of God is being poured out.

When we read these passages, they are there to prepare for mercy. They show the hopelessness of living away from God so that all will reject that way of life and follow Christ. They teach those who do follow Christ how to live by faith in a hostile world.

In Romans 15, Paul lists a series of quotes taken from these judgment passages, so that 'the Gentiles may glorify God for his mercy' (Rom. 15:9a).

And look how he finishes.

> 'The Root of Jesse will spring up,
> one who will arise to rule over the nations;

the Gentiles will hope in him.'
May the God of hope fill you with all joy and peace as you
trust in him, so that you may overflow with hope by the power
of the Holy Spirit (Rom. 15:12b-13).

Hope in a hopeless world. Jesus and all He is can be enjoyed by
anyone who turns from the judgment of God.

Israel the nation is judged

There are two main strands in the judgment passages. The first
is that Israel is to be judged for rejecting the real King, His law
and His prophets. But why so much emphasis on the judgment
of Israel when they have all the promises?

The Bible is clear that they certainly do have the gospel. They
have the gospel through the law. They have the gospel through
the temple. They have the gospel through the sacrifices. They
have the gospel through circumcision. But all of these gospel
signs do not make them trust Christ!

Because they have all of these things but still refuse to
believe in the Jesus they point to, they are judged.

Enjoying hearing the gospel preached but never repenting,
is turning a blessing into a curse. Having a Bible on your shelf
or attending a Bible church, but never trusting Jesus is turning
the blessing into a curse.

What we see is 'not all who are descended from Israel are
Israel' (Rom. 9:6). You must believe on Jesus before you can
enjoy all that God has for you. If you don't whatever you do is
condemned already. To obey the gospel is greater than sacrifice.
Not to obey the gospel is to miss the whole point of sacrifice.

The false prophets (false because they aren't sent by the
King) will be judged most severely for their lies. Their sole aim
is to tell people not to believe the gospel.

All the nations are judged

The other main strand in the latter prophets is judgment of the
nations. Jesus is their King as well.

Never forget, as terrible as these judgments are, they point to that great day of judgment when God's wrath is poured out on Jesus. How terrible a day it will be when people are judged for rejecting Him!

Note. The Old Testament calls these people 'the nations'. The New Testament calls them 'Gentiles'.

The purpose of these judgment passages is to bring people to believe on Jesus – this is the gospel that needs to be preached today.

7:4
The message: the righteousness of God

Every time we had a family wedding there would be a similar ritual. A good scrub, (I like most little boys hated water and despised soap even more) a shirt – and a tie attached to a piece of elastic. Elderly relatives would grab my cheek and say 'is it the same boy?' I felt like screaming 'Of course it is. I've just got to wear this ridiculous outfit.'

'You've got to dress up or everyone will stare at you,' Mum would say. The argument was just enough to convince even the scruffiest little boy.

I know it's a silly illustration but where can we get an outfit that will stop us feeling out of place and dirty before God? God says clearly we have nothing righteous in ourselves and we deserve only judgment and His anger. The situation seems hopeless and yet Jeremiah says:

> In his days Judah will be saved
> and Israel will live in safety.
> This is the name by which he will be called:
> The Lord Our Righteousness (Jer. 23:6).

This is remarkable. He, the Lord, will become our righteousness. As Romans makes clear this is the hope for everyone who has sinned, Jew or Gentile.

This righteousness from God comes through faith in Jesus Christ to all who believe. There is no difference, for all have sinned and fall short of the glory of God (Rom. 3:22-23).

It is the righteousness that Jesus gives that makes us right. Jonathan Edwards helps us to understand:

> Of these two, God's righteousness and his salvation, the one is the cause, of which the other is the effect. God's righteousness, or covenant mercy, is the root of which his salvation is the fruit.[1]

God's righteousness being revealed makes our salvation possible.

So how is it revealed?

▷The righteousness of God is revealed as He gathers a people and redeems them

> 'Hear the word of the Lord, O nations;
> proclaim it in distant coastlands:
> "He who scattered Israel will gather them
> and will watch over his flock like a shepherd."
> For the Lord will ransom Jacob
> and redeem them from the hand of those stronger than they'
> (Jer. 31:10-11).

Just as God gathered His people at Sinai and just as He gathers churches across the world.

▷The righteousness of God is revealed in a new covenant

> 'The time is coming,' declares the Lord,
> 'when I will make a new covenant with the house of Israel and with the house of Judah.
> It will not be like the covenant I made with their forefathers when I took them by the hand to lead them out of Egypt,
> because they broke my covenant, though I was a husband to them,' declares the Lord.
> 'This is the covenant that I will make with the house of Israel after that time,' declares the Lord,
> 'I will put my law in their minds and write it on their hearts.
> I will be their God, and they will be my people' (Jer. 31:31-33).

The old covenant was only a foreshadowing – this one deals with sin. Because of Jesus we will be able to keep this covenant.

▷The righteousness of God is revealed in a new Davidic King

'The days are coming,' declares the Lord,
'when I will raise up to David a righteous Branch,
a King who will reign wisely and do what is just and right in
    the land.
In his days Judah will be saved and Israel will live in safety.
This is the name by which he will be called:
The Lord Our Righteousness' (Jer. 23:5-6).

▷The righteousness of God is revealed in a new temple
This temple will provide life-giving water to everyone through Jesus and His church.

The man brought me back to the entrance of the temple, and I saw water coming out from under the threshold of the temple towards the east (for the temple faced east). The water was coming down from under the south side of the temple, south of the altar (Ezek. 47:1).

'but whoever drinks the water I give him will never thirst. Indeed, the water I give him will become in him a spring of water welling up to eternal life' (John 4:14).

'Whoever believes in me, as the Scripture has said, streams of living water will flow from within him' (John 7:38).

▷The righteousness of God will be revealed in a new creation

'Behold, I will create
new heavens and a new earth.
The former things will not be remembered,
nor will they come to mind' (Isa. 65:17).

▷The good shepherd Jesus will lead His sheep there

'For this is what the Sovereign Lord says: I myself will search for my sheep and look after them. As a shepherd looks after his scattered flock when he is with them, so will I look after my sheep. I will rescue them from all the places where they were scattered on a day of clouds and darkness. I will bring them out from the nations and gather them from the countries, and I will bring them into their own land. I will pasture them on the mountains of Israel, in the ravines and in all the settlements in the land (Ezek. 34:11-13 see also 34:26-31).

'I am the good shepherd. The good shepherd lays down his life for the sheep' (John 10:11 see also 2 Cor. 5:17).

▷ The righteousness of God will be revealed in the salvation of the nations

'I will keep you and will make you to be a covenant for the people and a light for the Gentiles, to open eyes that are blind, to free captives from prison and to release from the dungeon those who sit in darkness (Isa. 42:6b-7).

I will also make you a light for the Gentiles, that you may bring my salvation to the ends of the earth (Isa. 49:6b).

▷ The Lord's anointed will do all this and bring the righteousness of God

A shoot will come up from the stump of Jesse;
from his roots a Branch will bear fruit.
The Spirit of the Lord will rest on him –
the Spirit of wisdom and of understanding,
the Spirit of counsel and of power,
the Spirit of knowledge and of the fear of the Lord –
and he will delight in the fear of the Lord.
He will not judge by what he sees with his eyes,
or decide by what he hears with his ears;
but with righteousness he will judge the needy,
with justice he will give decisions for the poor of the earth.
He will strike the earth with the rod of his mouth;
with the breath of his lips he will slay the wicked
(Isa. 11:1-4, see also 42:1, 49:1-3, 50:4, 59:21, 61:1).

> **▷When Jesus is anointed everyone will see all righteousness is fulfilled**

Jesus replied, '…it is proper for us to do this to fulfil all righteousness'

…As soon as Jesus was baptised, he went up out of the water. At that moment heaven was opened, and he saw the Spirit of God descending like a dove and lighting on him. And a voice from heaven said, 'This is my Son, whom I love; with him I am well pleased' (Matt. 3:15-17).

Note: the way the Trinity are involved in the work of Jesus, in creation and in the new creation.

Robert M. McCheyne wrote a wonderful hymn teaching us our proper response to the Lord our Righteousness, 'Jehovah Tsidkenu' (Hebrew for 'The Lord Our Righteousness'):

I once was a stranger to grace and to God,
I knew not my danger, and felt not my load;
Though friends spoke in rapture of Christ on the tree,
Jehovah Tsidkenu was nothing to me.

I oft read with pleasure, to sooth or engage,
Isaiah's wild measure and John's simple page;
But e'en when they pictured the blood sprinkled tree
Jehovah Tsidkenu seemed nothing to me.

Like tears from the daughters of Zion that roll,
I wept when the waters went over his soul;
Yet thought not that my sins had nailed to the tree
Jehovah Tsidkenu—'twas nothing to me.

When free grace awoke me, by light from on high,
Then legal fears shook me, I trembled to die;
No refuge, no safety in self could I see—
Jehovah Tsidkenu my Saviour must be.

My terrors all vanished before the sweet name;
My guilty fears banished, with boldness I came
To drink at the fountain, life giving and free—
Jehovah Tsidkenu is all things to me.

Jehovah Tsidkenu! my treasure and boast,
Jehovah Tsidkenu! I ne'er can be lost;
In thee I shall conquer by flood and by field,
My cable, my anchor, my breast-plate and shield!

Even treading the valley, the shadow of death,
This "watchword" shall rally my faltering breath;
For while from life's fever my God sets me free,
Jehovah Tsidkenu, my death song shall be.

(ENDNOTES)
[1] History of Redemption, p.3

7:5
Still looking forward

When we go on holiday and stop at a petrol station en route, one child pipes up from the back of the car, 'Is this it?' To which I reply, 'Look around you. Do you really want to stay here?'

A petrol station is simply a means to an end.

After returning from the exile the people realize they are still not enjoying all that was promised, pale shadows, yes, but nothing like the complete promise.

The numbers are so small. The ten tribes of Israel are scattered among the nations or intermarried with foreigners, so their identity as the people of Israel is compromised. Only 42,360 returned (Ezra 2:64). That's a tiny number compared even with the numbers of the Exodus when 603,550 came out (Num. 1:45-46).

Neither figure is the 'countless' number of the 'stars of the sky' and the 'measureless' number of the 'sand on the seashore' promised to Jeremiah (33:22) and Abraham for that matter.

The temple that was rebuilt is nothing like the huge structure promised in Ezekiel. Listen to Haggai:

> 'Who of you is left who saw this house in its former glory? How does it look to you now? Does it not seem to you like nothing?' (Hag. 2:3).

Malachi ends this section and his message is clear. The people might have returned to the land. The temple, although smaller, might have been rebuilt. But the same problems remain. God hasn't changed but neither has sinful humanity.

> 'I the Lord do not change. So you, O descendants of Jacob, are not destroyed. Ever since the time of your forefathers you have turned away from my decrees and have not kept them. Return to me, and I will return to you,' says the Lord Almighty (Mal. 3:6-7).

But the hope is this – the Lord is coming.

Before He comes Elijah will prepare the way

> 'Remember the law of my servant Moses, the decrees and laws I gave him at Horeb for all Israel. See, I will send you the prophet Elijah before that great and dreadful day of the Lord comes. He will turn the hearts of the fathers to their children, and the hearts of the children to their fathers; or else I will come and strike the land with a curse' (Mal. 4:4-6).

The gospels start with a tremendous sense of anticipation. Where is the Lord's Anointed, the Christ? Each gospel starts with Elijah coming in the person of John the Baptist. And John baptizing Jesus shows how Jesus 'fulfils all righteousness'.

But let's listen to Jesus preaching the Old Testament:

> 'The Spirit of the Lord is on me,
> because he has anointed me to preach good news to the poor.
> He has sent me to proclaim freedom for the prisoners
> and recovery of sight for the blind, to release the oppressed,
> to proclaim the year of the Lord's favour.'

Then he rolled up the scroll, gave it back to the attendant and sat down. The eyes of everyone in the synagogue were fastened on him, and he began by saying to them, 'Today this scripture is fulfilled in your hearing' (Luke 4:18-21).

How wonderfully Paul sums up Jesus' ministry preached in the Old Testament.

For no matter how many promises God has made, they are 'Yes' in Christ (2 Cor. 1:20).

Some people believe that the prophets look forward and we look back. Even though there is some truth in this, it is open to misunderstanding. They did look forward to the cross but they also saw what the cross achieved. They looked forward to the renewed creation that we look forward to. They looked to Jesus as we do (Rom. 3:21-22).

Remember 'there is no difference'! What was written to them is written to us. The Spirit of Christ in them showed them they were serving us.

Conclusion

I was at a seminar in a ministers' conference recently. At the end came a remarkable quote.

'If you would like to understand a post-modern society and how to witness in it, I have two books to recommend.'

The speaker paused, and eager preachers got out their notebooks and pencils.

'One book is Isaiah and the other is Acts.'

Whatever your situation the latter prophets will help you understand the world you face.

> How firm a foundation you saints of the Lord
> Is laid for your faith in his excellent word
> What more can he say, than to you he has said–
> To you, who for refuge to Jesus have fled.

Part Eight
The writings

8:1
Introduction

After a prayer meeting one Wednesday night, we decided to have coffee in McDonald's across the road. I was a bit preoccupied – with one of those trivial problems that take up the mind of a minister in a city-centre church – when suddenly my assistant stopped me, 'Look it's some of the kids from Birchgrove'(the area where I used to work as a church planter).

As I went over to speak to them I could see they were no longer kids. They were teenage girls now, with dyed hair and provocative clothes – dressed for sex. At first I didn't know where to look. And then I remembered they were just kids who needed Jesus – quickly or they were going to get into all kinds of trouble.

I warned and encouraged them to turn to Jesus and to return to the church they used to attend where they were so loved. They listened – as they always did. There was the usual laughter but they were listening. As I walked off I was ecstatic, this is what I used to be doing all the time. This was the greatest thrill in the world.

I sat down in McDonald's with my mind racing and heart pounding. Then somebody made a comment about the way they dressed.

The thought crossed my mind like a punch in the stomach. This is what you *used to do*. You used to spend all your time talking to kids like that. What are you doing now?

I could see them out of the window. I remembered how I used to preach hope and how they would come and hear. I stared into the mess of their lives and where they were going.

What have you done? You've deserted kids like this and for what?

I was losing a grip of myself. Remember the hours of prayer, the abuse you faced, the thrill of Sunday nights as kids and teenagers marched in and swamped the congregation. Look where they've ended up.

I lost it. I never cry but now I was welling up. One of my elders saw as I turned and sobbed.

Afterwards I got control of myself again and went over to sit by the others, joking around as usual. As we were going home I turned to him and said how sorry I was for earlier. He grabbed my arm, looked me in the eye and said, 'Don't be. It was good.'

I must admit I didn't think it was good. In fact, to use a Swansea term, it 'freaked me out.' But he was right. If I was unmoved by what sin had done, what kind of person was I?

I'm not saying that every time a Christian walks into McDonald's he should cry! But being a Christian is more than saying we believe a number of doctrines in our heads, it has to touch us – every part of us.

A huge part of us is how we feel. If Christ is not Lord of our emotions, he is not Lord. How emotions are expressed is another matter but only a fool would deny we have them. It would be a strange thing to think that we are simply rational beings never touched by feelings.

Our feelings so often control what we do. They show what we really believe. We don't have lustful thoughts because we think it is a good idea, we have them because they are what our heart really desires. We don't covet because we think it is a good idea but because it is what our heart really desires.

What we say we believe does not always control the decisions we make in life. It is far more likely to be our emotions expressing what we believe in our hearts.

We need to understand our emotions to understand ourselves, and more importantly to rejoice in Christ. Look at this quote from Jonathan Edwards:

> I should think myself in the way of my duty, to raise the affections of my hearers as high as I possibly can, provided they are affected with nothing but truth, and with affections that are not disagreeable to the nature of what they are affected with.[1]

As we look at the writings, we see how they aim for our emotions so that we can enjoy Christ more. Of course this is true throughout the Bible, but is one of the great themes of the writings – to help us understand ourselves as whole people.

In the Psalms, the Christian through Christ, praises, cries, dances and shouts. In Job he is overwhelmed with sorrow. In Proverbs the emphasis is on desire. In Ecclesiastes there is frustration. In Ruth we see romance. In Lamentations we see weeping. In Daniel, suffering – but knowing hope.

Who can say the Christian life is cold or dull or lifeless!

(ENDNOTES)

[1] Works, Thoughts concerning the revival in the Great Awakening, p. 387

8:2
The Psalms

Before teaching my son how to ride a bike I felt it was essential to explain the importance of him using brakes, keeping his balance around corners and watching out for cars. Needless to say with my teaching abilities not being great, tears soon welled up, 'I can't do it.' After just a few attempts he was adamant, 'No-one can ride this bike.'

As family members stood around looking appalled, I realized there was only one thing for it. I (all fifteen stone of me) would have to ride the tiny bike to prove it could be done.

After that my son decided to have another go – if I promised never to let go. By the end of the holiday I weighed a lot less than fifteen stone. Chasing a bike is no easy task!

Learning to ride a bike is a lot easier if someone shows you how to do it rather than letting you get on with it yourself.

How does the church cope with life and all it brings? Jesus Christ in the Psalms shows us how.

The Psalms are an expression of the church and its life in this world – with all its joys, sorrows, hopes, fears and sufferings. And at the very centre of the church's life is her Christ – so we find His experience expressed in many of the psalms. His life is our life – His enemies are our enemies – His sufferings are experienced by us too. So we can stand with Him and learn from Him how to pray.

But how can He teach me to live in a hostile world? How can He teach me to think about God's Word all the time? How can He teach me to live a life that bears fruit? How can He teach me to pray?

The 'Man' who shows us how to live

This is where Psalm 1 starts. Notice that it doesn't start with 'the men', but **'the Man'** who shows us how to live[1]. Everyone else is lumped together with the wicked – **they** are like chaff that blows away, **they** do not stand; **their** life perishes.

> Blessed is the man who does not walk in the counsel of the wicked or stand in the way of sinners or sit in the seat of mockers. But his delight is in the law of the Lord, and on his law he meditates day and night. He is like a tree planted by streams of water, which yields its fruit in season and whose leaf does not wither. Whatever he does prospers (Ps. 1:1-3).

He is the one who can ascend the holy hill of the Lord. He is the only one 'who has clean hands and a pure heart, who does not lift up his soul to an idol'. He is the one we must look to for help (see Ps. 24:3-6).

Psalm 2

How can we cope when the world seems against us and it seems impossible to go on?

> Why do the nations conspire and the peoples plot in vain? The kings of the earth take their stand and the rulers gather together against the Lord and against his Anointed One (Ps. 2:1-2).

> 'I have installed my King on Zion, my holy hill.' I will proclaim the decree of the Lord: He said to me, 'You are my Son; today I have become your Father. Ask of me, and I will make the nations your inheritance, the ends of the earth your possession (Ps. 2:6-8).

Kiss the Son, lest he be angry and you be destroyed in your way, for his wrath can flare up in a moment. Blessed are all who take refuge in him (Ps. 2:12).

It is Christ, the Lord's Anointed, that we must put our trust in. It is Christ who wins. It is the Son that we must kiss and it is the Son who we must take our refuge in.

For God did not send his Son into the world to condemn the world, but to save the world through him. Whoever believes in him is not condemned, but whoever does not believe stands condemned already because he has not believed in the name of God's one and only Son (John 3:17-18). .

He shows us how to pray

How do we learn to pray in the Psalms? Well, how does Jesus pray?

My God, my God, why have you forsaken me? Why are you so far from saving me, so far from the words of my groaning? (Ps. 22:1).

All who see me mock me; they hurl insults, shaking their heads: 'He trusts in the Lord; let the Lord rescue him. Let him deliver him, since he delights in him' (Ps. 22:7-8).

My strength is dried up like a potsherd, and my tongue sticks to the roof of my mouth; you lay me in the dust of death. Dogs have surrounded me; a band of evil men has encircled me, they have pierced my hands and my feet. I can count all my bones; people stare and gloat over me. They divide my garments among them and cast lots for my clothing. But you, O Lord, be not far off; O my Strength, come quickly to help me (Ps. 22:15-19).

I will declare your name to my brothers; in the congregation I will praise you (Ps. 22: 22).

Hebrews makes it clear that it is Jesus praying in Psalm 22. So **Jesus** is not ashamed to call them brothers. He says,

'I will declare your name to my brothers; in the presence of the congregation I will sing your praises' (Heb. 2:11b-12).

Again Matthew (27:35, 39, 42-43, 46) Mark (15:29-30) and John (19:28) all show it is Jesus speaking in Psalm 22. As you read the psalm it becomes very clear, as with others where the psalmist talks about being blameless, that the speaker can only be Christ.

As we read we see Christ's sufferings and death. We see what it was like for Him, how He coped, how He prayed in the most intense suffering that has ever been. We can learn from Him how to pray in the darkest of hours.

Again we see Him pray in Psalm 16:

Keep me safe, O God, for in you I take refuge.... I have set the Lord always before me. Because he is at my right hand, I will not be shaken. Therefore my heart is glad and my tongue rejoices; my body also will rest secure, because you will not abandon me to the grave, nor will you let your Holy One see decay. You have made known to me the path of life; you will fill me with joy in your presence, with eternal pleasures at your right hand (Ps. 16:1, 8-11).

Acts (2:25-28, 31-32) makes it clear that Psalm 16 is Jesus' prayer given to us by the prophet David[2].

But these psalms are also for us. We can learn that whatever occurs in life and death, we will not be abandoned to the grave because of Jesus Christ. If He went before us through death into resurrection, then we can trust Him to bring us through as well.

David and the Psalms

Jesus uses Psalm 110 as a test to find out whether people understand that He is the Christ:

'What do you think about the Christ? Whose son is he?' 'The son of David,' they replied. He said to them, 'How is it then

> that David, speaking by the Spirit, calls him "Lord"? For he says, "'The Lord said to my Lord: "Sit at my right hand until I put your enemies under your feet."' If then David calls him "Lord", how can he be his son?' (Matt. 22:42-45; Mark 12:35-37; Luke 20:41-44).

The gospels tell us the Pharisees and the Sadducees could not answer a word (Matt. 22:46).

But in Acts 2 Peter tells us exactly what David knew and understood of the resurrection and ascension of Christ, and how then we are to understand the Psalms.

> But he was a prophet and knew that God had promised him on oath that he would place one of his descendants on his throne. Seeing what was ahead, he spoke of the resurrection of the Christ, that he was not abandoned to the grave, nor did his body see decay. God has raised this Jesus to life, and we are all witnesses of the fact. Exalted to the right hand of God, he has received from the Father the promised Holy Spirit and has poured out what you now see and hear. For David did not ascend to heaven, and yet he said, "'The Lord said to my Lord: "Sit at my right hand until I make your enemies a footstool for your feet."' Therefore let all Israel be assured of this: God has made this Jesus, whom you crucified, both Lord and Christ (Acts 2:30-36).

We understand the Psalms, and the Christ, as David did, only when we understand the death, resurrection and suffering of Jesus whom God has made both Lord and Christ.

Look at David writing Psalm 24, and explaining the ascension of Jesus, after His death and resurrection.

> Lift up your heads, O you gates; be lifted up, you ancient doors, that the King of glory may come in. Who is this King of glory? The Lord strong and mighty, the Lord mighty in battle. Lift up your heads, O you gates; lift them up, you ancient doors, that the King of glory may come in. Who is he, this King of glory? The Lord Almighty—he is the King of glory (Ps. 24:7-10).

The sinner's Psalm

We have seen how Jesus speaks in the Psalms as our sinless Saviour and we have seen how David writes about Him in His death, resurrection and ascension. But there is another kind of psalm where David speaks of his faith in Jesus.

Look at Psalm 51:

> Have mercy on me, O God, according to your unfailing love; according to your great compassion blot out my transgressions. Wash away all my iniquity and cleanse me from my sin (Ps. 51:1-2).

> Create in me a pure heart, O God, and renew a steadfast spirit within me. Do not cast me from your presence or take your Holy Spirit from me. Restore to me the joy of your salvation and grant me a willing spirit, to sustain me (Ps. 51:10-12).

> You do not delight in sacrifice, or I would bring it; you do not take pleasure in burnt offerings. The sacrifices of God are a broken spirit; a broken and contrite heart, O God, you will not despise. In your good pleasure make Zion prosper; build up the walls of Jerusalem. Then there will be righteous sacrifices, whole burnt offerings to delight you; then bulls will be offered on your altar (Ps. 51: 16-19).

David teaches us how to repent, to throw ourselves on God's mercy and our desperate need of the Holy Spirit in times of failure, sin and despair.

The sacrifices of God are a broken spirit, a contrite heart

We also get great insight into his understanding of the sacrificial system in this psalm. He realizes that it is not the sacrifices that God delights in, but the penitent believer who trusts in Christ's sacrifice.

He still longs for Zion to prosper and burnt offerings to be given that delight God. So is there a contradiction here?

A wife goes out at Christmas and to show her husband how much she loves him she buys him a computer game. Every time he sees that game she hopes he will see how much she loves him. Everything about the game is to show her love for him.

It doesn't take long before he is spending more time with the computer game than her and when his friends come around he talks more about the computer than her. At the beginning friends are told how amazing his wife is for buying it for him, but soon that face is forgotten and the game becomes everything. Trouble looms in the relationship.

The sacrifices delighted God when they pointed to Christ but not when they were trusted in themselves.

The law of the Lord

David's relationship with the law at first glance appears contradictory. He sacrifices and yet knows God does not delight in sacrifices. He eats the show bread which is not lawful. And yet he is concerned throughout his life for the temple to be built, and the sacrificial system to be set up.

But Jesus explains that David really understands the law.

> He answered, 'Haven't you read what David did when he and his companions were hungry? He entered the house of God, and he and his companions ate the consecrated bread – which was not lawful for them to do, but only for the priests. Or haven't you read in the Law that on the Sabbath the priests in the temple desecrate the day and yet are innocent? I tell you that one greater than the temple is here. If you had known what these words mean, "I desire mercy, not sacrifice," you would not have condemned the innocent. For the Son of Man is Lord of the Sabbath' (Matt. 12:3-8).

When David stared at the temple he could see one greater than the temple. When David enjoyed his Sabbath rest he enjoyed it because he enjoyed the Lord of the Sabbath. He loved the law only because Christ was the end of the law. The law never became an end in itself.

In Psalm 119 he is ecstatic about the law. He loves it, and in nearly every verse he tells us the reason he loves it – because it is 'the law of *the Lord*', 'it is *his* statutes', 'they are *your* decrees', '*your* commands'.

The law affects every part of David's life. It causes delight, it is his life preserver, his strength, it saves from shame and disgrace, it is his salvation, his hope, his freedom, comfort in suffering and contentment. It makes him discerning, rescues his soul, helps him cope with abuse, is better than money and the best food, it teaches him to encourage others, brings the love of God to him, makes him wise, guides his life, makes simple people wise, helps him know God's face shining on him, is a place of hope in a difficult world, gives understanding, hope for answered prayer, and causes him to praise.

It is little wonder he says, 'Oh how I love your law! I meditate on it all day long.'

Look at how he ends the psalm.

> I long for your salvation, O Lord, and your law is my delight.
> Let me live that I may praise you, and may your laws sustain
> me (Ps. 119:174-175).

David knows the Lord saves, not the law. The law's delight is that it is a schoolmaster to lead him to Christ. He ends the psalm praising the law. He longs to live to praise the Lord who gave it.

Throughout the Psalms the experience of the church is seen in the light of Christ and His wonderful law that teaches us about Him.

Jesus came that we might have life and life to the full. Learn to live it from Him and with Him.

(Endnotes)

[1] The great Augustine, church leader of the 4th century, begins his commentary on the Psalms by showing that Psalm 1 is all about Jesus. He begins: " 1. "Blessed is the man that hath not gone away in the counsel of the ungodly" (v. 1). This is to be understood of our Lord Jesus Christ, the Lord Man…. "And he shall be like a tree planted hard by the running streams of waters" (v. 3); that is Very "Wisdom," who vouchsafed to assume man's nature for our salvation"

[2] David is a prophet and a king

8:3
Job

Emma Freeman was a member of the first church I pastored. She was diagnosed with a brain tumour at the age of nine. Her hair fell out and it was thought she would not live very long. An unnecessary operation caused her to have a stroke.

One morning Emma was in her grandmother's house. Her Aunty Sue had popped in to see her and to help with lunch. Emma was sitting, bolstered on cushions in the faded armchair in the corner of the room.

'I don't know Emma, you will sit in my chair, and you know that's my favourite one. Are you ready for lunch yet?'

Sue draped a tea towel across her niece's front to act as a bib; eating was such a messy business these days.

'I'll just go and fix the dinner.'

Ten minutes later she brought in the tray of food. Emma was singing to herself, very softly, eyes closed. She drew a little nearer wondering what she was singing. Through the muffled words she could just make out the tune, then some of the words. She was singing a hymn. One of their favourite hymns

> I am not skilled to understand
> What God has willed
> What God has planned
> I only know at his right hand,
> Stands one who is my Saviour

She put the tray down, put her face in her hands and cried out to God. Not once had Emma been bitter, not once bad-tempered, always trusting in her Saviour. Only God's grace could have done that.[1]

How does God sustain Christians in terrible trials? Could He sustain me?

When his life fell apart, Job did not know the circumstances or reasons of his suffering. But as chapters 1-3 clearly show, he, like us, was called to show off God's manifold wisdom in Christ. Look what Ephesians says:

> His intent was that now, through the church, the manifold wisdom of God should be made known to the rulers and authorities in the heavenly realms, according to his eternal purpose which he accomplished in Christ Jesus our Lord (Eph. 3:10-11).

Job is brutally honest with God about how he feels. He understood what we must understand. Again look at the same passage in Ephesians:

> In him and through faith in him we may approach God with freedom and confidence (Eph. 3:12).

His prayers appear quite extreme, but he is coming boldly before God with freedom and confidence, because he is coming in Christ. This is his confidence. In suffering he can be painfully honest before God – because of Christ.

Job's Redeemer

Listen to his confession in the middle of his suffering:

> 'Oh, that my words were recorded, that they were written on a scroll, that they were inscribed with an iron tool on lead, or engraved in rock for ever!' (Job 19: 23-24).

I think we can safely say the next statement is important to him!

'I know that my Redeemer lives, and that in the end he will stand upon the earth' (Job 19: 25).

It is Jesus he looks to as his only Redeemer. Jesus is the one he knows.

'And after my skin has been destroyed, yet in my flesh I will see God; I myself will see him with my own eyes – I, and not another. How my heart yearns within me!' (Job 19: 26-27).

His great hope is the Second Coming of Christ and all that will bring.

Samuel Medley in 1775 captured the heart of Job's faith in Jesus Christ with his famous hymn:

I know that my Redeemer lives;
What comfort this sweet sentence gives!
He lives, he lives, who once was dead;
He lives, my ever living Head.

He lives to bless me with his love,
He lives to plead for me above.
He lives my hungry soul to feed,
He lives to help in time of need.

He lives triumphant from the grave,
He lives eternally to save,
He lives all glorious in the sky,
He lives exalted there on high.

He lives to grant me rich supply,
He lives to guide me with his eye,
He lives to comfort me when faint,
He lives to hear my soul's complaint.

He lives to silence all my fears,
He lives to wipe away my tears
He lives to calm my troubled heart,
He lives all blessings to impart.

He lives, my kind, wise, heavenly Friend,
He lives and loves me to the end;
He lives, and while he lives, I'll sing;
He lives, my Prophet, Priest, and King.

He lives and grants me daily breath;
He lives, and I shall conquer death:
He lives my mansion to prepare;
He lives to bring me safely there.

He lives, all glory to his Name!
He lives, my Jesus, still the same.
Oh, the sweet joy this sentence gives,
I know that my Redeemer lives!

This joyful faith in Jesus Christ is why Job in his suffering can cry triumphantly:

> 'The Lord gave and the Lord has taken away; may the name of the Lord be praised'(Job 1:21b).

The end of the book

At the end of the book his Redeemer encourages and humbles him with a series of questions which Job knows he has the answer to even if he does not. Let's choose one:

> 'Have the gates of death been shown to you? Have you seen the gates of the shadow of death?' (Job 38:17).

Job knows Jesus has. Seeing his Redeemer humbles him and brings great joy (see the final chapter). Because of his trust in Christ alone and because of his honesty in prayer, God says that Job has spoken 'what is right' (see Job 42:8).

Throughout his sufferings Job would not be turned by his friends' health, wealth and prosperity teaching – which we are told proved their unbelief (see Job 42:7-9).

They believed that his suffering was caused by personal sin. They are conclusively proved wrong at the end of the book. They witness the relentless slaughter as seven bulls suffer and die individually and seven rams suffer and die individually under the command of God and are consumed in the burnt offering.

What had they done to deserve such suffering? They were innocent victims of suffering for others.

The sacrifice, as with all the sacrifices, points to the sacrifice of the innocent Lamb of God who consumed the wrath of God against us, so that we, the guilty, can receive twice the blessing that we would have if we had never sinned! All this, if we put our trust in Him.

The lesson is obvious when we suffer we are to:

> Be patient, then, brothers, until the Lord's coming. See how the farmer waits for the land to yield its valuable crop and how patient he is for the autumn and spring rains. You too, be patient and stand firm, because the Lord's coming is near. Don't grumble against each other, brothers, or you will be judged. The Judge is standing at the door!
>
> Brothers, as an example of patience in the face of suffering, take the prophets who spoke in the name of the Lord. As you know, we consider blessed those who have persevered. You have heard of Job's perseverance and have seen what the Lord finally brought about. The Lord is full of compassion and mercy (James 5:7-11).

Our Redeemer is full of compassion and mercy. Trust Him and – as with Job in the final chapter – we will be rewarded when the Lord comes back.

(ENDNOTES)

[1] Clare Levy, Just an Orange, p.92

8:4
Solomon's books

Proverbs – Wisdom and godly living
As a boy playing football on the streets I would be right in the middle of the FA Cup Final:

'Last goal wins!' the cry would go up.

Then another voice could be heard.

'Steve, tea's ready!'

If it was Mum it was best to plead temporary deafness. But there was a voice that had to be listened to – if this was ignored there were dire consequences – Dad's!

In a world of many conflicting voices David advises his son Solomon (Prov. 1-9) to listen to one voice and reject all others – the voice of the person who is Wisdom.

> Christ Jesus, who has become for us wisdom from God (1 Cor. 1:30).

There are many other voices calling for our attention – especially when we are young. There are many ways that seem right to a man but they all end in death. Our desire must be for Wisdom and in this person all we need is found.

Proverbs 10-31 are a description (like the Sermon on the Mount) of life in harmony with Wisdom. Many of these proverbs make us smile but they touch all of life.

There is another theme that overarches the book and that is sex and its fulfilment in marriage and the home. This is the context for godly living. The book shows what the home and hospitality (the missing gift of the Western Christian church) can achieve. It is little wonder that the book ends with the description of the noble wife.

How many Christians have discovered how to live the Christian life while sitting in this kind of home, while talking over a meal or drinking a cup of coffee? If only more Christians would exercise this God-given gift, how much would be achieved for the kingdom!

The question is often asked – where are the godly men in the church – but where are the godly homes? And is this what we are teaching young Christians to aspire to?

Song of Songs – a greater marriage

When I read this book as an eleven-year-old for the first time, I'll confess I thought someone had 'sneaked it in' and in 2,000 years nobody had noticed!

Then someone told me it was about marriage and only marriage, which I thought was great as in it the husband is without sin and everything that goes wrong is the woman's fault.

When I got married I was sure I would find that I was sinless, my wife would be the cause of all our problems and I would lovingly restore her. Actually I realized that couldn't be right – but we all like to live in fantasy land occasionally!

In Hosea we are shown a marriage to reflect a greater marriage – Hosea and his prostitute wife Gomer – reflecting Christ and His love for the church. Also in Ephesians 5, as Paul is talking about rules for marriage and intimacy he says:

This is a profound mystery – but I am talking about Christ and the church (Eph. 5:32).

Marriage is God-given but it is not an end in itself. It exists to reflect a greater marriage between Christ and the church. Just as the godly home in Proverbs is not an end in itself but to reflect the home Jesus is making for us in heaven.

Hudson Taylor the great missionary was right in his excellent commentary on this book, *'It is the marriage love between Jesus and his church'.[1]*

It is as we see the intimacy that Jesus has for the church that we can make sense of the passionate and what some might see as extreme language He uses towards His people's adultery in Ezekiel, Jeremiah and Hosea. He longs for intimacy. He is appalled at His people's unfaithfulness. We are to reject all others and enjoy Him.

Jesus wants us to know His love. He doesn't want to be outside knocking on the door (Song. 5:2-6 and Rev. 3:20).

Ecclesiastes

I knew a student in Bible college who when listening to a long dull lecture on Ecclesiastes shouted out, 'Isn't there a time for coffee?'

This book is so negative it can get you down. It simply states the opposite to Proverbs – especially Proverbs 8. Proverbs tells us to seek Wisdom. Ecclesiastes says it is foolish (or stupid) not to follow Christ your creator. All other voices are futile.

Remember Him while you are still young. Remember Him before you make a fool of yourself.

(ENDNOTES)
[1] Union and Communion, The Marriage of Love between Jesus and His Church

8:5
The exiled, the outsider and the persecuted

Lamentations – living in a hopeless world
Lamentations is a book about the mess sin has caused – the mess of exile from God – and facing it. It is a heart-rending book. When everything is laid waste, where is Jesus then?

> Because of the Lord's great love we are not consumed, for his compassions never fail. They are new every morning; great is your faithfulness. I say to myself, 'The Lord is my portion; therefore I will wait for him' (Lam. 3:22-24).

How can this hope be known in the context of such suffering and despair? Listen again:

> The Lord's anointed, our very life breath, was caught in their traps (Lam. 4:20a).

Christ, the Lord's Anointed, is their very life breath and He understands. He too was a man of sorrows and knew constant grief.

If our 'life breath' is with us we can face a terrible world and even a failing church.

Daniel – living in a hostile world
Is there anything harder than going into a workplace or classroom when you are the only Christian – when the people around you are so different to you? You know at some point you are going to have to speak out – and it will cost.

If you've faced this, then Daniel is the book for you.

We see Shadrach, Meshach and Abednego making a great stand and knowing fellowship in Christ's sufferings. Who can forget the Son of Man joining them in the fiery furnace? We see them, and Daniel, glorying in – even embracing – sufferings for Christ.

Look at Daniel before the threat of the lion's den.

> Now when Daniel learned that the decree had been published, he went home to his upstairs room where the windows opened towards Jerusalem. Three times a day he got down on his knees and prayed, giving thanks to his God, just as he had done before (Dan. 6:10, see also 3:16-18).

Was that wise? But they knew the beginning of wisdom is to fear the Lord. That is how the wise live.

Unlikely conversions

We also see the most unusual person being converted – Nebuchadnezzar the destroyer of Jerusalem.

> Now I, Nebuchadnezzar, praise and exalt and glorify the King of heaven (Dan. 4:37a).

In the early part of the book we see how God speaks to unbelievers in different ways. Because they don't hear what he is saying they are left confused and fearful (Dan. 5:9). The same thing happens to Nebuchadnezzar before he is converted.

However hard it may be in a hostile world, 'There is a God in heaven.' He is always closer than we think and the world is never out of his control.

Glorious visions

The book finishes with a series of glorious visions.

It is said that when astronauts go into space they never return feeling the same. When asked why, one of the astronauts gave this reply:

In space the world looks so small. If you place your hand in front of it, it all disappears – everything – the great empires, the pyramids, the USA, the cities and towns you know so well. Everything is gone! You cannot live life the same way again once you have seen the world like that!

So it is with the visions. They are meant to change the way you look at the world around you, whether your classroom or workplace or neighbourhood, because:

Blessed is the one who waits for and reaches the end… (Dan. 12:12a).

Kingdoms and rulers – as powerful as they may seem – all eventually pass away, because there is a God in heaven and there is only one kingdom that lasts.

'In my vision at night I looked, and there before me was one like a son of man, coming with the clouds of heaven. He approached the Ancient of Days and was led into his presence. He was given authority, glory and sovereign power; all peoples, nations and men of every language worshipped him. His dominion is an everlasting dominion that will not pass away, and his kingdom is one that will never be destroyed' (Dan. 7:13-14).

In a hostile world, this is how to live.

Nehemiah and Ezra – both building for Christ
In the Hebrew Bible these were one book – and as you read them the reasons become obvious.

Ezra is concerned with building the temple and Nehemiah is concerned with rebuilding Jerusalem – they worked together in these great tasks.

Both wanted to build something God had appointed – to show off the glory of Christ in the gospel. Both emphasize the importance of prayer in the task. Both emphasize the importance of God's law. Both emphasize the need to confess sin and know forgiveness in Christ. Both of them know all kinds of persecution while carrying out their tasks.

In Ezra even though the temple is to be rebuilt as a witness, everyone sees that the glory does not descend (as happened with the previous temple). They know the temple is just a shadow.

We see in Ezra, as is always the case with God's people, their lives are to reflect the gospel. And in Nehemiah it is clear that all the people, whatever their background, are to make every effort to help in gospel work as they are taught to live lives that glorify God.

We too are in the business of building to show off the glory of God – but it is churches we must get involved in building up now:

> And in him you too are being built together to become a dwelling in which God lives by his Spirit (Eph. 2:22).

Why the lists?

In Nehemiah there are a number of lists. Why?

In Junior School once, I broke my elbow in three places and was banned from playing football for four months. That 'four month' date was circled in red on my wall planner. The date arrived, the doctor declared me fit and I let the teacher know.

I remember vividly the names of the team going up on the notice board…

Central midfield – Stephen Levy

Sure I was only eleven, but seeing my name there made that piece of paper probably the most precious piece of paper in my entire school life. To an outsider it was just a list of names but to me it was so much more.

And so we need to be careful how we read these lists in Nehemiah. If we are believers our names have gone up on the board as well. How precious to know your name is written in the 'Lamb's book of life' (Rev. 21:27, see also Ps. 87).

We have much to learn from Nehemiah and Ezra.

Ruth – hope for the outsider

Ruth is an outsider in every sense of the word. The book emphasizes how vulnerable she is. She marries a man who should never have left the land of blessing and who certainly shouldn't have married a Gentile like her. Then he dies and leaves her as a young widow. But in spite of all this she wants her mother-in-law's God to be her God (see Ruth 1:16).

Boaz chooses to buy her back out of her situation and into his people – even though he doesn't have to. Jesus also chooses to buy her back.

And who can argue that this woman belongs to God's people when we see in print that she is David's great-grandmother (Ruth 4:18-22).

There is hope for the outsider in the gospel – when Jesus is your kinsman redeemer.

Esther – when God's name isn't even mentioned

How is life to be lived for Christ when everybody in the world ignores him?

The people are exiled and the name of God is not spoken of. There are even people out to destroy them. In a situation like this how should they live for God? How are His purposes worked out?

The book of Esther shows the wise way to live in a world where God's name is never even mentioned.

Where does the real power lie?

The book begins with a description of the man who is supposed to be ruling the world, Xerxes. And what a great man he is.

> 'Xerxes who ruled over 127 provinces stretching from India to Cush.' (Esther 1:1).

He throws a party to show what a powerful man he is:

> For a full 180 days he displayed the vast wealth of his kingdom and the splendour and glory of his majesty (Esther 1:4).

It is all very impressive and he appears to be all-powerful. He is the one who rules. But when he asks his wife to come in and join them she refuses point-blank, 'No' (1:1). He is humiliated in front of everyone.

So where does the real power lie?

He is furious but he is 'told' by his advisers to take a new wife. He ends up selecting the godly Mordecai's step-daughter Esther (2:7).

Despite his grand introduction he seems to have very little control over his private life, let alone the lives of the people in the 127 provinces he is supposed to rule.

Haman, who hates Mordecai and God's people, gains power and tricks the king into a plot to destroy them (chapter 3). Again, it is not the king in control but those who scheme and plot – the enemies of God's people.

So where does the real power lie?

God's people humble themselves and cry out to him (4:1-3) and the gallows prepared to hang Mordecai are used to hang Haman. Many Gentiles see where the real power lies and join God's people.

Many people of other nationalities 'became Jews because fear of the Jews had seized them' (Esth. 8:17b).

Those who plot against God's people find their end is always the opposite of their plans (9:2).

Mordecai is promoted to second in the kingdom (10:2-3) and he works for the welfare of God's people. He knows the only thing worth living for is God and God's people.

Mordecai knows Christ who has been raised from the dead and is seated in 'heavenly realms':

> far above all rule and authority, power and dominion, and every title that can be given, not only in the present age but also in the one to come. And God placed all things under his feet and appointed him to be head over everything for the church, which is his body, the fulness of him who fills everything in every way' (Eph. 1:21-23).

In a world that ignores God when power and influence seem to lie elsewhere, in a world where Christ is ignored and not named, his purposes do not fail.

Live for Him and you will find that the kingdoms of this world will end and become the 'kingdom of our Lord and of his Christ' (Rev. 11:15).

This is the wise way to live! The people of the nations saw it (Esther 8:15-16). Mordecai saw it. Esther saw it. Have you?

8:6
Chronicles – a huge overview

Lloyd Jones says, 'Repetition is the key to great teaching.'

I'll say that again. Repetition is the key to great teaching!

Usually when I start a talk with this quote, there is a terrible groan from the congregation. And yet repetition is key in Scripture.

As we have seen, the core truth of the whole Bible is found in the first three verses of the Bible. Every time we read we seem to see something new but the gospel doesn't change when you read through the Bible. Jesus isn't greater at the end than he is at the beginning. The end of the Bible tells us that.

Ask any Christian, do they love Jesus more now than they did when they were first saved, and they will say yes. Ask them, do they know more about Jesus now than they did when they were first saved, and they will say yes. So is Jesus greater now than then? Of course not. All that has happened is understanding has increased.

Jesus is no greater now than He has ever been.

When He is held up as Creator at the beginning of the Bible all we needed to know about His creative and redemptive power was seen. But like a diamond held up, it is one thing to see it the first time, how much greater to study it and see and appreciate its beauty from every angle. The diamond has not changed, but our appreciation has.

Chronicles is the last book of the Law, the Prophets and the Writings. It really is a huge overview and is full of repetition – yet in it all we see the glory of Jesus again.

God keeps His promises

1 Chronicles starts with Adam in verse 1. There is a brief history of all the nations of the known world (1 Chron. 1:5-16). All these are remembered and are part of God's good purpose.

We see how God has not only been faithful in providing a seed for Adam, but how He has been faithful in keeping the line of Abraham. He has provided for the twelve tribes. He has provided a line for David, for the High Priests and the Levites. God is interested in the details of all His promises, and not one of His promises fails.

The exile comes right at the start of the book (1 Chron. 9:1-34). God makes sure we know at the outset, He is still in control, and the promised Messiah will come.

No-one can doubt that, having seen the detail he gives at the beginning of Chronicles.

An overview of David

David who points to the coming Messiah, is reintroduced, gathering around him his mighty warriors. Many are from the nations, for example Uriah the Hittite (11:41) and Ithmah the Moabite (11:46). The Messiah is for the nations.

The theme of the ark is introduced, because it is where the one who is enthroned between the cherubim sits and the people can enquire of the Lord. It is where the real decisions get made (13:3); where the real King sits. Listen to David's prayer when the ark is restored to the centre of God's people:

> Ascribe to the Lord, O families of nations, ascribe to the Lord glory and strength, ascribe to the Lord the glory due to his name. Bring an offering and come before him; worship the Lord in the splendour of his holiness. Tremble before him, all the earth! The world is firmly established; it cannot be moved. Let the heavens rejoice, let the earth be glad; let them say among the nations, 'The Lord reigns!' (1 Chron. 16:28-31).

David's great desire is that the family of nations might praise the King enthroned between the cherubim; the King whose ark is but a symbol of His authority. He wants heaven and earth to join together in joy and gladness because the Lord reigns and He should be praised by all. He is worth it.

The great Messianic prophecy occurs in chapter 17.

> I will set him over my house and my kingdom for ever; his throne will be established for ever (1 Chron. 17:14).

And the nations submit to David who reflects his greater Son (chs. 18–20).

The temple revisited

Then comes the great cosmic picture of the heavens and earth – the temple the Messiah will rule over (1 Chron. 21-29).

David is clearly excited about the temple and all it points to, but he knows who the real King over heaven and earth is.

> David praised the Lord in the presence of the whole assembly, saying, 'Praise be to you, O Lord, God of our father Israel, from everlasting to everlasting. Yours, O Lord, is the greatness and the power and the glory and the majesty and the splendour, for everything in heaven and earth is yours. Yours, O Lord, is the kingdom; you are exalted as head over all' (1 Chron. 29:10-11).

Life on this present earth is not it, as all the believers in the Old Testament knew so well:

> We are aliens and strangers in your sight, as were all our forefathers. Our days on earth are like a shadow, without hope (1 Chron. 29:15).

The temple dominates the first ten chapters of 2 Chronicles. The main part of the temple (2 Chron. 3:4-7) is still cut off from the ark. This is still in the Most Holy Place, behind the curtain with cherubim, guarding sinners from seeing God's rule (2 Chron. 3:14). The priests and sacrifices are still there to break through the curtain (1 Chron. 23-24 and 2 Chron. 5).

Heaven and earth are still divided – waiting for the Christ to come.

Solomon clearly rejoices in the temple. He like his father could see the gospel illustrated in the temple and yet see that the temple **was only** an illustration.

> But will God really dwell on earth with men? The heavens, even the highest heavens, cannot contain you. How much less this temple that I have built! (2 Chron. 6:18).

The rest of the book is dominated by David's sons, who are clearly not the Christ, and the declining state of the temple, again pointing to the new heavens and earth.

The people are constantly reminded not only to look forward to the coming Saviour but to look back and trust the same Saviour of their fathers.

No easy ride

One of the constant problems of the Christian life is our continued disappointment with ourselves.

'Why do I feel so low as a Christian?'

'Why can't the times I'm close to God last?'

Behind this thinking is the myth that the Christian life is to be lived with every day being a little better than the day before.

If only the Christian life was like cycling in Holland – flat and steady! My Christian life is like cycling in the Alps – sometimes faster than I can cope with, sometimes so hard I have to get off and push, and sometimes even going backwards.

I have to add here I've never even been to Holland or the Alps, let alone cycled there! My views are formed on hearsay – which only seems to reinforce the point. Expectations for the Christian life are often based on books that cannot be checked out or travelling preachers and their stories.

The Bible describes the Christian life as full of highs and lows, ups and downs. And this is clearly seen in 2 Chronicles in the period between Solomon and the exile.

The pattern is not dissimilar to the highs and lows at the beginning of Judges or Numbers, to the lives of Abraham or David, or to the pattern of church history.

From Solomon there is no gradual slide into exile 345 years later. The church does not go silently into the night, it rages and fights hard to enjoy God blessings.

Occasionally the people of God repent and cry out to God and there are great revivals. Occasionally there are kings like David and apostles like Paul who can say 'Follow me as I follow Christ'.

One such revival occurs in Israel's darkest hour – halfway through Manasseh, the most godless king's reign (2 Chron. 33:15).

The church of Jesus Christ can never be written off.

The greatest revival

But the most remarkable of these revivals is found in 2 Chronicles 34-35 under the rule of Josiah. It takes place after one of the darkest times in Israel's history and just before the exile, *the* darkest time in the church's history. It is the greatest revival of all (2 Chron. 35:18).

Because God has done this in the past the Latter Prophets can pray 'revive your work in the middle of the years'. If He did it in the darkest hour He can do it again.

Do you despair of the ups and downs in your Christian walk? Do you despair of the ups and downs in your own church? Pray for revival.

Remember, when Paul talks of running the race he is not talking about a treadmill in an air-conditioned health club or in a stadium with a soft track and athletic spikes to help you run. He speaks of running a marathon in Greece, with a spectacular view but with hard work, never being sure what is around the corner, feeling like giving up but knowing you need to press on.

Pray that God will revive you.

The end of the Old Testament as Jesus knew it
The end of the Old Testament is extraordinary – a Gentile king, Cyrus, who clearly recognizes the division between heaven and earth, issues this command:

> 'This is what Cyrus king of Persia says: "The Lord, the God of heaven, has given me all the kingdoms of the earth and he has appointed me to build a temple for him at Jerusalem in Judah. Anyone of his people among you – may the Lord his God be with him, and let him go up"' (2 Chron. 36:23).

But the question still remains.

Where is the Messiah who rules the heavens and earth and tears down the curtain? Where is the Messiah whose Kingdom will never end? Where is the Christ who brings the Gentiles in? Where is the Christ who is the Lord of all history?

This is why the New Testament starts with one question:

'Are you the Christ?'

Part Nine
The gospels

9:1
What's really going on?

My aunt had a picture on her wall of an old lady in church – or so it appeared.

'What do you see?' she would ask me.

'An old lady in church.'

'Anything else?'

'She looks a bit smug.'

'Anything else?'

'There's another old lady sitting behind her.'

'Look closely at her outfit.'

'She's dressed as if she's better than everyone else?'

Then she pointed it out – the shape of the devil in her shawl.

From then on whenever I looked at that picture I could see the woman for the hypocrite she was. But I never would have seen it unless my aunt had pointed it out to me.

Sometimes we see things straight away – sometimes we need help.

A similar thing (although with quite the opposite point) happens in the gospels. Jesus is born to a fearful, troubled young woman in the stench of a cattle shed. Most people don't notice or care enough to provide even a room. But from another vantage point angels rejoice, a star is created, and those who understand bow down and worship Him as God with us.

What is going on? It is as clear as day to those who can see, but as black as night to those who can't – and there appears to be no in-between.

A running commentary

Throughout the gospels there is a commentary going on – documentary-style – to help us understand there is often more than meets the eye taking place. The stories are broken up with phrases such as, 'All this took place to fulfil what the Lord had said through the prophet' or, 'It is written'.

It soon becomes clear that the Old Testament is our guide to what is unfolding in the gospels, pointing out things we might otherwise never see. Very often the Old Testament is quoted without any explanation – there is simply an assumption we will know the background.

This is a commentary we are supposed to already know, because it is a salvation that has already been clearly promised.

Sometimes Jesus' language is even stronger. He acts because He must 'fulfil all righteousness'. Isn't He God? Can't He do what He likes?

But God cannot lie. The Old Testament believers put their trust in the Jesus of Scripture. He has to fulfil all that Scripture speaks about Him for the salvation of their souls.

A timeless commentary

Often the Old Testament passages quoted seem plucked out of their time. Jesus quotes from one of Isaiah's sermons, for example, and yet He says clearly that this is a direct prophesy about His listeners.

'You hypocrites! Isaiah was right when *he prophesied about you:*

> "These people honour me with their lips, but their hearts are far from me. They worship me in vain; their teachings are but rules taught by men"'(Matt. 15: 7-9).

So what's going on? Is Jesus taking Isaiah's words out of context and applying them to his hearers? To imply such a thing would be blasphemy. So what are we to make of these and other quotes?

There is a simple answer. God's Word is timeless. What applied in Isaiah's time is a word for Jesus' time and a word for ours – no explanation needed.

Sin hasn't changed. Salvation in Jesus hasn't changed. The point is this: if you know the Scriptures and understand them you will believe on Jesus.

One message

The whole Bible commands us to believe on Jesus, as Jesus Himself points out:

> 'These are the Scriptures that testify about me, yet you refuse to come to me to have life… If you believed Moses, you would believe me, for he wrote about me. But since you do not believe what he wrote, how are you going to believe what I say?' (John 5:39b-40, 46-47).

The more you read the Old Testament the more the gospels make sense – after all they are written with the same purpose.

> But these are written that you may believe that Jesus is the Christ (John 20:31a).

The fact is we need both Old and New Testaments.

> 'Do not think that I have come to abolish the Law or the Prophets; I have not come to abolish them but to fulfil them' (Matt. 5:17).

The Old Testament makes sense of the New. The New Testament makes sense of the Old. Many Christians only read the New Testament but this is a mistake. When you meet Jesus and see Him as the key, the response is obvious. You will want to read the whole Bible.

Listen to the two people on the road to Emmaus:

> 'Were not our hearts burning within us while he talked with us on the road and opened the Scriptures to us?' (Luke 24:32b).

It would be strange to think that having had such an experience they never read the Old Testament again.

We can be sure of this; they never read the Old Testament again without seeing Jesus as its centre. And my suspicion is they read it more and more because they had met the risen Christ.

The Pharisees, Sadducees and scribes

I remember as a boy being taken to the pantomime at Christmas. Whenever the villain entered the stage the booing and whistling was so loud most of what he said couldn't be heard. I used to feel a bit sorry for him.

The Pharisees, Sadducees and scribes usually provoke a similar reaction. One man in a church, after hearing a sermon on the 'Pharisee and the Tax Collector' prayed at the communion table:

'Lord, we thank you we are not like the Pharisees.'

And so many of us secretly feel the same.

So why are these groups here? Why do the gospels and Acts make so much of them? And why when they believe such different things are they placed together?

They are there to show that it is possible to completely misunderstand the Bible.

If we are honest with ourselves we all do this in part. In fact many authors and preachers are fully paid-up-members of the 'Pharisee society' of the twenty-first century!

So what are they like?

The Pharisees loved to be asked to pray in meetings and admired people who took part in services. They felt strongly about worshipping God correctly and were deeply disturbed when others got it wrong. They were concerned about political action, sexual purity and the condition of the poor. They had an extraordinary knowledge of the contents of the Bible.

Their problem was twofold. They knew the Bible but they didn't understand it – or more to the point they wouldn't understand it. And they refused to see the law was about Jesus.

They could not understand that Jesus met Abraham. They get incredibly annoyed when Jesus says He is the 'I am'. They even want to kill Him for making such a claim.

The reason they do not understand the Scripture is because they do not understand themselves or their condition.

Wrong diagnosis, wrong cure

As I write this I am taking part in a medical exam. Young, very young (!) student doctors are examining me and others with unusual medical conditions.

They have to do two things. They must tell the examiners what is wrong with me and they must state the cure. If they get the diagnosis wrong it is quite possible they could seriously harm me with the wrong cure.

The Pharisee says, 'I don't need a Saviour. I'm okay. I keep the law.'

But you cannot read the law like that. It brings the knowledge of sin. It shows that what is inside makes us unclean. It brings us to the end of ourselves. It makes us realize we cannot keep it, but Christ can.

The Pharisee says, 'If that is true, then the law doesn't make me feel great about myself or the fact I can trace my family line back to Abraham. It makes me feel terrible. I can't bear feeling bad about myself.'

It is interesting to note that the sinners and the tax collectors accept Jesus. They already know they are wrong. They are delighted someone has explained why and delighted to accept the cure.

Jesus answered them, 'It is not the healthy who need a doctor, but the sick. I have not come to call the righteous, but sinners to repentance' (Luke 5:31-32).

Jesus leaves the sheep who think they are okay in the wilderness. It is the lost ones who are found and taken home.

You don't need to know the law to know you are a lost sinner – the law simply diagnoses more symptoms.

The disease is sin. It results in death. The cure is Christ.

Tragically wrong

The Pharisees, Sadducees and scribes believed the Old Testament was about Abraham, about Moses looking for an earthly land, and about putting your faith in sacrifices. They invested everything in this.

Anyone who believed differently was attacking all they had put their trust in. Jesus and all who preached about Him had to be stopped.

They disagreed on so much, but on this they were agreed. They could not see their sin or their need of a Saviour.

That is why they are placed together in the Bible. That is why they are all tragically wrong.

Beware of the leaven of the Pharisees

I couldn't be like that.
I couldn't twist Scripture.
I love Jesus too much.
I thank God I'm not like the Pharisee.

I came home the other day to find my eight-month-old baby crawling up the stairs. At eight months babies shouldn't crawl up stairs. Whether they should or shouldn't – this one did.

Babies and toddlers need to be watched and you cannot predict what will happen with them next.

Our hearts are unpredictable and they end up in dangerous places before we know it.

At one time, every month at our house we would meet for Bible study. The congregation would have read the same book of the Bible and we would share what we had learnt together. One week we were on Philippians:

'Unity of the church.'
'Joy.'
'Suffering.'
'Dancing.'

'Dancing!' Whatever book of the Bible we looked at dancing would be in there somewhere! It turned out that even Nahum's destruction of Nineveh could be about dancing!

We will twist the Bible and make it about anything we want as long as it isn't about my sin and Jesus my Saviour. But it is easy to see flaws in others.

I must cry out, 'God, have mercy on me, a sinner'(Luke 18:13).

9:2
Understanding the contents

My little boy was asked to draw a christening card in school. The teacher passed it over to me with a concerned look. The front was okay – a little baby in a crib with a mum and dad – but inside there was a fierce sword fight taking place!

In fact the only time his eyes lit up was when swords were mentioned. Any subject and I mean any subject could be brought round to one main point – sword fighting. I a Baptist was a proud dad!

The gospels are not exhaustive records. There were many other miracles that Jesus performed and many areas of interest that are not recorded. These incidents have been selected and written with one purpose. They are about Jesus the Christ who suffered and rose again. They always have been. They always will be. It is amazing how children see this and amazing so many adults do not.

How can you be someone who is not blind to what angels see? Believe on Jesus.

Why four gospels?
Each book has a different purpose but there is one dominating theme throughout – Jesus is the Christ – the Christ who must suffer and rise again.

Matthew
Matthew's gospel shows how Jesus fulfils the promise to Abraham, David and the prophets of the exile. There are more Old Testament quotes in Matthew than in all the other gospels.

Key verses:

> Thus there were fourteen generations in all *from Abraham* to David, fourteen from David to the exile to Babylon, and fourteen from the exile *to the Christ* (Matt. 1:17).

> Therefore go and make disciples *of all nations*, baptising them in the name of the Father and of the Son and of the Holy Spirit (Matt. 28:19).

The promise to Abraham is that all nations of the earth will be blessed through his seed. It is through the gospel of Jesus Christ that this is achieved.

Mark

Mark is a simple introduction to the gospel of Jesus Christ.

Key verse:

> The beginning of the gospel about Jesus Christ, the Son of God (Mark 1:1).

Luke

Luke shows how Jesus is the second Adam and how He brings real saving hope to individuals.

Key verses:

> the son of Adam, the son of God (Luke 3:38b).

> But the angel said to them, 'Do not be afraid. I bring you good news of great joy that will be for all the people. Today in the town of David a Saviour has been born to you; he is Christ the Lord (Luke 2:10-11).

> For the Son of Man came to seek and to save what was lost (Luke 19:10).

John

John tells us simply why he wrote his gospel:

Key verse:

> But these are written that you may believe that Jesus is the Christ, the Son of God, and that by believing you may have life in his name (John 20:31).

Jesus the Christ (Messiah – the Anointed one)

Jesus is the Christ who reveals the work of the Trinity.

The same Trinity working in creation and through the Old Testament is seen to be working here in the New.

Each gospel begins by showing the Trinity's involvement in the work of Jesus at his baptism – at the start of his ministry.

Later on it is emphasized that it is through Jesus God is known.

> 'Anyone who has seen me has seen the Father. How can you say, "Show us the Father"?' (John 14:9b).

Both Jesus and the Father give the Holy Spirit.

> When the Counsellor comes, whom I will send to you from the Father, the Spirit of truth who goes out from the Father, he will testify about me (John 15:26).

9:3
The Christ and His kingdom

When I started in my new church there were a number of Iranian families attending and one family asked us to their home for a meal. We arrived and inside the door there was a large pile of shoes. Thinking it was a Middle Eastern custom we quickly removed ours.

When the food was ready we sat down. Iranian food, I soon discovered, is the best I have ever tasted and we ate and ate – eventually even I stopped.

'That was the first course,' Ali announced with a smile and taking the plates.

'In our culture there are another six courses – and it's rude not to eat them all.'

I panicked. I had stuffed myself with the first course and I really didn't have any room for more. There was an awkward pause and then a burst of laughter.

'I'm just joking.'

The reason for my panic was my ignorance of Iranian culture. I didn't know how to behave. I didn't know what was deemed rude. I knew I was in a place where there was a different way of doing things – a place with different rules.

Jesus' first recorded sermon in the gospels is about the kingdom of God – a completely different kind of kingdom – and how to join it.

The King arrives!

There is nothing startlingly new about the kingdom of God. People repented and believed and were part of it long before this point.

In Exodus, God says to Moses:

'Although the whole earth is mine, you will be for me a kingdom of priests and a holy nation' (Exod. 19:5b-6).

And David says:

'he has chosen my son Solomon to sit on the throne of the kingdom of the Lord over Israel...I will establish his kingdom for ever' (1 Chron. 28:5b-7).

The difference is – now the King has arrived!

Listen to that great Christmas passage:

'You will be with child and give birth to a son, and you are to give him the name Jesus. He will be great and will be called the Son of the Most High. The Lord God will give him the throne of his father David, and he will reign over the house of Jacob for ever; his kingdom will never end' (Luke 1:31-33).

The great hope of the world and history: God Himself comes in flesh. The Old Testament believer longed to see the time and circumstances when the real King would arrive. Now all their hopes are fulfilled.

When we see how God the Son appeared to certain people in the Old Testament, we might wonder how different it was when He became flesh. All we can say is that in the Old Testament he was never one of the Israelites. He was never a mortal, subject to the weaknesses and limits of our human life. He was never born under the law. He was never born of a woman. He never became flesh. He was the all-glorious Lord of hosts and when He appeared to someone His glory could shake the building and all but kill a man (see Isaiah 6 for just one example).

In the incarnation, He laid aside His glory and lived among us with such inconceivable humility. He took upon Himself the poverty of our existence and learned obedience, even to the ultimate test of the cross. Even after He ascended back to His Father's glory, He did not cease to be one of us. Yes, the eternal Son who sits at his Father's side is actually our human brother![1]

The famous carol, 'O Little Town of Bethlehem' sums it up so well:

The hopes and fears of all the years are met in thee tonight.

Trust only the King

When the Bible speaks about the kingdom of God the emphasis is on King Jesus. It is He who will be great, He is the Son of the Most High and it is His throne.

We often refer to the stories of the wise men or Nicodemus or the leper, but the truth of the matter is Jesus dominates them all. Each story is about Him and how to find faith in Him.

The greatest thing about the kingdom of God is the King and the only way you can enter is by trusting Him.

He does what only God can do

This king is the King of the universe – God Himself. He does what only God can do.

▷He stills the sea:

> Then they cried out to the Lord in their trouble, and he brought them out of their distress. He stilled the storm to a whisper; the waves of the sea were hushed (Ps. 107:28-29).

▷He walks on the sea in the storm:

> 'He alone stretches out the heavens and treads on the waves of the sea' (Job 9:8).

▷He feeds the people in the wilderness:

> He gave you manna to eat in the desert (Deut. 8:16).

> **He sees what people are thinking:**

'He who forms the mountains, creates the wind, and reveals his thoughts to man, he who turns dawn to darkness, and treads the high places of the earth — the Lord God Almighty is his name' (Amos 4:13).

> **He raises the dead:**

Our God is a God who saves; from the Sovereign Lord comes escape from death (Ps. 68:20).

> **He opens the eyes of the blind:**

the Lord gives sight to the blind, the Lord lifts up those who are bowed down, the Lord loves the righteous (Ps. 146:8).

> **He heals the sick:**

Praise the Lord, O my soul, and forget not all his benefits – who forgives all your sins and heals all your diseases (Ps. 103:2-3).

> **He controls and limits Satan** (see Job 1-2).

Who can join the kingdom?

Glyn Morris had been the minister of a large city-centre church in Swansea. He often went on preaching tours to many of the most famous churches in America and Canada. On one occasion he preached to the entire Cabinet of the St Lucia government. Now an old man I was speaking to him about his ministry.

He mentioned having a phone call one afternoon from the local hospital. A lady had asked to see him. He didn't recognize the name and when he arrived at the ward he didn't recognize her. He was informed by hospital staff that she was dying.

He sat beside her bed and she poured out her story. She was a prostitute. On Sunday nights she would slip up to the gallery of the church during the first hymn – and as the last hymn was sung she would sneak out. She didn't want anyone to see her but she enjoyed his sermons.

'Well my dear, have you accepted Jesus as your own personal Saviour?'

'No.'

So he opened up the Bible and led her to the Saviour. He went back to see her in hospital a number of times. A couple of weeks later he had a phone call from the undertaker informing him she had died. Did he want to take her funeral?

'Of course.'

At the service, it was just himself, the coffin and the undertaker. He preached and when he finished the undertaker grabbed his hand and told him it was the most remarkable funeral he had ever been to.

'You know Steve I don't think I have ever preached better. Not to the big congregations in America or Canada or even to the dignitaries in St Lucia.'

Isn't that typical of God? That lady meant so much to him. Imagine the reception in heaven when she got there!

The gospels show us that individuals matter – the leper, the lame, the blind, the centurion, the religious leader, the woman who slept around – all get God's best in Jesus. All really matter.

He touches the unclean, is patient with the bitter, listens to the confused. He walks their walk, he feels their pain.

For we do not have a high priest who is unable to sympathize with our weaknesses, but we have one who has been tempted in every way, just as we are – yet was without sin (Heb. 4:15).

And He is more. He is the solution to all their needs. In fact it is clear that He is, 'God with us.'

When the kingdom of God comes these are the kinds of people who join.

Living the kingdom life

There is one special group that reflect His gathering of different kinds of people – the twelve apostles. Jesus spends three years explaining the gospel to them so that when He leaves they will be able to teach the gospel to the church.

He is not only concerned with teaching how people can become part of His kingdom, but how this kingdom life is to be lived.

The Sermon on the Mount is a great example of this.

Can everyone know how to live the kingdom life?

Jesus uses a style of teaching which is often misunderstood because it is so exclusive. He teaches what the kingdom life is like by using parables. Their purpose is not to make clear how to live for God but the very opposite.

'This is why I speak to them in parables:

> "Though seeing, they do not see; though hearing, they do not hear or understand"' (Matt. 13:13).

Why does He use this approach?

The answer is found in Isaiah 6. Jesus tells Isaiah that it is when everything is destroyed, when all that is left is Jesus (the holy seed), then can people see, hear and understand.

When we trust only Jesus and have turned from everything else, when he is the only King – only then can we understand the kingdom life.

Nicodemus has to stop trusting his religion. Zacchaeus has to stop trusting in money. The Samaritan woman has to stop trusting in her relationships and her religion.

The leper who recognizes he is completely unclean and throws himself on the mercy of Jesus is instantly made clean.

We must destroy everything of self and trust in Christ alone.

(ENDNOTES)
[1] Paul Blackham, Frequently Asked Questions, at the end of the book

9:4
The suffering King

A few years ago I was in the local school helping children who attended my church. Some had speech problems and had no-one to do drill work with them so necessary to help them to speak. Some were on the verge of being expelled because of their bad behaviour.

A lady visiting the school commented, 'I guess this is the most important part of your job.'

I could only reply, 'The only job I have is to preach Jesus. This is simply putting my sermons into practice.'

How often people fail to distinguish between Jesus' purpose in coming – His death and resurrection – and the application of that.

Jesus' intended suffering and death is the main theme of the gospels. It casts a shadow over His birth in Matthew. Three times while teaching in Mark, he tells of His impending suffering and death. In John there is constant reference to 'his hour' that will come.

Christ the anointed King had to suffer and die for our sin. It is this death that looms over the whole of His life, teaching and birth (Luke 2:35).

People say His final week takes up a third of the gospels. But that can actually give the wrong impression. His suffering for our sins, His death on the cross and His resurrection dominate every part of the gospels.

In fact none of the Bible can be understood without seeing its end and point in the death and resurrection of Jesus.

Why did He die?

> He himself bore our sins in his body on the tree, so that we might die to sins and live for righteousness; by his wounds you have been healed (1 Peter 2:24).

He died to set us free from sin. He died to set us free to live for Him. But best of all:

> For Christ died for sins once for all, the righteous for the unrighteous, *to bring you to God* (1 Peter 3:18a).

> 'But this has all taken place that the writings of the prophets might be fulfilled' (Matt. 26:56a).

The temple is rendered useless because the curtain is torn apart. All it pointed to is fulfilled in the death of Jesus. The darkness that descends when God is judging sin in the Exodus descends on Christ on the cross. The fulfilments go on and on.

When Jesus has risen he summarizes all his teaching in the gospels:

> He said to them, 'This is what I told you while I was still with you: Everything must be fulfilled that is written about me in the Law of Moses, the Prophets and the Psalms.'

> Then he opened their minds so they could understand the Scriptures. He told them, 'This is what is written: The Christ will suffer and rise from the dead on the third day, and repentance and forgiveness of sins will be preached in his name to all nations, beginning at Jerusalem. You are witnesses of these things' (Luke 24:44-48).

Motivated by love

We must be very careful when we look at the death of Jesus Christ to realize that it was all motivated out of God's deep love – for you who are reading this right now:

> You see, at just the right time, when we were still powerless, Christ died for the ungodly... But God demonstrates his own

love for us in this: While we were still sinners, Christ died for us (Rom. 5:6-8).

He had you in mind when He left glory to come to this world. He had you in mind when He set His face like flint to go to Jerusalem. He had you in mind when He sweat great drops of blood in the garden. He had you in mind when he handed Himself over to sinful men to be crucified. He felt all the pain you have ever felt and ever will feel for your sin when He hung on that cross.

Do you think He went there blindly, not knowing what you've done?

He died to save the man that you've become.[1]

The risen King

Jesus is not left in death. The Spirit raises Him from the dead. The angels appear at the tomb showing that the one enthroned between the cherubim is now risen.

▷Because He lives we can know new birth into a living hope

In his great mercy he has given us new birth into a living hope through the resurrection of Jesus Christ from the dead (1 Pet. 1:3b).

▷Because He lives we have proof we can be rescued from the coming wrath

and to wait for his Son from heaven, whom he raised from the dead – Jesus, who rescues us from the coming wrath (1 Thess. 1:10).

▷Because He lives he is able to save us completely and we know He is always praying for us

Therefore he is able to save completely those who come to God through him, because he always lives to intercede for them (Heb. 7:25).

▷The same Spirit who raised Jesus from the dead works in us

> …and his incomparably great power for us who believe. That power is like the working of his mighty strength, which he exerted in Christ when he raised him from the dead and seated him at his right hand in the heavenly realms (Eph. 1:19-20).

Jesus hasn't left us. He has left us His Spirit who helps and works through us. He confronts this world we live in and brings faith in Jesus.

The beginning of the end

In Jesus we see an end to the shadows of the Old Testament worship which centred around Jerusalem and the temple – because 'one greater than the temple is here' (Matt. 12:6).

The temple, spectacular as it was, must now be destroyed (see Mark 13:1-2). But this is only the beginning of the end. There will be many disasters like this one until Jesus returns and the world is judged. The old heaven and earth will pass away, but his kingdom will endure for ever.

> 'At that time men will see the Son of Man coming in clouds with great power and glory. And he will send his angels and gather his elect from the four winds, from the ends of the earth to the ends of the heavens (Mark 13:26-27).

It then His kingdom will have come. This is the blessed, happy hope of the church – the glorious appearing of our great God and Saviour, Jesus Christ.

Spurgeon says every morning we should open our curtains and be disappointed that Jesus hasn't come back yet.

So how are we to live until then? And what is the guarantee that we are going to enjoy His kingdom in all its fullness?

> And you also were included in Christ when you heard the word of truth, the gospel of your salvation. Having believed, you were marked in him with a seal, the promised Holy Spirit, who is a deposit guaranteeing our inheritance until the

redemption of those who are God's possession – to the praise of his glory (Eph.1:13-14).

We are not there yet. There may be terrible days to be lived through. But Jesus is coming back. We can be sure we will be with Him if we have received the Holy Spirit.

But you are only included in the kingdom if you have believed.

(ENDNOTES)
[1] From a song by Haydn Jenkins

Part Ten
Acts and the church

10:1

The gospel worked out today

At the beginning of Acts Jesus leaves and ascends to heaven to an extraordinary welcome:

> Lift up your heads, O you gates;
> lift them up, you ancient doors,
> that the King of glory may come in.
> Who is he, this King of glory?
> The Lord Almighty –
> he is the King of glory (Ps. 24: 9-10).

We'll let Daniel describe the purpose of the ascension:

> 'In my vision at night I looked, and there before me was one like a son of man, coming with the clouds of heaven. He approached the Ancient of Days and was led into his presence. He was given authority, glory and sovereign power; all peoples, nations and men of every language worshipped him. His dominion is an everlasting dominion that will not pass away, and his kingdom is one that will never be destroyed' (Dan. 7:13-14).

Jesus is given people of every nation, tribe and language who will worship Him. One day He will come back in the same way as He ascended and everyone will see His Kingdom come.

In the rest of the Bible this truth above all other truths must be remembered.

The beginning and end

He is the beginning and end of everything that follows.

›He is the one who commands the disciples to preach to the nations

Then Jesus came to them and said, 'All authority in heaven and on earth has been given to me. Therefore go and make disciples of all nations, baptising them in the name of the Father and of the Son and of the Holy Spirit'(Matt. 28:18-19).

›He is to be the subject of their sermons

For I resolved to know nothing while I was with you except Jesus Christ and him crucified (1 Cor. 2:2).

›He, with the Father, is the one who will give the Holy Spirit. The Spirit's work is to point to and apply the work of Jesus

When the Counsellor comes, whom I will send to you from the Father, the Spirit of truth who goes out from the Father, he will testify about me (John 15:26).

He is often described by Paul as the 'Spirit of Christ'.

›It is Jesus' apostles who write the letters to the churches

Paul, an apostle of Christ Jesus by the will of God (Eph. 1:1a).

›It is Jesus who is the head of every church that is formed in every tribe and nation and language

Christ is the head of the church, his body, of which he is the Saviour (Eph. 5:23b).

Note how often Paul in his letters uses the phrase 'in Christ Jesus' – that is the church in Christ, in Christ alone!

The rest of the Bible is Jesus reaping the rewards of His sufferings.

Sent by Jesus

Just as the prophets before them, it is essential we see the letters' authority is found in the fact that they are written by apostles sent from Jesus.

Because Jesus sends Paul, Peter, James and John, because they are servants of Jesus we must listen to them.

It is the same King who sits on the throne. He spoke through the prophets and now speaks through the apostles.

Paul makes this point very clearly as we have seen at the end of Acts but he makes it again in the letters.

'I thank God, whom I serve, as my forefathers did' (2 Tim. 1:3).

Not only does he serve the same God in the same way; he also preaches the same message:

'Paul, a servant of Christ Jesus, called to be an apostle and set apart for the gospel of God – the gospel he promised beforehand through his prophets in the Holy Scriptures' (Rom. 1:1-2).

It might be Paul or Peter or Jude speaking but it is Jesus who sends them – to His churches.

10:2
The gospel preached to the nations

I had never had any desire to preach outside Swansea and the idea of being a 'celebrity preacher' always repulsed me. However a couple from America arrived in the church and asked if I would be interested in preaching in New York State.

The more I heard the more I liked the idea. A tape was dispatched to the pastor of one of the largest churches there and we waited for the reply. It soon came back:

'Have you got any tapes of him preaching in English?'

My career as an international preacher devastated! My Welsh accent apparently made me impossible to understand!

Language is a huge dividing barrier for the nations; a barrier set by the curse of sin. How can they go and make disciples of all nations when they cannot even make themselves understood?

Power to preach to the nations
Before Jesus ascends he tells them how:

> 'But you will receive power when the Holy Spirit comes on you; and you will be my witnesses in Jerusalem, and in all Judea and Samaria, and to the ends of the earth' (Acts 1:8).

There are many barriers to them preaching in Jerusalem – after all this is where Christ was crucified. Judea and Samaria were hardly easy – after all 'Jews do not associate with Samaritans' (John 4:9b).

How on earth can they know the curse of God on *nations* being broken down?

Pentecost – the gospel to the world

In the Old Testament some people of the nations were saved. Rahab, Ruth, Uriah the Hittite and Naaman were all saved through faith in Jesus (see Hebrews 11). But they had to go to the physical land of Israel in order to be blessed.

But what happens now is on a completely different scale. Jesus explains what will happen when the Holy Spirit comes. He will reach the world with the message of Jesus:

> 'When he comes, **he will convict the world** of guilt in regard to sin and righteousness and judgment: in regard to sin, because men do not believe in me; in regard to righteousness, because I am going to the Father, where you can see me no longer; and in regard to judgment, because the prince of this world now stands condemned' (John 16:8-11).

At Pentecost the barriers all come down. The Holy Spirit will convict the world – not just Israel – of sin and righteousness and judgment. And Jesus commands His disciples to go out of Israel into 'all the' world with the gospel.

This is exactly what the gospel preached in advance to Abraham was – the nations hearing and believing the gospel.

> Consider Abraham: 'He believed God, and it was credited to him as righteousness.' Understand, then, that those who believe are children of Abraham. The Scripture foresaw that God would justify the Gentiles by faith, and announced the gospel in advance to Abraham: 'All nations will be blessed through you.' So those who have faith are blessed along with Abraham, the man of faith (Gal. 3:6-9).

Now the Gentiles too can be justified by faith.

Kicking the barriers down

How can anyone fail to be impressed when they see a fireman running into a burning house? It doesn't matter what is in the way – axes and sledgehammers crash through it – every obstacle must be removed so that people inside can be rescued.

Acts 2 is where we see God kicking every barrier down so people can be saved.

⊳ The barrier of language

> Now there were staying in Jerusalem God-fearing Jews from every nation under heaven. When they heard this sound, a crowd came together in bewilderment, because each one heard them speaking in his own language (Acts 2:5-6).

⊳ The barrier of nations

> "'In the last days", God says, "I will pour out my Spirit on all people'" (Acts 2:17a).

> The circumcised believers who had come with Peter were astonished that the gift of the Holy Spirit had been poured out even on the Gentiles (Acts 10:45).

⊳ The barrier of age and sex

> "'Your sons and daughters will prophesy,
> your young men will see visions,
> your old men will dream dreams'" (Acts 2:17b).

⊳ The barrier of time

The privilege David had and spoke of in the Old Testament is ours:

> 'But he was a prophet and knew that God had promised him on oath that he would place one of his descendants on his throne. Seeing what was ahead, he spoke of the resurrection of the Christ, that he was not abandoned to the grave, nor did his body see decay' (Acts 2:30-31).

▷ That greatest of all barriers – sin

> 'God has made this Jesus, whom you crucified, both Lord and Christ' (Acts 2:36b).

Imagine if one of the men who lied about Jesus was listening to the sermon. Imagine if the one who punched Jesus was there. Imagine if one of the priests who plotted was there. Imagine if the soldier who flogged him, or the soldier who drove the nails through his hands was there.

Even their barrier can be broken down – if they repent and are baptized in the name of Jesus.

Look who is preaching the sermon – Peter – the man who only weeks before had lied, sworn and denied Jesus. If his barrier is broken down then there is hope for anyone.

Everyone – wherever you live, however old you are, whether man or woman – 'everyone who calls on the name of the Lord will be saved' (Acts 2:21).

Is that it?

After the Spirit of God is poured out, after the end of the curse of Babel is seen – Christ is preached. The people accept the message, are baptized and 3,000 are added to their number.

And a church is formed!

10:3
A church is formed

'Did you enjoy the day?' I asked the exhausted bride.

'The preparation took it out of me. I was too tired to enjoy it properly.'

God is not like that. He has broken all the barriers down, He has prepared the way and now He delights in His church.

The model church

A church is formed where:

> They devoted themselves to the apostles' teaching and to the fellowship, to the breaking of bread and to prayer. Everyone was filled with awe, and many wonders and miraculous signs were done by the apostles. All the believers were together and had everything in common. Selling their possessions and goods, they gave to anyone as he had need. Every day they continued to meet together in the temple courts. They broke bread in their homes and ate together with glad and sincere hearts, praising God and enjoying the favour of all the people. And the Lord added to their number daily those who were being saved (Acts 2:42-47).

Surely the most exciting thing the world has ever seen – an actual living, breathing community, which day by day shows that the barriers between race, age, nationality and background are all broken down. A place where the poor in the church are helped. A place where the greatest barrier of all is broken down – sin.

Welcome to church!

Something new?

Stephen as he preaches refers to the gathering of believers in the Old Testament as 'the church'. He uses the word '*ekklesia*' which is translated 'church' in the KJV.

> 'He was in the *assembly* (ekklessia) in the desert, with the angel who spoke to him on Mount Sinai, and with our fathers' (Acts 7:38a).

The same angel (sent one) – the same church.

This church had the struggles and temptations of the world, but also had the glory of God in the middle of it. This church throughout the Old Testament had to endure persecution from the nations, but also had the glorious privilege of shining hope to the nations.

Each new church formed knows the same trials, persecutions, challenges, difficulties, the same joys, fellowship and pleasures – and the same God.

The hope of the world throughout the Old Testament, which sinful humanity could become part of, is now available for us too.

Church for the Gentiles too

It is the same church but it is growing – fast.

As Acts moves on we see the gospel is for the Gentiles as well. No longer is the church based in Israel and worship centred around Jerusalem. Jesus makes this really clear:

> Jesus declared, 'Believe me, woman, a time is coming when you will worship the Father neither on this mountain nor in Jerusalem. You Samaritans worship what you do not know; we worship what we do know, for salvation is from the Jews. **Yet a time is coming and has now come when the true worshippers will worship the Father in spirit and truth,** for they are the kind of worshippers the Father seeks. God is spirit, and his worshippers must worship in spirit and in truth' (John 4:21-24).

Apostle to the Gentiles

But who will go to the Gentiles and be their apostle?

God raises up the worst sinner – Paul – the one-time enemy of the Christian church. Why? So that Christ Jesus might display his unlimited patience as an example for those who would go on to believe in Him and receive eternal life.

> But for that very reason I was shown mercy so that in me, the worst of sinners, Christ Jesus might display his unlimited patience as an example for those who would believe on him and receive eternal life (1 Tim. 1:16).

Every time we see Paul's name it reminds us of God's unlimited patience in Christ.

Planting churches

So we see Paul planting churches.

Why? Because it is through churches that God's manifest wisdom is known. This is how it has always been. This is God's eternal plan. And now they are reaching into all the world. This is the mystery that was not always seen until now. Paul says:

> This mystery is that through the gospel the Gentiles are heirs together with Israel, members together of one body, and sharers together in the promise in Christ Jesus (Eph. 3:6).

> … this grace was given me: to preach to the Gentiles the unsearchable riches of Christ, and to make plain to everyone the administration of this mystery, which for ages past was kept hidden in God, who created all things. **His intent was that now, through the church, the manifold wisdom of God should be made known** to the rulers and authorities in the heavenly realms, according to his eternal purpose which he accomplished in Christ Jesus our Lord (Eph. 3:8b-11).

> …for the sake of his body, which is the church. I have become its servant by the commission God gave me to present to you the word of God in its fullness – the mystery that has been

kept hidden for ages and generations, but is now disclosed to the saints. To them God has chosen to make known among the Gentiles the glorious riches of this mystery, which is Christ in you, the hope of glory (Col. 1:24b-27).

It is so important we see this. Each church is there to make plain the unsearchable riches of Christ. If you see it – it might just change the way you look at the people you meet with Sunday by Sunday!

The only institution which God has promised to bless is the local church.

Join one and enjoy the exciting and sometimes hair-raising ride that believers have enjoyed throughout the Bible.[1]

(ENDNOTES)

[1] Most of the earliest Christian writings after Scripture written by some people who would have known the apostles themselves are taken up with the running and ordering of churches eg the letter of Polycarp to the Philippians, the Didache, the letters of Clement etc.

10:4
The gospel on the move

After Babel and the division of the nations, the righteousness that comes by faith in Christ is seen **only in the family of Abraham** and those who join him. He knows the nations will be blessed through him but he sees very little of it himself.

The light shines from one family

In the Exodus, the righteousness that comes by faith in Christ is seen **in Egypt and in the wilderness**. With the exception of the Egyptians and the surrounding peoples, the nations don't see it.

The light shines from the people around the tabernacle

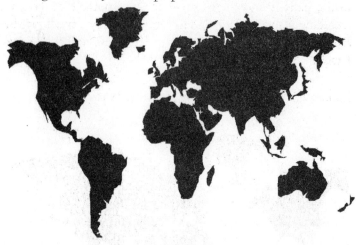

In the former prophets, the righteousness that comes by faith in Christ is clearly seen **in the land** with the exception of a few individuals – Rahab, Ruth, and the Queen of Sheba amongst others. The nations surrounding the land (but not the whole world) know more than before.

The light shines from Jerusalem and the temple

In the latter prophets, the exile causes the gospel to be preached to the nations and there are some quite notable conversions including Nebuchadnezzar. However, still only a small number are saved and the people return to Jerusalem and the land of Israel.

Light of the gospel preached by the prophets in exile

In Acts, the mystery hidden in the past, spoken of in the prophets, is seen being made known.

> Now to him who is able to establish you by my gospel and the proclamation of Jesus Christ, according to the revelation of the mystery hidden for long ages past, **but now revealed and made known through the prophetic writings** by the command of the eternal God, **so that all nations might believe** and obey him – to the only wise God be glory for ever through Jesus Christ! Amen (Rom. 16:25-27).

The gospel preached in Acts

There is clearly a progress in the Bible – as the knowledge of God fills the whole earth. Notice how the light of the gospel starts to cover the whole earth. The mystery they heard spoken of we now see.

They had to go to Jerusalem and worship Christ in physical ways to look forward to His coming. But in the many thousands of churches that meet across the world we now worship Him in spirit and truth as the day of our redemption draws near.

> 'stand up and lift up your heads, because your redemption is drawing near'(Luke 21:28b).

Each generation is more privileged than the last. Every time you meet new believers, every time you see or hear of a gospel church, you know a little more of the mystery spoken of in the Bible being revealed.

Salvation does not unfold

Let's be clear here – the way of salvation doesn't unfold through time. It was set before the foundation of the world.

Jesus answered, 'I am the way, and the truth, and the life. No-one comes to the Father except through me' (John 14:6).

But the outworking, the results of this eternal salvation unfold all the time.

This is why Paul rejoices to hear of churches he has never even been to, almost as much as he rejoices over the churches he has planted (Romans 1:8-10).

How much more privileged we will be in eternity when we see our redemption fulfilled and every believer brought in.

The gospel today
NB. There are thousands more churches than can be represented on this map however there are still many areas that remain unreached.

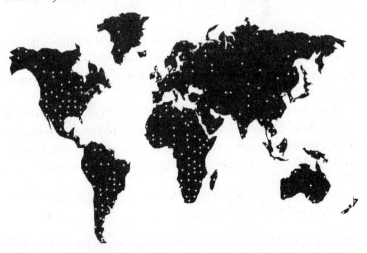

We are to wake up every morning and realize we are closer to the fulfilment of our redemption.

This is why Paul plants churches!

10:5
Learning how everything works

When my daughter was born, every cough or rash resulted in a phone call to my mother. Why? Because compared to her experience of raising four children, our knowledge was minimal.

So it is with the church. We are to learn from Christians who had the same experience as us in the past. We are to read the Old Testament to see how everything works.

We are not simply to stand in awe and amazement at the Old Testament church's experience of God and each other. We are to exercise faith, read the Scriptures and enjoy so much of what they enjoyed – in our church life.

Just like them...
▷**It is the Father who gathers His church, purely out of His grace – just as in Deuteronomy**

> 'After the Lord your God has driven them out before you, do not say to yourself, "The Lord has brought me here to take possession of this land because of my righteousness"... Understand, then, that it is not because of your righteousness that the Lord your God is giving you this good land to possess, for you are a stiff-necked people' (Deut. 9:4,6).

> Once you were not a people, but now you are the people of God; once you had not received mercy, but now you have received mercy (1 Pet. 2:10).

⊳ It is Christ who redeems the church – just as in Exodus

'I am the Lord, and I will bring you out from under the yoke of the Egyptians. I will free you from being slaves to them, and I will redeem you with an outstretched arm and with mighty acts of judgment' (Exod. 6:6b).

For he has rescued us from the dominion of darkness and brought us into the kingdom of the Son he loves, in whom we have redemption, the forgiveness of sins (Col. 1:13-14).

In him we have redemption through his blood, the forgiveness of sins, in accordance with the riches of God's grace…(Eph. 1:7).

⊳ God speaks to His church – just as in Exodus 19

⊳ The Spirit of God lives in the church – just as in Exodus

Then the cloud covered the Tent of Meeting, and the glory of the Lord filled the tabernacle (Exod. 40:34).

Don't you know that you yourselves are God's temple and that God's Spirit lives in you? (1 Cor. 3:16).

And in him you too are being built together to become a dwelling in which God lives by his Spirit (Eph. 2:22).

⊳ Each church is to look like God – just as in the Law

'Speak to the entire assembly of Israel and say to them: "Be holy because I, the Lord your God, am holy"' (Lev. 19:2).

But just as he who called you is holy, so be holy in all you do; for it is written: 'Be holy, because I am holy' (1 Pet. 1:15-16).

⊳ Each church is to exercise a priest's ministry – just as in the Law

'Although the whole earth is mine, you will be for me a king-dom of priests and a holy nation' (Exod. 19:5b-6).

But you are a chosen people, a royal priesthood, a holy nation, a people belonging to God, that you may declare the praises of him who called you out of darkness into his wonderful light (1 Pet. 2:9).

▷Each church is to remove sin from the camp – just as in the Law

'Everyone who does any of these detestable things – such persons must be cut off from their people' (Lev. 18:29).

Since we have these promises, dear friends, let us purify ourselves from everything that contaminates body and spirit, perfecting holiness out of reverence for God (2 Cor. 7:1).

The middle wall of partition – gone
When you go to church realize there are no barriers.

– remember that at that time you were separate from Christ, excluded from citizenship in Israel and foreigners to the covenants of the promise, without hope and without God in the world. But now in Christ Jesus you who once were far away have been brought near through the blood of Christ.
For he himself is our peace, who **has made the two one** and has destroyed the barrier, the dividing wall of hostility... (Eph. 2:12-14).

Peace and mercy to all who follow this rule, even to the **Israel of God** (Gal. 6:16).

You are all sons of God through faith in Christ Jesus, for all of you who were baptised into Christ have clothed yourselves with Christ. There is neither Jew nor Greek, slave nor free, male nor female, for you are all one in Christ Jesus. If you belong to Christ, then you are Abraham's seed, and heirs according to the promise (Gal. 3:26-29).

No difference!
When Jesus and the apostles want us to understand the gospel and the church they take us back to the Old Testament – and usually right back to the beginning. At no point do we read that Abraham had only a 'bit' of truth and Moses 'a bit more' and Solomon 'a bit more'.

For everything that was written in the past was written to teach us, so that through endurance and the encouragement of the Scriptures we might have hope (Rom. 15:4).

Paul is saying nothing new as he so clearly states towards the end of Acts:

'I am saying **nothing beyond what the prophets and Moses said would happen** – that the Christ would suffer and, as the first to rise from the dead, would proclaim light to his own people and to the Gentiles' (Acts 26:22b-23).

Those who believed in Jesus in the Old Testament find their forgiveness in exactly the same place as us:

for all have sinned and fall short of the glory of God, and **are justified freely by his grace through the redemption that came by Christ Jesus**. God presented him as a sacrifice of atonement, through faith in his blood. He did this to demonstrate his justice, because in his forbearance he had left the sins committed beforehand unpunished – he did it to demonstrate his justice at the present time, so as to be just and the one who justifies those who have faith in Jesus (Rom. 3:23-26).

This righteousness from God comes through faith in Jesus Christ to all who believe. **There is no difference** (Rom. 3:22).

10:6
Defending the faith

Why does Paul stop planting?

The apostle Paul knows tremendous success in church planting and then appears to do the strangest thing.

Instead of continuing with this great work he heads back to Jerusalem. Everyone warns him this will end in certain death and he clearly knows this is true (Acts 21:13).

So why does he go? He goes to Jerusalem because he has a truth to defend – a truth of huge significance.

The first place he goes is to the church in Jerusalem where he is told that those who believe in Jesus are 'all' still 'zealous for the law' (Acts 21:20) – which is hardly surprising as it is all about Jesus.

He then returns to the temple itself, the centre of Old Testament worship (Acts 21:26), causes a riot and is arrested.

Why?

Paul's defence – the same faith!

The closing chapters of Acts answer the question – he wants to show his faith is the same as the Old Testament believer.

He explains it is the 'God of our fathers' who has called him to plant churches:

'The God of our fathers has chosen you to know his will and to see the Righteous One and to hear words from his mouth. You will be his witness to all men of what you have seen and heard'(Acts 22:14b-15 see also 24:14-15, 25:8, 26: 6-7 and 26:22-23).

He tells them the reason for his imprisonment is his hope in the Old Testament:

'And now it is because of my hope in what God has promised our fathers that I am on trial today. This is the promise our twelve tribes are hoping to see fulfilled as they earnestly serve God day and night. O King, it is because of this hope that the Jews are accusing me'(Acts 26:6-7).

'It is because of the hope of Israel that I am bound with this chain' (Acts 28:20b).

The false teachers who are behind his imprisonment accuse him of turning Jews 'from Moses' (Acts 21:21). By the way these are the same Pharisees and Sadducees who cannot agree on even the basics of the Old Testament (Acts 23:1-11).

He argues strongly that he is doing nothing against the temple, the people, the customs of the ancestors or the law:

Paul made his defence: 'I have done nothing wrong against the law of the Jews or against the temple...'(Acts 25:8 see also Acts 28:17).

In fact the opposite is true. He believes in and preaches the Jesus of the law and the prophets.

'However, I admit that I worship the God of our fathers as a follower of the Way, which they call a sect. I believe everything that agrees with the Law and that is written in the Prophets, and I have the same hope in God as these men, that there will be a resurrection of both the righteous and the wicked' (Acts 24:14-15).

From morning till evening he explained and declared to them the kingdom of God and tried to convince them about Jesus from the Law of Moses and from the Prophets (Acts 28:23b).

One magnificent sermon

He sums up his calling in one magnificent sermon:

> the Lord replied…'I will rescue you from your own people
> and from the Gentiles. I am sending you to them to open
> their eyes and turn them from darkness to light, and from the
> power of Satan to God, so that they may receive forgiveness
> of sins and a place among those who are sanctified by faith in
> me' (Acts 26:17-18).

This is not just an argument about religion as Felix and Festus
saw it, this is a battle for the souls of mankind.

This is why he makes such a courageous stand:

> 'That is why the Jews seized me in the temple courts and tried
> to kill me. But I have had God's help to this very day, and so
> I stand here and testify to small and great alike. I am saying
> nothing beyond what the prophets and Moses said would
> happen – that the Christ would suffer and, as the first to rise
> from the dead, would proclaim light to his own people and to
> the Gentiles' (Acts 26:21-23).

It is worth going to Jerusalem – the city where everything,
especially the temple, points to the gospel for mankind. It is
worth going to jail. It is worth dying in Rome – the city that
represents everything opposed to the gospel (Rev. 17:9).

This is a battle worth fighting.

This battle continues in the letters. Each church must fight
to reflect the light to the nations just as the church in the Old
Testament was meant to.

As we read on in the letters they tell us that the Old Testament writers are serving us (1 Pet. 1:10-13). If we are struggling
in our walk with God and feeling discouraged is it because we
are not using the Scriptures God has given us, that so clearly
apply to us in our church life.

Listen again to Paul in Romans:

For everything that was written in the past was written to teach us, so that through endurance and the encouragement of the Scriptures we might have hope (Rom. 15:4).

Reported all over the world

What joy and excitement to be in Jesus' church where the unsearchable riches of Christ are made known to the nations.

To the church of the Thessalonians (1 Thess. 1:1).

The Lord's message rang out from you not only in Macedonia and Achaia – your faith in God has become known everywhere (1 Thess. 1:8a).

First, I thank my God through Jesus Christ for all of you, because your faith is being reported all over the world (Rom. 1:8).

It is only in this context that the nations can be reached. It is the best context for reaching neighbours and friends. This is God's way.

If we are going to go around like St George trying to slay the dragon; if we are going to go around like a knight from the round table against the devil – we're asking for trouble. The New Testament doesn't see a Christian like that at all. The picture in the Bible is not some lone hero, some super spiritual saint going to fight the devil. No, no. The picture of the New Testament is of a trained disciplined army standing together against the foe. This is so important. God's provision for us is the church.[1]

(ENDNOTES)
[1] A sermon preached in Grove Chapel by DN Jones

Part Eleven
The church in Revelation

11:1
Precious to God

Often at Christmas a mother receives a present made by her child. It may be the cheapest thing – and nearly falling apart – but it moves her every time she looks at it. It reminds her of her child's heart. It is not to be mocked, despised or ignored. It is to have pride of place.

So it is with the church in the Old and the New Testament. It is precious to the Father – He even calls it the 'apple of his eye'.

He holds churches up and shows them off because they have something of Jesus about them.

What is striking in the closing books of the Bible is that these churches are spreading to such diverse parts of the world.

The time really has come where people worship God in Spirit and truth.

▷Jesus in the centre
Notice the importance God places on these churches – they each have an 'angel' and Jesus is in the middle of them.

> 'Write on a scroll what you see and send it to the seven churches: to Ephesus, Smyrna, Pergamum, Thyatira, Sardis, Philadelphia and Laodicea.'
> I turned round to see the voice that was speaking to me. And when I turned I saw seven golden lampstands, and **among the lampstands was someone 'like a son of man'**, dressed in a robe reaching down to his feet and with a golden sash round his chest (Rev. 1:11-13).

The mystery of the seven stars that you saw in my right hand and of the seven golden lampstands is this: The seven stars are the angels of the seven churches, and the seven lampstands are the seven churches (Rev. 1:20).

▷ Everything is for the church – everything!

And God placed all things under his feet and appointed him to be head over everything for the church, which is his body, the fulness of him who fills everything in every way (Eph. 1:22-23).

▷ God shows off His wisdom – through the church

His intent was that now, through the church, the manifold wisdom of God should be made known to the rulers and authorities in the heavenly realms (Eph. 3:10).

Not super churches!
What are they like?

The first thing to note is that they are not full of super Christians! They are places where ordinary people are valued. James talks about welcoming all kinds of people into church and note the lists of names at the end of the letters, particularly Romans 16.

Imagine one Sunday morning you travel back in time to Philippi 2,000 years ago.

In the congregation is a beautiful slave girl – she used to be demon-possessed. Near her is a hard-looking man with his family – the Philippian jailer. You glance around and there is a smart businesswoman – Lydia. Two other godly, hard-working women are there – Euodia and Syntyche – probably sitting apart as they are not getting on as they should.

They sing together, pray together and hear God's Word together. They strive together in a 'crooked and perverse generation' to 'shine like stars'.

You might be surprised how different things are. But, as you find whenever you meet up in church, most things are just the same.

Each church had problems – just like ours: problems of people not getting on, (Philippians), problems of leadership, finance and morality (1 Corinthians). Problems with heresy are referred to in nearly all the letters. Even the letters which are not specifically written to churches have a great deal in them about church life.

Sticking to the task

It is the job of the Bible teachers to make sure the people are taught by God and to rebuke them for false doctrine – so that the church can fulfil its purpose and be God's delight.

> 'Therefore, I declare to you today that I am innocent of the blood of all men. For I have not hesitated to proclaim to you the whole will of God. Keep watch over yourselves and all the flock of which the Holy Spirit has made you overseers. Be shepherds of the church of God, which he bought with his own blood. I know that after I leave, savage wolves will come in among you and will not spare the flock. Even from your own number men will arise and distort the truth in order to draw away disciples after them. So be on your guard! Remember that for three years I never stopped warning each of you night and day with tears.
>
> Now I commit you to God and to the word of his grace, which can build you up and give you an inheritance among all those who are sanctified' (Acts 20:26-32).

It is astonishing how many of the letters are written to defend churches against false teaching.

Churches must be of enormous significance if the devil makes such efforts to attack them with false teaching – and if the Scriptures make such efforts to teach us how to defend them.

We should be congregations who pray that those who teach the Bible will teach it fearlessly (Eph. 6:19).

11:2
Reflecting heaven

There is a famous story of a little boy drawing. His teacher asked him:

'What are you drawing?'

'I'm drawing God.'

'But nobody knows what God looks like.'

'Well they know now.'

The Bible tells us all that can be known about God is found in Jesus. It also tells us it is possible to know what *heaven is like* by looking at the church.

We know that those God has gathered He will redeem and those He redeems He will glorify:

> And those he predestined, he also called; those he called, he also justified; those he justified, he also glorified (Rom. 8:30).

But it is not just that we will get to heaven one day. We are to taste heaven now and reflect it to the world around us.

This is true of the church in the Old Testament but as we draw closer to the return of Christ it becomes the dominant theme in the New.

Never forget that the great vision of the final days – the book of Revelation – which ends in the new heaven and the new earth, was written to churches with struggles just like ours.

We are all looking for a place of rest, a place where God's purposes can be seen to work out, a place where Jesus Christ is seen at the centre, a place of love, a place that reflects heaven on earth.

God has set up one institution, and one institution alone, which anyone can join if they have trusted Jesus as their Lord and Saviour – the local church.

▷Church is a place gathered by God to reflect the great gathering in heaven

According to the Lord's own word, we tell you that we who are still alive, who are left till the coming of the Lord, will certainly not precede those who have fallen asleep. For the Lord himself will come down from heaven, with a loud command, with the voice of the archangel and with the trumpet call of God, and the dead in Christ will rise first. After that, we who are still alive and are left will be caught up together with them in the clouds to meet the Lord in the air. And so **we will be with the Lord for ever** (1 Thess. 4:15-17).

> After this I looked and there before me was **a great multitude that no-one could count**, from every nation, tribe, people and language, standing before the throne and in front of the Lamb. They were wearing white robes and were holding palm branches in their hands. And they cried out in a loud voice:
>
> 'Salvation belongs to our God, who sits on the throne, and to the Lamb' (Rev. 7:9-10).

▷We are gathered around the Lamb who was slain

As churches we are gathered around the cross but when He returns we will be gathered around Him for ever:

> while we wait for the blessed hope – the glorious appearing of our great God and Saviour, Jesus Christ, who gave himself for us to redeem us from all wickedness and to purify for himself a people that are his very own, eager to do what is good (Titus 2:13-14).

▷We will hear him speak

God speaks to each church He gathers. He speaks of the hope to come. When we get to heaven we will hear Him speak more clearly than ever before. And in heaven because we are made perfect we will not misunderstand or misuse His Word ever again.

'And I heard a loud voice from the throne saying...' (Rev. 21:3).

▸We will be with Him
The Holy Spirit lives in each church He gathers – but at the moment we only have a deposit in heaven:

Having believed, you were marked in him with a seal, the promised Holy Spirit, who is a deposit guaranteeing our inheritance until the redemption of those who are God's possession – to the praise of his glory (Eph. 1:13b-14).

Then we will be with Him:

'Now the dwelling of God is with men, and he will live with them. They will be his people, and God himself will be with them and be their God' (Rev. 21:3b).

The city does not need the sun or the moon to shine on it, for the glory of God gives it light, and the Lamb is its lamp (Rev. 21:23).

They will see his face… (Rev. 22:4).

▸The real thing
Each church is to look like God by being 'a place of love' (Jonathan Edwards once described heaven as this). But as much as we show love in church life on earth, because of the curse, at best our efforts are a poor reflection of the real thing.

Now we see but a poor reflection as in a mirror; then we shall see face to face. Now I know in part; then I shall know fully, even as I am fully known (1 Cor. 13:12).

In heaven:

No longer will there be any curse. The throne of God and of the Lamb will be in the city, and his servants will serve him.

277

They will see his face, and his name will be on their foreheads (Rev. 22:3-4).

▶We are being transformed

Our desire is to see God constantly changing us.

> But our citizenship is in heaven. And we eagerly await a Saviour from there, the Lord Jesus Christ, who, by the power that enables him to bring everything under his control, will transform our lowly bodies so that they will be like his glorious body'(Phil. 3:20-21).

Our desire is that we will be able to see, and that others will be able to see, that we are seated in the heavenly realms; that we will enjoy the incomparable riches of his grace (Eph. 2:6-7).

How passionately we should read the Bible to understand what this means and to make our churches like heaven on earth.

How hard we should pray that first part of the Lord's Prayer – 'Our Father in heaven, hallowed be your name, your kingdom come, your will be done **on earth as it is in heaven**…'

This is no carrot that God merely dangles in front of us.

This is written about in Scripture to show us how we can know this reality in our own local fellowships.

11:3
The final victory

Catherine Booth, granddaughter of William Booth, was being interviewed on television. She recalled how she came back once from an open-air meeting and her grandfather asked her how it had gone.

'We did our best.'

Sternly he had glared at her.

'Catherine you can do better than your best in Christ.'

Why is it so hard for church life to reflect heaven on earth?

> For our struggle is not against flesh and blood, but against the rulers, against the authorities, against the powers of this dark world and against the spiritual forces of evil in the heavenly realms (Eph. 6:12).

It is so hard because the church has to fulfil its destiny of fighting the devil – the devil who was behind the fall.

Is it too great a task? No. Note the promise given in Genesis 3:15 will be fulfilled in the church.

> The God of peace will soon crush Satan **under your feet** (Rom. 16:20a).

> Therefore we do not lose heart. Though outwardly we are wasting away, yet inwardly we are being renewed day by day. For light and momentary troubles are achieving for us an eternal glory that far outweighs them all. So we fix our eyes not on what is seen, but on what is unseen. For what is seen is temporary, but what is unseen is eternal (2 Cor. 4:16-18).

The battle will reach its completion

One of the hardest things when we are in the heat of the battle in the Christian life and in church life is the feeling that our trials and struggles will never end.

Will Satan ever be defeated? Will sin ever be finished? Is there any point in keeping on going? It sometimes seems to make so little difference that we do.

> The great dragon was hurled down – that ancient serpent called the devil, or Satan, who leads the whole world astray. He was hurled to the earth, and his angels with him.
>
> Then I heard a loud voice in heaven say:
>
> 'Now have come the salvation and the power and the kingdom of our God, and the authority of his Christ. For the accuser of our brothers, who accuses them before our God day and night, has been hurled down. They overcame him by the blood of the Lamb and by the word of their testimony; they did not love their lives so much as to shrink from death.
>
> Therefore rejoice, you heavens and you who dwell in them! But woe to the earth and the sea, because the devil has gone down to you! He is filled with fury, because he knows that **his time is short**' (Rev. 12:9-12).

The fight the church is involved in is severe but it will end soon.

More than conquerors

The Bible teaches we will not collapse into heaven, glad that all our battles are over, but we will enter triumphantly.

We will rejoice that we had the privilege of being involved in the struggles and trials of church life.

We will not just be conquerors, but we will hold up our enemies and use their defeat for the glory of God. We will be more than conquerors, rejoicing eternally that we had the privilege of being in the battle we are now in, so that God could give victory through us in Christ for evermore.

This hope should keep us going through all the work and trials that we are now going through.

And they sang a new song:
'You are worthy to take the scroll
and to open its seals,
because you were slain,
and with your blood you purchased men for God
from every tribe and language and people and nation.
You have made them to be a kingdom and
priests to serve our God,
and they will reign on the earth' (Rev. 5:9-10).

How it will all finish up

I was stewarding in a Christian conference. A fire regulation had been issued stating that only those with tickets could enter the building. We were told in no uncertain terms if the safety officer came and found someone without a ticket in the building he would stop the meeting.

Inside a thousand voices could be heard singing. A girl came up and asked if she could be let in. I knew the fire safety officer was on the premises and explained the situation.

'But it's my Uncle Sel preaching.'

'I'm sorry.'

'But he's my favourite preacher. I've known him since I was a small girl.'

'I'm sorry.'

▸How awful it will be for those who don't know Jesus

Then I saw a great white throne and him who was seated on it. Earth and sky fled from his presence, and there was no place for them. And I saw the dead, great and small, standing before the throne, and books were opened. Another book was opened, which is the book of life. The dead were judged according to what they had done as recorded in the books. The sea gave up the dead that were in it, and death and Hades gave up the dead that were in them, and each person was judged according to what he had done. Then death and Hades were thrown into the lake of fire. The lake of fire is the second death. If anyone's name was not found written in the book of life, he was thrown into the lake of fire (Rev. 20:11-15).

> ## How wonderful for those who do

But how wonderful this gathering will be – a greater Eden, a greater Israel, a greater Jerusalem, a greater temple, a greater church and a greater heavens and earth will have come!

> Then I saw a new heaven and a new earth, for the first heaven and the first earth had passed away, and there was no longer any sea. I saw the Holy City, the new Jerusalem, coming down out of heaven from God, prepared as a bride beautifully dressed for her husband. And I heard a loud voice from the throne saying, 'Now the dwelling of God is with men, and he will live with them. They will be his people, and God himself will be with them and be their God. He will wipe every tear from their eyes. There will be no more death or mourning or crying or pain, for the old order of things has passed away.'
>
> He who was seated on the throne said, 'I am making everything new!' (Rev. 21:1-5a).

I did not see a temple in the city, because the Lord God Almighty and the Lamb are its temple. The city does not need the sun or the moon to shine on it, for the glory of God gives it light, and the Lamb is its lamp. The nations will walk by its light, and the kings of the earth will bring their splendour into it. On no day will its gates ever be shut, for there will be no night there. The glory and honour of the nations will be brought into it. Nothing impure will ever enter it, nor will anyone who does what is shameful or deceitful, but only those whose names are written in the Lamb's book of life.

Then the angel showed me the river of the water of life, as clear as crystal, flowing from the throne of God and of the Lamb, down the middle of the great street of the city. On each side of the river stood the tree of life, bearing twelve crops of fruit, yielding its fruit every month. And the leaves of the tree are for the healing of the nations. No longer will there be any curse. The throne of God and of the Lamb will be in the city, and his servants will serve him. They will see his face, and his name will be on their foreheads. There will be no more night. They will not need the light of a lamp or the light of the sun, for the Lord God will give them light. And they will reign for ever and ever (Rev. 21:22– 22:5).

⊳Shadow to reality

How we should long for this day – when church life will be no more because the shadow will have broken into reality. How we should long for our churches to reflect this great hope.

> 'The kingdom of the world has become the kingdom of our Lord and of his Christ, and he will reign for ever and ever' (Rev. 11:15b).

> Then I heard what sounded like a great multitude, like the roar of rushing waters and like loud peals of thunder, shouting:
> 'Hallelujah!
> For our Lord God Almighty reigns.
> Let us rejoice and be glad and give him glory!
> For the wedding of the Lamb has come,
> and his bride has made herself ready.
> Fine linen, bright and clean, was given her to wear.'
> (Fine linen stands for the righteous acts of the saints.)
> (Rev. 19:6-8).

Why is it going to be so amazing? Because Jesus is there!

Conclusion

I was a young student on a church placement. I was given the task of reading the end of Romans 8. I got rather nervously to verse 38:
'For I am convinced…'
'Me too!' came a voice from the congregation.
I was thrown. It's not the sort of thing they prepare you for in Bible college. I started the verse again:
'For I am convinced…'
'Me too!' boomed the voice again.
George Jenkins was a large man in every sense of the word. Now retired, he had spent his working life cleaning the underside of lorries. He was dramatically converted in his late twenties

and stories of his wild behaviour (getting into fist fights with hecklers in open-air meetings etc) were well known. Also he was not averse to shouting down preachers he didn't like.

Later that year I knocked every door in his village asking people if they wanted Bible notes. When I came to Tabernacle Street, where he lived, I was startled by the response.

At the first house:

'I know all about the blood of Jesus. If I wanted to go to church I'd go with George.'

The next person opened the door:

'If I was going to go to church I would go with George. He's told me all about it.'

And on it went down the street.

I have never felt so humbled as one by one, neighbours explained how George had told them about the blood of Christ and how they knew they were going to hell if they did not believe.

What a great man he was.

I have read many commentaries on Romans 8 – I have nine on my shelves in front of me now – but no scholar understood Romans 8 like George.

When reading Scripture we should feel like shouting out loud, 'Me too!'

Because the Bible is about Jesus it is to be our food, our hope, our life. It is where we go when we fail; it is where we go when we are happy. If we come to the Bible like this we will find it really is all about Jesus.

When we read it, lives will be changed

The thrill of this living!
A minister I heard once, when preaching, stopped, held up his Bible and with tears in his eyes said to the congregation:

'This is what this book has done for me. This book has been the introduction to behold the glory of my Lord. Young people I want you to get the thrill of this living.'

Oh that we all would get the thrill of this living!

Appendices

Appendix 1
Frequently Asked Questions
(Written by Paul Blackham)

1. *Do we need the New Testament? If the gospel was set out in the Old Testament and the ancient church was saved by that revelation, then is the New Testament ultimately necessary?*

The Old Testament presents the gospel of the Promised Messiah, looking **forward** to his birth, life, death, resurrection and ascension. The New Testament is the fulfilment of that 'forward-looking' gospel. The New Testament contains the eye-witness accounts announcing that all the promises and predictions of the Old Testament have been fulfilled just as the ancient saints hoped.

If there were no New Testament then the prophecies of the Old Testament would be left hanging in the air. It is vital for us to know how and when all the predictions concerning the divine Messiah are fulfilled.

The knowledge of the Saviour is prophesied in the Old Testament, but his actual work of redemption is recorded in the New Testament.

Does a sign require a destination? Does a shadow need to be cast by somebody? Does a prophecy need a fulfilment?

Then of course the Old Testament requires the New Testament.

2. *Weren't the writers of the Old Testament trying to work out what they had written, according to 1 Peter 1:10-12?*

Sometimes people read 1 Peter 1:10-12 and assume that Peter is saying something that he is not. When we take time to read carefully what he actually says we see that Peter is making the very opposite point!

> Concerning this salvation, the prophets, who spoke of the grace that was to come to you, searched intently and with the greatest care, trying to find out **the time and circumstances** to which the **Spirit of Christ** in them was pointing when he predicted **the sufferings of Christ and the glories that would follow**. It was **revealed** to them that they were not serving themselves but you, when they spoke of the things that have now been told you by those who have preached the gospel to you by the Holy Spirit sent from heaven.

First, notice that these prophets spoke because the Spirit of Christ was in them.

Second, they were not trying to understand what they were prophesying about. Sometimes people have suggested that these ancient prophets almost fell into strange trances and uttered words that they could not understand. However, Peter tells us that the prophets were carefully and intently searching to find out when and how their prophecies would be fulfilled.

Third, the Old Testament prophets wanted to know when and how Christ would suffer and then enter into His glory. This is so important. They knew that the Christ would suffer and that His glory would only come after that suffering.

Furthermore, they also knew that their prophecies did not merely refer to the events of their own day and circumstances. It was revealed to them that their prophecies referred to a future time, the time of the Messiah.

3. Did the writers of the Hebrew Scriptures understand what they were writing?
Do I understand what I'm writing right now? I am trying to communicate certain ideas to you using these words. Perhaps I'm confused about what I want to say or perhaps you think that I don't understand the subject. However, all we can deal with is the actual words that I have written. I hope that these words accurately convey what I am trying to say.

The same is true of the Old Testament writers. We have their words as they wrote them. The meaning of these words can be understood by studying the grammar and context of the Scriptures. When they wrote these words they intended to convey specific meaning. Our job is simply to faithfully and carefully explain what the authors originally intended to say.

So, when Jesus referred to David's intention in writing Psalm 110, Jesus simply said,

'Why is it said that the Messiah is the son of David? David himself declares in the Book of Psalms: The Lord said to my Lord: "Sit at my right hand until I make your enemies a footstool for your feet." David calls him 'Lord.' How then can he be his son?' (Luke 20:41-44).

Jesus assumes that David intended to refer to the Messiah as 'Lord' – so we must assume that David understood that the Messiah was the Lord. We have to trust that the Old Testament writers meant what they said and said what they meant. If we deny this then it seems that we enter into a maze of personal opinion and speculation.

4. How much did the Old Testament saints really know about the person and work of Jesus Christ?

We cannot know what was going on in the minds of those people thousands of years ago – other than by looking at the text of Scripture. Whether every saint understood or believed all that God had spoken to them is highly unlikely, just as many Christians today do not understand all that the Bible contains.

However, if we look at the text of the Scriptures we can see that the living God revealed a great deal about the gospel of His promised Messiah. There was never a time when the knowledge of Christ was not held before His church.

Remember that the apostles presented the person and work of Jesus Christ by quoting the Old Testament writings. If the apostles told people to study Moses and Isaiah and David in order to understand who Jesus is and what He has done, then there must have been lots of important information about Jesus Christ in the Old Testament writings.

Jesus Himself summarized the content of the Old Testament in Luke 24:44-47:

> He said to them, 'This is what I told you while I was still with you: Everything must be fulfilled that is written about me in the Law of Moses, the Prophets and the Psalms.' Then he opened their minds so they could understand the Scriptures. He told them, 'This is what is written: The Christ will suffer and rise from the dead on the third day, and repentance and forgiveness of sins will be preached in his name to all nations, beginning at Jerusalem.'

5. According to Hebrews 1:1-3, didn't God have a different revelation in the Old Testament?

Hebrews chapter 1 is one of the most fascinating chapters in the whole Bible. If you were going to explain the relationship between the Father and the Son in the Trinity how would you do it? We might well turn to various parts of John's gospel, but the writer of Hebrews takes us through a selection of Old Testament quotations. This writer was convinced that the writers of the Old Testament had plenty to say about the true divine nature of God the Son.

In fact the whole book of Hebrews is packed full of explanations of the person and work of Jesus Christ taken from the Old Testament Scriptures. So, it seems certain that there is no fear that the Old Testament has a different revelation than the New Testament!

However, as we read in the opening verses of Hebrews chapter 1, the way in which God has delivered his gospel revelation had a major change in the incarnation of God the Son. In the Old Testament we see God the Son appearing, briefly, to all kinds of individuals and they in turn shared that revelation with others. The Angel of the Lord used many different 'middle-men' or mediators to convey the revelation to others. If you wanted to know the Word of the Lord you went to the priests and the prophets. However, in the incarnation it is as if God pushed aside all these middle-men and speaks for Himself. God the Son became one of us and spoke these truths for Himself, as a citizen of planet earth!

How awesome this is! The One who appeared to a select few in the Old Testament becomes flesh and is touched and handled and questioned by anybody and everybody. The Lord who previously sent messengers with His gospel – now became the divine Messenger speaking for Himself with no mediators.

As Hebrews 1:1-3 puts it, even though He made the universe, even though He is the exact copy of the Father's glory, even though He sustains the universe by His mere word – yet, He became flesh to speak His message for Himself.

The message is essentially the same from Genesis to Revelation, but there never was such a time before when the infinite and eternal Son spoke this message with our human lips!

6. *If the Old Testament church knew so much what was the point of the incarnation?*
If we think about Moses or Abraham or David or Isaiah we can see that they really did know the Living God. Yet, in spite of that, it was necessary for God the Son to become flesh. Why?

The Scriptures tell us that the heart of the incarnation is redemption. Those Old Testament saints knew God and also knew that the Lord God had promised to accomplish a glorious redemption one day. Those ancient saints looked forward to the birth of the Messiah, trying to find out the time or circumstances when He would be born among them.

In one sense we could say that God the Son had to become flesh precisely because the Old Testament church had been trusting in His future work for their own salvation. If he didn't become flesh to accomplish their redemption, then their faith in His salvation would have been empty and futile!

In chapter 8 of the Westminster Confession, this is expressed perfectly:

> 6. Although the work of redemption was not actually wrought by Christ till after His incarnation, yet the virtue, efficacy, and benefits thereof were communicated unto the elect, in all ages successively from the beginning of the world, in and by those promises, types, and sacrifices, wherein He was revealed, and signified to be the seed of the woman which should bruise the serpent's head; and the Lamb slain from the beginning of the world; being yesterday and to-day the same, and for ever.

7. *What difference did the incarnation make to God the Son? How did the incarnation affect Him?*

At face value this is an impossible question! The incarnation of God the Son is a marvel beyond all human comprehension. How can we know anything of the infinite and omnipresent God being contained within the limits of finite human flesh? How can we understand how the One who made us and sustains us with His mere word could ever actually be one of us? How can the eternal Creator become a historical creature?

However, when we see how God the Son appeared to certain people in the Old Testament, we might wonder how different it was when He became flesh. All we can say is that in the Old Testament He was never one of the Israelites. He was never a mortal, subject to the weaknesses and limits of our human life. He was never born under the law. He was never born of a woman. He never became flesh. He was the all-glorious Lord of hosts and when he appeared to someone His glory could shake the building and all but kill a man (see Isa. 6 for just one example).

In the incarnation, he laid aside His glory and lived among us with such inconceivable humility. He took upon Himself the poverty of our existence and learned obedience, even to the ultimate test of the cross. Even after He ascended back to His Father's glory, He did not cease to be one of us. Yes, the eternal Son who sits at his Father's side is actually our human brother!

8. In Hebrews 11:40, doesn't it seem as if the Old Testament church was imperfect until the New Testament church came along?

Hebrews 11 shows us how the ancient church had the same gospel of faith in Christ, from the very beginning of the world. In Hebrews 11:8-10 we learn that Abraham was looking forward to life in the city of God, not any temporary life in any earthly city. The same truth is emphasized in verses 13-16. These Old Testament saints were not trusting in earthly promises concerning earthly rewards. Just like us, they were looking forward to life in the new creation, life in the heavenly city.

In Hebrews 11:26 we learn that Moses turned away from the staggering earthly wealth and power of Egypt because he was trusting in Christ and the reward of eternal life in Christ. Hebrews 11 shows us that the Old Testament church had no inheritance in this passing age. They rejected the treasures of this age, even enduring terrible sufferings, because they were looking forward to the coming age, the coming city of God, the day of resurrection when Christ returns in glory.

The chapter concludes by telling us that they kept looking forward to that final glory, just as we also do now. The church of the Old Testament was looking forward to that glorious future, and the church of the New Testament does the same. However, one day, on the day when Jesus returns, the whole church of every age will inherit that promised city of God together.

Article 7 of the 39 Articles of the Church of England explains that the Old Testament saints were not looking for merely earthly rewards, but were looking forward to everlasting life just as we are:

> The Old Testament is not contrary to the New: for both in the Old and New Testament everlasting life is offered to Mankind by Christ, who is the only Mediator between God and Man, being both God and Man. Wherefore they are not to be heard,

which feign that the old Fathers did look only for transitory promises.

We are still waiting – and one day we will all be made perfect together!

9. *According to Exodus 6:2-3, did Abraham know the name of the Lord?*
In many translations of Exodus 6:2-3, it seems as if the name of the Lord was unknown to the saints in the book of Genesis.

> God also said to Moses, 'I am the Lord. I appeared to Abraham, to Isaac and to Jacob as God Almighty, but by my name the Lord I did not make myself known to them. I also established my covenant with them to give them the land of Canaan, where they lived as aliens. Moreover, I have heard the groaning of the Israelites, whom the Egyptians are enslaving, and I have remembered my covenant.'

There are many translation issues in these verses. In the footnotes in many Bibles you will see an alternative translation of verse 3: 'and by my name the Lord did I not let myself be known to them?'

So, which is the right way to translate the verse? In one, Abraham knew the name of the Lord and in the other he did not! Perhaps the best way of deciding this is to turn back to Genesis to see whether the people in Genesis actually did know the name of the Lord.

It might come as a surprise to see that in Genesis 4:1, the first woman, Eve, speaks the name of the Lord. So, she knew the name of the Lord! In addition we see that the name of the Lord is used all the way through the book of Genesis from the very beginning. At the end of Genesis chapter 4 we a re specifically told that man began to call on the name of the Lord. Lamech speaks of the Lord in 5:29. In Genesis 9:26 Noah uses the name of the Lord. In Genesis 14:22 we have proof that Abraham knew that his God was called the Lord. In Genesis 15:7 the Lord actually tells Abraham 'I am the Lord'!

As we go on we read of Abraham using the name of the Lord on many occasions. In Genesis 26:25 we are told that Isaac called on the name of the Lord and then in 27:7 Isaac used the name of the Lord. Jacob himself knows the name of the Lord in 27:20 – even while he is lying to his father!

So, when we study the actual text of Genesis we see that many people knew the name of the Lord, including Abraham, Isaac and Jacob.

Therefore, it seems that we have to translate Exodus 6:3 as 'by my name the Lord did I not let myself be known to them?' in order to be consistent with the book of Genesis.

10. When Jeremiah spoke about a 'new covenant' was he looking forward to a different way of salvation?

In Jeremiah 31:31 the Lord declared that a time was coming when He would make a 'new covenant' with Israel. Like Ezekiel in Ezekiel 36:24-27, this 'new covenant' would bring a new heart and a new spirit for the Lord's people, a heart with the law of God written into it.

However, if we go back to the beginning of the prophecy of Jeremiah we see that the people were urged to get just such a heart at that time.

In Jeremiah 4:4 the Lord says, 'Circumcise yourselves to the Lord, **circumcise your hearts…**' This idea of hearts being spiritually renewed does not begin with Jeremiah, but goes right back to Moses at the beginning of the Bible.

Deuteronomy 10:14-16 sets the eternal God before us with His eternal covenant:

> To the Lord your God belong the heavens, even the highest heavens, the earth and everything in it. Yet the Lord set his affection on your forefathers and loved them, and he chose you, their descendants, above all the nations, as it is today. Circumcise your hearts, therefore, and do not be stiff-necked any longer.

In Ezekiel 18:31 we see again how the Lord God challenged His ancient church to be born again, to receive the regenerating benefit of His covenant right then in ancient times: 'Rid your-selves of all the offences you have committed and get a new heart and a new spirit. Why will you die, O house of Israel?'

So, what is the old covenant if we can find the new covenant throughout the whole Bible?

If we turn to Jeremiah 31:31-32 we are told plainly what the old covenant is:

> 'The time is coming,' declares the Lord, 'when I will make a new covenant with the house of Israel and with the house of Judah. It will not be like the covenant I made with their forefathers when I took them by the hand to lead them out of Egypt...'

The old covenant is the covenant made at Sinai, the system of law given through Moses. So why is it called 'old' when the 'new' covenant is older?

The covenant of Sinai is 'old' because it was just a temporary shadow and sign pointing towards the person and work of Jesus Christ. It was 'old' because it had a fading and a time-limited glory. Its purpose was not to save anybody but to point people forward to the time when the redemption of the new covenant would be accomplished by the promised Messiah. The blood of bulls and goats in the 'old' covenant was never able to save anybody, but it was a schoolmaster teaching the ancient people about the person and work of the promised Messiah.

In one sense we can say that the 'new' covenant is older than the 'old' covenant! The new covenant is everlasting and ever new, remaining the same in Christ yesterday, today and forever. The 'old' covenant belonged to a specific historical time and has now finished its work.

To summarize all this we again turn to the Westminster Confession, which explains how there is just one eternal covenant as the foundation for the whole Bible. Here is how this is expressed in Chapter 7 of the Confession:

> 3. Man, by his fall, having made himself incapable of life by that covenant, the Lord was pleased to make a second, commonly

called the covenant of grace; wherein He freely offereth unto sinners life and salvation by Jesus Christ; requiring of them faith in Him, that they may be saved, and promising to give unto all those that are ordained unto eternal life His Holy Spirit, to make them willing, and able to believe.

4. This covenant of grace is frequently set forth in Scripture by the name of a testament, in reference to the death of Jesus Christ the Testator, and to the everlasting inheritance, with all things belonging to it, therein bequeathed.

5. This covenant was differently administered in the time of the law, and in the time of the gospel: under the law it was administered by promises, prophecies, sacrifices, circumcision, the paschal lamb, and other types and ordinances delivered to the people of the Jews, all foresignifying Christ to come; which were, for that time, sufficient and efficacious, through the operation of the Spirit, to instruct and build up the elect in faith in the promised Messiah, by whom they had full remission of sins, and eternal salvation; and is called the Old Testament.

6. Under the gospel, when Christ, the substance, was exhibited, the ordinances in which this covenant is dispensed are the preaching of the Word, and the administration of the sacraments of Baptism and the Lord's Supper: which, though fewer in number, and administered with more simplicity, and less outward glory, yet, in them, it is held forth in more fullness, evidence, and spiritual efficacy, to all nations, both Jews and Gentiles; and is called the new Testament. There are not therefore two covenants of grace, differing in substance, but one and the same, under various dispensations.

11. What are the differences between the church in the Old Testament and the church in the New Testament? What are the areas of continuity and discontinuity?

The Old Testament looked forward to the person and work of Jesus Christ, through all the signs and shadows that the Lord God gave to them. These signs and shadows came to an end when Christ came to fulfil them.

The New Testament Church looks back to the completed work of Jesus Christ. The signs and the shadows have come to an end now that Jesus Christ has fulfilled them.

Salvation has only ever come through faith in Christ – whether that was through the Old Testament signs or the New Testament testimony.

Chapter 7 of the Westminster Confession, quoted above, expresses this truth so very well.

12. We just speak about 'Jesus' all the time, but what name did the Old Testament saints use to refer to God the Son?

The Scriptures contain many titles and names of God the Son, and if we have limited ourselves to just one or two of these then it might be good for us to expand our vocabulary a little!

We find the ancient church using many different titles to refer to the second person of the Trinity. Of course we find titles like the Angel of the Lord or the Messiah occurring quite often, but there are many more.

> Commander of the Lord's army - Joshua 5:14
> Arbitrator - Job 9:33
> Counsellor - Isaiah 9:6
> Sun of righteousness - Malachi 4:2
> Witness; Friend; Intercessor – Job 16:19-21
> The Lord's Servant – Isaiah 52:13
> Prince of Peace – Isaiah 9:6
> The Seed – Genesis 3:15
> Man of Sorrows - Isaiah 53:3
> Shiloh – Genesis 49:10 (see footnote in most translations)
> The Rock – Deuteronomy 32:4

As we get to learn the many and glorious titles of God the Son, as our Christian ancestors did, so we will get more used to recognizing when the Old Testament saints are speaking about Him.

13. What is the meaning of the day of Pentecost in Acts 2? Is it 'the birth of the church' or perhaps 'the coming of the Spirit'?

Although in popular Christianity sometimes people describe the Day of Pentecost as 'the birth of the church' or 'the coming of the Spirit', actually the Bible never speaks of Pentecost in those terms. The Holy Spirit did not begin His work halfway through the New Testament! Remember how Simeon (Luke 2:25-27) was moved by the Spirit when Jesus was a child. He wasn't a prophet, priest or king, yet the Holy Spirit was upon him. Again, in John 14:15-18, Jesus tells the disciples that they not only already know the Holy Spirit but also that the Holy Spirit would continue to be with them forever.

The 'church' did not begin on the Day of Pentecost. Stephen spoke about the 'church in the desert' (Acts 7:38 – the Greek word for 'assembly' is *ekklesia*) when he spoke of the church during the life of Moses. If the Old Testament saints were not in the church then they were not saved at all!

In John 3:5, Jesus assumes that any teacher of Israel knew that no-one can enter the kingdom without the Spirit. In Romans 8:9 we are reminded that 'if anyone does not have the Spirit of Christ, he does not belong to Christ.'

So, what is the meaning of Pentecost? Well, that is the very question asked by the amazed and perplexed people from across the world in Acts 2:12. Peter answered by taking them back to the prophet Joel. It is helpful to see the bit just before the verses that Peter quoted. Consider Joel 2:27-28 – 'Then you will know that I am in Israel, that I am the Lord your God, and that there is no other; never again will my people be shamed. And afterwards, I will pour out my Spirit on all people...' Notice that the blessing of the Spirit will be given not only to 'my people' but to 'all people'. In Joel 2:32 the same point is made very clear. Not just Jews, but all nations will find salvation: 'Everyone who calls on the name of the Lord will be saved....'.

This is why Acts 2:1-11 emphasizes the international character of the crowds in Jerusalem. The apostles were enabled to speak all these different international languages, showing that the church would no longer be a single nation but a community spread throughout all the nations of the world.

So, in Acts 10:44-45, the Holy Spirit came upon all, Jews and Gentiles. The circumcised believers were not surprised at the presence of the Spirit as such, but that 'the gift of the Holy Spirit had been poured out even on the Gentiles.'

14. Why does Paul speak about the 'mystery' that was not revealed to people in the past as it has now been revealed in the New Testament?
First we need to gather together the verses where Paul speaks of this 'mystery'. First Romans 16:25-26:

> 'Now to him who is able to establish you by my gospel and the proclamation of Jesus Christ, according to the revelation of the **mystery** hidden for long ages past, but now revealed and made known through the prophetic writings by the command of the eternal God, so that all nations might believe and obey him.'

In this conclusion to his letter to the Romans, Paul indicates that the hidden mystery is made known through the prophetic writings. The mystery, then, seems to be something that was not generally known to the world, but is known in the ancient prophetic writings. The result of making the mystery known through the prophetic writings is that 'all nations might believe and obey him'.

The mystery, then, seems to have relevance to all the nations and is known through the ancient prophets.

In the next Scripture, Paul actually defines what this mystery is. In Ephesians 3:4-6:

> 'In reading this, then, you will be able to understand my insight into the **mystery** of Christ, which was not made known to men in other generations as it has now been revealed by the Spirit to God's holy apostles and prophets. This **mystery** is that through the gospel the Gentiles are heirs together with Israel, members together of one body, sharers together in the promise in Christ Jesus.'

Through the prophets and apostles this mystery is being made known to humanity as never before. So what is the mystery? It is the good news that the nations, the Gentiles, are accepted by the living God just as if they were Jews. The time of division between the Jews and all the other nations of the world was just a temporary arrangement and now the barrier has been destroyed. Jews and Gentiles form one body, equal members of Israel, sharing together in Jesus.

In all the time since Moses, the different nations of the world were excluded from the church. The Gentiles had to become Jews in order to join Israel (see Deut. 23:7-8). When Jesus died the Law and all its regulations were nailed to the cross and the dividing wall of the Law was pulled down.

And Colossians 1:25-27:

> 'I have become its servant by the commission God gave me to present to you the Word of God in its fullness – the **mystery** that has been kept hidden for ages and generations, but is now disclosed to the saints. To them God has chosen to make known **among the Gentiles** the glorious riches of this **mystery**, which is Christ in you, the hope of glory.'

15. *Why do so many Christians think that the Angel of the Lord is God the Son?*
In different parts of the Hebrew Scriptures we come across the figure of the Angel of the Lord. Down the centuries most Christians have understood Him to be a special appearance of God the Son before He became flesh (the pre-incarnate Son). There is a lot to be said for this view.

In Genesis 16 the Angel of the Lord spoke to Hagar and in verse 13 she gave this name to the Lord who spoke to her: 'You are the God who sees me,' for she said, 'I have now seen the One who sees me.'

In Genesis 48:15-16, the elderly Jacob thinks of the Angel of the Lord as the God of Abraham and Isaac. 'May the God before whom my fathers Abraham and Isaac walked, the God who has been my shepherd all my life to this day, the Angel who has delivered me from all harm – may he bless these boys.'

Finally, in Judges 2:1-2, the Angel of the Lord claims to have been the God of the patriarchs and Redeemer of Israel: 'The Angel of the Lord went up from Gilgal to Bokim and said, "I brought you up out of Egypt and led you into the land that I swore to give to your forefathers..."'

The word 'angel' simply means 'one who is sent' or 'messenger'. So, 'the Angel of the Lord' means 'the One sent from the Lord'. On the evidence of the Scriptures it seems highly likely that the Angel of the Lord is not only God but is also sent by God. This seems to be a fair definition of the person of Christ, the Son of God.

16. Is the Word of the Lord in the Old Testament the same as the Word of God in John 1? Is the Word of the Lord a title for Jesus in the Old Testament?

When the apostle John speaks of 'the Word of God' he is referring to God the Son. When the apostle Paul speaks of the Word of God, he seems to be referring to the Scriptures. We find the same variety in the Hebrew Scriptures. Perhaps Moses is more like John and uses the phrase 'the Word of God' to refer to God the Son. It could be argued that the same pattern is found in the prophet Jeremiah. However, when we read the prophet Haggai, he seems to use the phrase to refer simply to a message given to him from the Lord.

So, sometimes 'the Word of the Lord' is one of Jesus' titles in the Old Testament – but not in every case.

It seems wisest to be sensitive to the way each Biblical writer uses language. Forcing a systematic framework onto the Biblical text may seem easier but it will obscure the original meaning of the authors. We have to keep asking what does 'the Word of the Lord/God' mean for this author in this context?

17. Are we in a more privileged position today than the Old Testament saints?

Yes. The Old Testament church was looking forward to the death of Jesus and beyond that to the final day of the Lord Jesus. We can look back to see the wonderful way that Jesus fulfilled all that the prophets predicted about him. He did everything that they foresaw, exactly as they prophesied! It is such a privilege to have this thrilling confirmation of the Messianic prophecies.

In addition to all this, as we have seen, the geographical/ ethnic limitations of the church have been removed. Now, whether we are Jew or Gentile, no matter where in the world we live, we are together the one body of Christ across the whole world. The prophets knew that such a day of global blessing would happen, but we have the privilege of enjoying this time.

18. Is the revelation of God 'progressive'?
Yes. The living God reveals so many aspects of Jesus Christ throughout the Bible. Although the gospel itself remains the same from first to last, yet it is expressed and filled out in so many rich ways down the ages. The promise of the Seed given to Eve is carried forward to Abraham, Isaac and Jacob. The Law is preached and explained by the latter prophets. The gospel of the promised Messiah received fresh expressions as the Biblical story unfolded.

As the 39 Articles of the 16th century so helpfully express it, 'the Old Testament is not contrary to the New, for in both the Old and New Testaments eternal life is offered to mankind through Christ.' Yes, the gospel of faith alone in Christ alone is the same from Genesis to Revelation, yet surely Moses could describe more about the theology of atonement than the earlier saints? Surely the prophet Isaiah could speak more fully of the sufferings of the divine Servant?

However, we must be careful not to imagine that after the New Testament was written the Old Testament has become irrelevant. The apostles in the New Testament emphasize that they are preaching only the truth that the Law and the Prophets already proclaimed (Acts 26:22).

19. In Matthew 11:11, doesn't Jesus say that even the least New Testament Christian is greater than the greatest Old Testament prophet, John the Baptist?
'I tell you the truth: Among those born of women there has not risen anyone greater than John the Baptist; yet he who is least in the kingdom of heaven is greater than he.'

Our first question is simply this: was John the Baptist in the kingdom of heaven? This is a very serious question because if we follow Jesus' teaching through the rest of Matthew, anyone who is not in the kingdom of heaven will be cast into hell. Consider Matthew 13:37-43. The sons of the kingdom are the righteous who shine like the sun in the kingdom of their Father. However, those outside the kingdom are the sons of the evil one who will be thrown into the fiery furnace, where there will be weeping and gnashing of teeth.

If we think that Jesus is contrasting John the Baptist with people who are in the kingdom of heaven, then we are saying that John the Baptist will be thrown into the fiery furnace!

However, John the Baptist was himself a minister of the kingdom of heaven. In Matthew 3:1-2 we see that John's entire preaching ministry centred on calling people to the kingdom of heaven.

Now, John was a very impressive and charismatic leader. In Matthew 3:4-6 we learn of the impact he made on the entire nation. He must have been intimidating and awe-inspiring and people flocked to see him (Matt. 11:7-10). Jesus seems to be acknowledging this in his words of Matthew 11:11. The phrase 'born of women' seems to simply refer to natural human birth and natural human ability. When the apostle Paul is referring to the fact that Jesus truly became one of us he too uses the phrase 'born of a woman' (Gal. 4:4). Jesus was saying that John the Baptist was an extraordinary human being with more natural human ability than anyone else.

In other words, Jesus is saying that although John the Baptist was a hugely gifted human being, yet his message about the kingdom of heaven is infinitely more important than the prophet. There was no point in all the crowds going out to watch the phenomenon of John the Baptist if they were not actually listening to the kingdom preaching of John! Instead of being fascinated by John, they needed to enter into the kingdom and get something infinitely greater than all the natural gifts and charisma of John.

What use is it if someone gets all the natural gifts in the whole world?

20. Can the gospel of Christ really be understood from the Old Testament as well as the New Testament?

Jesus Himself gave Bible studies that explained his person and work from the Old Testament. See Luke 24:45-47:

> Then he opened their minds so they could understand the Scriptures. He told them, 'This is what is written: The Christ will suffer and rise from the dead on the third day and repentance and forgiveness of sins will be preached in his name to all nations, beginning at Jerusalem...'

The apostles preached the gospel of Jesus Christ from the Old Testament. Consider Peter's sermon in Acts 2. He asks his hearers to remember what these Old Testament writers meant when they spoke about the resurrection and ascension of Jesus Christ.

In Peter's speech to the crowd at Solomon's Colonnade, he gives a quick summary of the whole Old Testament as he explains the gospel of Jesus. The whole of Acts 7 is Stephen's thorough presentation of the same message. When Philip meets the Ethiopian in Acts 8:26-40, the man is reading Isaiah 53:7-8 and Philip 'began with that very passage of Scripture and told him the good news about Jesus.' In Acts 13:13-48 the apostle Paul explained the gospel of Jesus Christ form the Old Testament.

In Acts 17:2-3:

> As his custom was, Paul went into the synagogue, and on three Sabbath days he reasoned with them from the Scriptures, explaining and proving that the Christ had to suffer and rise from the dead. 'This Jesus I am proclaiming to you is the Christ.'

If both Jesus and his apostles preached his gospel from the Old Testament, then it seems to be the right thing to do. The gospel can certainly be understood in the Old Testament just as in the New Testament.

However, we should remember that unless a person will turn to Jesus in repentance and trust, their vision will remain veiled and they will not understand the gospel of Jesus whether it is presented from the Old Testament or the New Testament (see 2 Cor. 3:14-16). The Pharisees not only failed to understand the gospel in the Old Testament but even when Jesus the Lord God of Israel was standing right in front of them, they still failed to see him!

21. Did every believer in the Old Testament have a personal meeting with the Angel of the Lord?
No. The appearances of the Angel of the Lord were not very common. We see him appear to various people in the book of Genesis and to Moses in the book of Exodus. He meets with particular people in the book of Judges, but after that his presence is extremely rare. For those leaders who were granted this special encounter, it must have been an incredible, life-changing event. However, the overwhelming majority of believers in the Old Testament did not have a direct, personal, visible encounter with the Angel of the Lord.

22. How can we speak of the 'church' in the Old Testament when that word is never used in the Old Testament?
The English word 'church' is used to translate the Greek word *ekklesia*. This is not a word that is only used after the day of Pentecost. Jesus himself speaks of the church in Matthew 18:17. Stephen describes Israel during the Exodus as the 'church (*ekklesia*) in the wilderness' (Acts 7:38).

In fact, this Greek word *ekklesia* was used before the New Testament was written, before Jesus was born. Three hundred years before the birth of Jesus the Hebrew Scriptures were translated into Greek. This translation was called The Septuagint [LXX]. When the Hebrew Scriptures speak about the assembly of Israel the Greek translators often used the word *ekklesia* to translate this.

In other words, the *ekklesia* or 'the church' was a common way of describing the people of God hundreds of years before the New Testament was written.

'Church' is an Old Testament word which is used in the New Testament.

' You will see that many of our Christian ancestors frequently use the word 'church' when they are writing about the saints in the Old Testament. For example, Andrew Bonar's great commentary on the Psalms, originally published in 1859, was simply called 'Christ and His Church in the Book of Psalms'.

23. Why did the early church think that Jesus was in Proverbs 8?

The ancient Christians believed that the figure of Wisdom in the book of Proverbs is actually God the Son or a personified symbol of the Son. Although many modern readers of Proverbs may miss this, it is worth considering.

In the first nine chapters of Proverbs, Wisdom is described in many ways. Could this figure by a kind of symbol of Christ? Make a list of all the qualities of Wisdom and all the blessings to be received from Wisdom.

Wisdom saves from wickedness. Wisdom is more valuable than all the treasure in the world. Wisdom grants eternal life. Wisdom is the tree of life. Whoever grasps Wisdom is blessed. Through Wisdom the heavens and the earth were created. Wisdom will protect you. If you love Wisdom, you will be guarded. The grace of God comes to you if you embrace Wisdom. The way of Wisdom is the straight path of life. Wisdom speaks what is right and just. Wisdom hates pride and governs all the rulers of the world. Wisdom says 'I love those who love me, and those who seek me find me. With me are riches and honour, enduring wealth and prosperity… I walk in the way of righteousness, along the paths of justice, bestowing wealth on those who love me… Whoever finds me finds life and receives favour from the Lord. But whoever fails to find me harms himself; all who hate me love death.'

So, when Proverbs 8:22-31 records a speech of the craftsman of Creation, the One who is older than all creatures, the One who has been present with the Lord in all his works, the One who eternally rejoices in His presence – it is understandable that the ancient Christians concluded that the figure of Wisdom is yet another way of depicting the eternal Son.

In addition to this, we can note that the apostle John describes Jesus as the eternal Word of God, through whom everything was created. Many have suggested that what John means by 'Word', Solomon/David means by 'Wisdom'. In 1 Corinthians 1:30 the apostle Paul does seem to suggest that Jesus is the wisdom from God.

24. Do all Christians understand the Old Testament in this way?

There are Christians who see the promises in the Old Testament as physical and earthly, and see those promises of God as speaking of nothing beyond earthly land, kings and signs. This perspective sees the Old Testament people as trusting in these promises, without knowing of the person of Christ.

However, it seems to us that the best way to understand the Old Testament is around the person and work of Jesus Christ. In all the promises and signs of the Old Testament, Jesus Christ was presented to his church. The great creeds and confessions of the historic Christian church tend to take this view of the Old Testament.

The Heidelberg Catechism (1563)
Question 19. Whence knowest thou this?
Answer: From the holy gospel, which God himself first revealed in Paradise; (a) and afterwards published by the patriarchs (b) and prophets, (c) and represented by the sacrifices and other ceremonies of the law; (d) and lastly, has fulfilled it by his only begotten Son.

The 39 Articles of the Church of England (1571) – Article 7
The Old Testament is not contrary to the New, for in both the Old and New Testaments eternal life is offered to mankind through Christ. Hence he, being both God and man, is the only mediator between God and man. Those who pretend that the Patriarchs only looked for transitory promises must not be listened to.

The Westminster Confession (1647) – Chapter 7

This covenant of grace is frequently set forth in scripture by the name of a testament, in reference to the death of Jesus Christ the Testator, and to the everlasting inheritance, with all things belonging to it, therein bequeathed. This covenant was differently administered in the time of the law, and in the time of the Gospel: under the law it was administered by promises, prophecies, sacrifices, circumcision, the paschal lamb, and other types and ordinances delivered to the people of the Jews, all foresignifying Christ to come; which were, for that time, sufficient and efficacious, through the operation of the Spirit, to instruct and build up the elect in faith in the promised Messiah, by whom they had full remission of sins, and eternal salvation; and is called the Old Testament.

Baptist Confession of Faith (1689) – Article 7

3. This covenant is revealed in the gospel; first of all to Adam in the promise of salvation by the seed of the woman, and afterwards by farther steps, until the full discovery thereof was completed in the New Testament; and it is founded in that eternal covenant transaction that was between the Father and the Son about the redemption of the elect; and it is alone by the grace of this covenant that all the posterity of fallen Adam that ever were saved did obtain life and blessed immortality, man being now utterly incapable of acceptance with God upon those terms on which Adam stood in his state of innocency. (Gen. 3:15; Heb. 1:1; 2 Tim. 1:9; Titus 1:2; Heb. 11;6, 13; Rom. 4:1, 2, &c.; Acts 4:12; John 8:56).

Appendix 2
Quotes from church history
(Selected by Steve Levy)

JC Ryle says:
> 'Enoch believed that God had graciously provided a way of
> salvation, that He had appointed a great Redeemer to bear our
> sins and carry our transgressions and bruise the serpent's head.
> He saw clearly that without this he had not the slightest chance
> of being saved, whatever he might do; he looked far forward,
> and in his mind's eye he saw a long way off the Messiah that
> was yet to come to pay the ransom of the world, and he built all
> his hopes on Him. Enoch believed in the Lord Jesus Christ.'
>
> **Heading for heaven, p.18**

> '...The plain truth is, that we are too apt to forget that there
> never was but one way of salvation, one Saviour, and one hope
> for sinners, and that Abraham and all the Old Testament saints
> looked to the same Christ that we look to ourselves.'
>
> **Expository thoughts, John 8:48-59**

CH Spurgeon says:
> 'Before the First Advent, all the types and shadows pointed
> one way – to Christ. To Him all believers looked with hope.
> Those who lived before Christ were not saved with a different
> salvation than the eternal salvation that will come to us. They
> exercised faith just as we must. Their faith struggled as ours
> struggles, and their faith obtained its eternal reward just as
> ours will. Comparing the spiritual life of the believer now with
> the spiritual life of David is like comparing a man's face with a
> reflection of that face.

Sometime, when you are reading the book of Psalms, forget for an instant that you are reading about the life of someone who lived a long time ago. You might suppose that David wrote only yesterday. Even in what he wrote about Christ, it seems as though he lived after Christ, instead of before. Furthermore, both in what he saw of himself and of his Saviour, he sounds more like a New Testament believer who has found his Messiah than an Old Testament Israelite still awaiting the Christ. What I am saying is that, living before Christ, he had the same joys and the same sorrows. He had the same impression of his blessed Redeemer that you and I have in these times. Jesus was the same yesterday as He is today, as far as being an anointed Saviour to His people. They received from Him similar precious gifts. If the good prophets could have been here today, they would all testify that in every office, He was the same in their time as He is today.'

The Joy of the Lord, pages 107-109

RM McCheyne says:

'Jesus is called "the Lamb slain from the foundation of the world." No sooner had man fallen than God pointed him to Jesus. Even before He pronounced the curse on man He preached the gospel to man. ...And was it not the same gospel that gentle Abel believed...And did not Noah believe the same gospel...Job went this way; and Aaron; and Jacob too, halting on his thigh. This way went Isaiah, hymning Immanuel's praise; and Jeremiah too, weeping along this narrow path. This way went Matthew the publican, and Zacchaeus the hoary-headed swindler; and the thief that died believing.'

Sermon on Hebrews, page 10

'some of the features of the priesthood of Aaron and his sons... were intended by God to be a great mirror to reflect the image of Jesus, the great High Priest who was to come. The believing Jew in those days could see in the features of Aaron, in his glorious garments, his breastplate etc...a bright representation of Jesus the High Priest and Saviour of sinners...The Jewish priesthood was the shadow which the coming Saviour cast before Him.'

Sermon on Hebrews, page 63

John Newton says:

'The Lord Jesus Christ was promised under the character *of the seed of the woman,* as the great deliverer who should repair the breach of sin, and retrieve the ruin of human nature. From that hour, he became the object of faith, and the author of salvation, to every soul that aspired to communion with God, and earnestly sought deliverance from guilt and wrath.'

'That the patriarchs and prophets of old were in this sense *Christians,* that is to say, that their joy and trust centred in the promised Messiah, and that the faith, whereby they overcame the world, was the same faith in the same Lord with ours, is unanswerably proved by St. Paul in several passages; particularly in Hebrews 11…'

Works volume 3, page 3

George Whitefield says:

'By the *seed of the woman,* we are here to understand, the Lord Jesus Christ, who though very God of very God, was, for us men and our salvation, to have a body prepared for him by the Holy Ghost, and to be born of a woman who never knew man, and by his obedience and death make an atonement for man's transgression, and bring in an everlasting righteousness, work in them a new nature, and thereby bruise the serpent's head. That is, destroy his power and dominion over them. By the *serpent's seed,* we are to understand, the devil and all his children, who are permitted by God to tempt and sift his children. But, blessed be God, he can reach no further than our heel. It is not to be doubted but Adam and Eve understood this promise in this sense.'

Sermons volume 2

Jonathan Edwards says:

'When we read of God's appearing after the Fall, from time to time, in some visible form or outward symbol of his presence, we are ordinarily, if not universally, to understand it of the second person of the Trinity: which may be argued from John 1:18, ' No man has seen God at any time; the only begotten Son, which is in the bosom of the Father, he hath declared him.' He is therefore called, 'the image of the invisible God' (Col. 1:15).'

History of Redemption, page 23

'God gives forth a law of nothing else but various and innumerable typical representations of good things to come, by which that nation were directed how, every year, month, and day, in their religious actions, and in their conduct of themselves, in all that appertained to their ecclesiastical and civil state, to show forth something of Christ; one observance showing one thing, exhibiting one doctrine, or one benefit; another, another; so that the whole nation by this law was, as it were, constituted a typical state. Thus, the gospel was abundantly held forth to that nation; so that there is scarce any doctrine of it, but it is particularly taught and exhibited by some observance of this law, though it was in shadows.'

History of Redemption, page 80
(Speaking of the Psalms, Edwards said of David)

'Joyfully did this holy man sing of those great things of Christ's redemption that had been the hope and expectation of God's church and people from the beginning of the church of God on earth; and joyfully did others follow him in it.'

History of Redemption, page 111

'The Christian church which has been since Christ's ascension is manifestly the same society continued within the church that was before Christ came. The Christian church is grafted on their root. They are built on the same foundation…The church before the Flood was built on the foundations of those revelations of Christ which were given to Adam, Abel, and Enoch, of which we have an account in the former chapters of Genesis.'

History of Redemption, pages 355–356

John Bunyan says:
'Now the promise of grace, being this, that the seed of the woman, which is Christ, should destroy the power of the devil; by this Abel saw that it was Christ that should abolish sin and death by himself, and bring in "everlasting righteousness" for sinners.'

Works, page 395

'all the ordinances of worship under the Old Testament preached to them that were under it, Christ, as yet to come.'

Works, page 433

Richard Sibbes says

The prophet Isaiah being lifted up and carriesdwith the wing
of prophetical spirit, passes over all the time between him
and the appearing of Jesus Christ in the flesh. Seeing with
the eye of prophecy, and with eye of Faith, Christ as present,
he presents him in the name of God, to the spiritual eye of
others,

Bruised reed page 1 (Banner of Truth paperback)

John Owen says:

'Speaking of their attitude towards keeping the externals of the
law…they knew and believed in faith that all spiritual good was
concealed beneath the shadows of these legal ceremonies, and
that all was summed up in eternal life through the Messiah yet
to be revealed. So it is that Christ Himself affirms that Moses,
and Moses' interpreters the prophets, all gave testimony to
Him, and to His work as *Mediator.* The Apostles also asserted
that, by preaching the death and resurrection of Christ and
the eternal life which flows therefrom, they were teaching
nothing else but what had been written before in Moses and
the prophets.'

Biblical Theology, page 376

'no sacrifice of animals was able, by itself, to effect the removal
of sin, or allow man to approach God, gain His favour, and
emerge from the sacrifice purged of guilt. For this reason,
these sacrifices had to be performed in such a way as to pre-
figure another and outstanding sacrifice.'

Hebrews, page 436

'The Christian church is not another church, but the very same
that was before the coming of Christ, having the same faith
with it, and interested in the same covenant.'

Hebrews, page 123

'The Faith of the Church under the Old Testament in and concerning the Person of Christ... that the faith of all believers, from the foundation of the world, had a respect unto him, I shall afterwards demonstrate; and to deny it, is to renounce both the Old Testament and the New. But that this faith of theirs did principally respect his person, is what shall here be declared. Therein they knew was laid the foundation of the counsels of God for their deliverance, sanctification, and salvation.'

Christologia, chapter 8

Turretin says

We maintain that Christ was not only predicted but also promised to the fathers and *by his grace they were saved under the Old Testament no less than we are saved under the New*; nor was any name given under heaven from which salvation could be hoped for (Acts 4:12) and that too according to the inviolable promise of the gratuitous covenant.

5th Q: 6

Peter testifies, "To Christ give all the prophets witness, that through his name whosoever believeth in him shall receive remission of sins" (Acts 10:43). *Nor can it be objected that the faith of the ancients was general in God, not special in Christ (the Saviour), because the opposite is evident* from many considerations. (a)No faith can be saving unless founded upon Christ. (b)He speaks of the faith by which they looked to God as their God (Heb. 11:16) and to heaven as their native country. Now this cannot be done without Christ. (c)Of the faith by which they looked to Christ himself and preferred his reproach to all treasures (Heb. 11:26). (d)*Not only a general but also a special command of faith in Christ is found in the Old Testament* (Exod. 23:20-21; Deut. 18:18; Ps. 2:12; Isa. 53:1, 5). If the faith of the ancients were not the same as ours, it would be improperly proposed for our imitation (Heb. 12:1, 2; Rom. 4:12). Paul could not argue with sufficient strength from the faith of the father of believers and his justification to ours (Gal. 3:6, 7; Rom. 4:16).

5th Q: 14

The Geneva Bible notes 1599 says

The power of Christ showed itself through all former ages in the fathers, for they saw in the promises that he would come, and very joyfully laid hold of him with a living faith.

Comments on John 8:56

In effect the ordinances of the old fathers were all one with ours, for they respected Christ alone, who offered himself to them in different forms.

Comments on 1 Corinthians 10:2

By these words "His voice" he shows that David meant the preaching of Christ, who was then also preached, for Moses and the prophets honoured no one else.

Comments on Hebrews 4:2

Church of England homilies (1562) says

All these Fathers, Martyrs, and other holy men, whom Saint Paul spake of, had their faith surely fixed on God, when all the world was against them. They did not only know God to be the Lord, Maker, and Governor of all men in the world: but also they had a special confidence and trust, that he was and would be their God, their comforter, aider, helper, maintainer, and defender. This is the Christian faith; which these holy men had, and we also ought to have. And although they were not named Christian men, yet was it a Christian faith that they had, for they looked for all benefits of God the Father, through the merits of his Son Jesus Christ, as we now do. This difference is between them and us, for they looked when Christ should come, and we be in the time when he is come. Therefore saith S. Augustine, "The time is altered and changed, but not the faith. For we have both one faith in one Christ." The same Holy Ghost also that we have, had they, saith St. Paul

True, lively, and Christian faith

John Calvin says:

'the God who of old appeared to the patriarchs was no other than Christ.'

Institutes Book 1, page 156

'I merely want to remind my readers that the hope of all the godly has ever reposed in Christ alone. All the other prophets also agree...God willed that the Jews should be so instructed by these prophecies that they might turn their eyes directly to Christ in order to seek deliverance...apart from Christ the saving knowledge of God does not stand. From the beginning of the world he had consequently been set before all the elect that they should look unto him and put their trust in him.'

Institutes, Book 1, pages 345, 346 and 347

(Calvin says of even the sacrificial system) 'by this sacrifice the minds of the people were directed to Christ.'

Comm. Exodus 29:38

'The covenant made with all the patriarchs is so much like ours in substance and reality that the two are actually one and the same... Here we must take our stand on three main points. First, we hold that carnal prosperity and happiness did not constitute the goal set before the Jews to which they were to aspire. Rather, they were adopted into the hope of immortality; and assurance of this adoption was certified to them by oracles, by the law, and by the prophets. Secondly, the covenant by which they were bound to the Lord was supported, not by their own merits, but solely by the mercy of the God who called them. Thirdly, **they had and knew Christ as Mediator, through whom they were joined to God and were to share in his promises.'**

Institutes, Book 1, page 429

'Who, then, dares to separate the Jews from Christ, since with them, we hear, was made the covenant of the gospel, the sole foundation of which is Christ? Who dares to estrange from the gift of free salvation those to whom we hear the doctrine of the righteousness of faith was imparted? Not to dispute too long about something obvious – we have a notable saying of the Lord: "Abraham rejoiced that he was to see my day, he saw it and was glad" (John 8:56). And what Christ there testified concerning Abraham, the apostle shows to have been universal among the believing folk when he says: "Christ remains, yesterday and today and forever"

(Heb. 13:8). Paul is not speaking there simply of Christ's everlasting divinity but of his power, a power perpetually available to believers...If the Lord, in manifesting his Christ, discharged his ancient oath, one cannot but say that the Old Testament always had its end in Christ.'

Institutes, Book 1, page 431

Martin Luther says:

'The faith of the fathers in the old testament era, and our faith in the new testament are one and the same faith in Christ Jesus, although times and conditions may differ... The faith of the fathers was directed at the Christ who was to come, while ours rests in the Christ who has come. Time does not change the object of true faith, or the Holy Spirit. There has always been and always will be one mind, one impression, one faith concerning Christ among true believers whether they live in times past, now, or in times to come. We too believe in the Christ to come as the fathers did in the old testament, for we look for Christ to come again on the last day to judge the quick and the dead.'

Galatians chapter 3:6-7

'The only difference between Abraham's faith and ours is this: Abraham believed in the Christ who was to be manifested, but we believe in the Christ who has already been manifested; and by that faith we are all saved.'

Volume 3, page 26

Cyril says

Moreover, that you may be sure that this is He who was seen of Moses, hear Paul's testimony, when he says, *For they all drank of a spiritual rock that followed them; and the rock was Christ.* And again: *By faith Moses forsook Egypt,* and shortly after he says, *accounting the reproach of Christ greater riches than the treasures in Egypt.* This Moses says to Him, *Shew me Thyself.* Thou seest that the Prophets also in those times saw the Christ, that is, as far as each was able.

lecture 10 on the clause and in one Lord Jesus Christ

Leo the great says

> **The blessings of the Incarnation stretch backwards as well as reach forward.**
>
> …What the apostles foretold, that the prophets announced: nor was that fulfilled too late which has always been believed. …And so it was no new counsel, no tardy pity whereby GOD took thought for men: but from the constitution of the world He ordained one and the same Cause of Salvation for all. For the grace of GOD, by which the whole body of the saints is ever justified, was augmented, not begun, when Christ was born: and this mystery of GOD's great love, wherewith the whole world is now filled, was so effectively presignified that those who believed that promise obtained no less than they, who were the actual recipients.

3. 4. - on the feast of nativity

Jerome says

> Jerome then speaks of the unity of the sacred books. "Whatever," he asserts, "we read in the Old Testament we find also in the Gospel; and what we read in the Gospel is deduced from the Old Testament. There is no discord between them, no disagreement. In both Testaments the Trinity is preached."

Letters to Pope Damascus

Augustine says

> He Shows by the Example of Abraham that the Ancient Saints Believed in the Incarnation of Christ. For it must not be supposed that those saints of old only profited by Christ's divinity, which was ever existent, and not also by the revelation of His humanity, which had not yet come to pass. What the Lord Jesus says, "Abraham desired to see my day, and he saw it, and was glad," meaning by the phrase *his day* to understand *his time*, affords of course a clear testimony that Abraham was fully imbued with belief in His incarnation.

Chapter 32 – pages 444-445

Ambrose says

> …Christ speaks to Abraham: "By Myself have I sworn."… Christ had, therefore, none greater, and for that cause sware

He by Himself. Moreover, the Apostle has rightly added, "for men swear by one greater than themselves," forasmuch as men have one who is greater than themselves, but God hath none.

...For the Father did not appear to Abraham, nor did Abraham wash the feet of God the Father, but the feet of Him in Whom is the image of the man that shall be. Moreover, the Son of God saith, "Abraham saw My day, and rejoiced." It is He, therefore, Who sware by Himself, [and] Whom Abraham saw.

Book 2 chapter 8

Chrysostom says

they that before Christ's coming pleased God, are "one body." How so? Because they also knew Christ. Whence does this appear? "Your father Abraham," saith He, "rejoiced to see My day, and he saw it, and was glad." (John 8:56) And again, "If ye had believed Moses," He saith, "ye would have believed Me, for he wrote of Me." (John 5:46) And the prophets too would not have written of One, of whom they knew not what they said; whereas they both knew Him, and worshiped Him.

Homily 10 – Ephesians 4:4

Concerning the Patriarch Christ Himself speaks by name, "that your father Abraham rejoiced to see My day, and he saw it, and was glad." (c. viii. 56) And concerning David, confuting the Jews He said, "How then doth David in spirit call Him Lord, saying, the Lord said unto my Lord, Sit Thou on My right hand." (Matt. 22:43; Mark 7: 36; Luke 20:42) And in many places, disputing with them, He mentions Moses; and the Apostle (mentions) the rest of the prophets; for Peter declares, that all the prophets from Samuel knew Him, and proclaimed beforehand His coming afar off, when he says, "All the prophets from Samuel and those that follow after, as many as have spoken, have likewise foretold of these days." (Acts 3:24) But Jacob and his father, as well as his grandfather, He both appeared to and talked with, and promised that He would give them many and great blessings,

Homily 8 - John 1:9

Eusebius Pamphilius says:

> 'the great servant Moses and before him in the first place Abraham and his children, and as many righteous men and prophets as afterward appeared, have contemplated him with the pure eyes of the mind, and have recognized him and offered to him the worship which is due him as Son of God.'

Chapter 2

> 'The Religion Proclaimed by Him to All Nations Was Neither New Nor Strange… Abraham himself back to the first man, were Christians in fact if not in name, he would not go beyond the truth…they also clearly knew the very Christ of God; for it has already been shown that he appeared unto Abraham, that he imparted revelations to Isaac, that he talked with Jacob, that he held converse with Moses and with the prophets that came after.'

Chapter **Church History, Life of Constantine, Oration in praise of Constantine**

Athanasius when arguing that Jesus is both God and man clearly states the Son of God was known and worshipped by the patriarchs. Discourse 2: 13, Discourse 1 40, Letter 6, section 8

Tertullian says

> Moses and the prophets declare one only God, the Creator, and His only Christ, and how that both awards of everlasting punishment and eternal salvation rest with Him,

Anti-Marcion Book 4 Chapter 34

> Now we believe that Christ did ever act in the name of God the Father; that He actually from the beginning held intercourse with (men); actually communed with patriarchs and prophets; was the Son of the Creator; was His Word;

Anti-Marcion Book 2 Chapter 27

Clement of Alexandra says

> But our Instructor is the holy God Jesus, the Word, who is the guide of all humanity. … the Scripture exhibited the Instructor in the account it gives of His guidance.

Again, when He speaks in His own person, He confesses Himself to be the Instructor: "I am the Lord thy God, who brought thee out of the land of Egypt." Who, then, has the power of leading in and out? Is it not the Instructor? This was He who appeared to Abraham,

Book 2 The Instructor page 308 ff

Ireneus says:

'John 5:39-40 How therefore did the Scriptures testify of Him, unless they were from one and the same Father, instructing men beforehand as to the advent of His Son, and foretelling the salvation brought in by Him? "For if you had believed Moses, you would also have believed Me; for he wrote of Me;" John 5:46 (saying this,) no doubt, because the Son of God is implanted everywhere throughout his writings: at one time, indeed, speaking with Abraham, when about to eat with him; at another time with Noah, giving to him the dimensions (of the ark); at another; inquiring after Adam; at another, bringing down judgment upon the Sodomites; and again, when He becomes visible, and directs Jacob on his journey, and speaks with Moses from the bush. Exodus 3:4, etc. And it would be endless to recount (the occasions) upon which the Son of God is shown forth by Moses. Of the day of His passion, too, he was not ignorant.'

Book 4 chapter 10

Justin Martyr dialogue with Trypho:

'they shall be saved through this Christ in the resurrection equally with those righteous men who were before them, namely Noah, and Enoch, and Jacob, and whoever else there be, along with those who have known this Christ, Son of God'
Chapter 45

'it was prophesied by Jacob the patriarch that there would be two advents of Christ, and that in the first He would suffer, and that after He came there would be neither prophet nor king in your nation (I proceeded), and that the nations who believed in the suffering Christ would look for His future appearance.'

Chapter 52

And Trypho said…'For you utter many blasphemies, in that you seek to persuade us that this crucified man was with Moses and Aaron, and spoke to them in the pillar of the cloud; then that he became man, was crucified, and ascended up to heaven, and comes again to earth, and ought to be worshipped. Then I answered, "I know that, as the word of God says, this great wisdom of God, the Maker of all things, and the Almighty, is hid from you."'

Chapter 38

Igniatius says

…as the Lord teaches us when He says, "If ye had believed Moses, ye would have believed Me, for he wrote of Me;" and again, "Your father Abraham rejoiced to see My day, and he saw it, and was glad; for before Abraham was, I am;" how shall we be able to live without Him? The prophets were His servants, and foresaw Him by the Spirit, and waited for Him as their Teacher, and expected Him as their Lord and Saviour, saying, "He will come and save us."

volume 1 page 131

Appendix 3
Bible readings and questions

Part One – What the Bible says about itself – Bible passages to read
Study 1 Colossians 2:1-10 and 2 Peter 1:2-4
 What do these verses tell us we have in Jesus?

Study 2 Luke 24:13-27 and Luke 24:44-47
 Which verses tell us the subject of all the Scripture?

Study 3 Acts 26: 11-23
 Which verses tell us the message Paul was given and where it could be found?

Study 4 2 Timothy 3:14-17
 What two things can the Bible do for us?

Study 5 Psalm 1 and Psalm 19:7-14
 What do these verses tell us the Bible does for the Christian?

Study 6 Romans 4:1-25
 Were Abraham and the Old Testament saints saved in a different way to us?
 What verses back up your answer?

Study 7 Hebrews 11:23 – 12:2
 What is the main lesson we can learn from the Old Testament Christians?

Summary question:
 A young Christian asks, 'Why do we read the Bible?' What is your answer?

Part Two – Creation to new creation – Bible passages to read
Study 1 John 1:1-3 and Colossians 1:15-20, 3:1-4
 Who is the centre of creation?

Study 2 Genesis 1
 What are the recurring phrases?

Study 3 Genesis 2
    What kind of place was the Garden of Eden to live in?

Study 4 Genesis 3
    What is the final result of their sin?

Study 5 Romans 5
    What does Jesus give that Adam lost?

Study 6 Deuteronomy 6
    What is their home going to be like?
    What happens to the enemies of God and His people?

Study 7 Revelation 21:1-9 and Revelation 22:1-5
    How is the new creation like Eden?
    What happens to the unbelieving?

Part Three – Father Abraham – Bible passages to read
Study 1 John 8:33-58
    How is Jesus greater than Abraham?

Study 2 Romans 4:1-25
    How was Abraham saved?

Study 3 Hebrews 11:1-22
    What can we copy from Abraham's faith?

Study 4 Galatians 3:6 – 4:5
    What do the true children of Abraham have?

Study 5 Genesis 12
    Who will make sure Abraham is blessed (v. 1-3)?
    What do you think of Abraham's response (see rest of chapter)?

Study 6 Genesis 15
    What does God do when Abraham doubts?

Study 7 Genesis 18:1-15
    What does Abraham do when Jesus calls?

Part Four – Redemption – Bible passages to read
Study 1 Exodus 3:1-17 and Deuteronomy 18:14-22
    What is so special about Moses?

Study 2 Exodus 12:21-51
    Why is there a Passover?

Study 3 Exodus 24:1-28
    What is God like (vv. 5-9)?
    What does God give His people (vv. 10-28)?

Study 4 Exodus 40
>What do they build (vv. 1-33)?
>What does God do (vv. 34-38)?

Study 5 Leviticus 16
>What is the Day of Atonement for?

Study 6 John 1:16-18 and Hebrews 3:1-6
>How is Jesus greater than Moses?

Study 7 Hebrews 9:23 – 10:18
>How are we to look at the sacrificial system?
>How did the Old Testament Christian look at the sacrificial system?

Part Five – Promised land – Bible passages to read
Study 1 1 Corinthians 10:1-13
>What did the people have to protect and keep them in the book of Numbers (vv. 1-4)?
>What happened to the people in the book of Numbers (vv. 5-13)?

Study 2 Matthew 4:1-11
>How does Jesus succeed where Israel fails?

Study 3 Deuteronomy 28:58-68
>What will God do if the people disobey?

Study 4 Deuteronomy 30:11-22 and Romans 10:4-13
>How is it possible to enjoy the blessings of God?

Study 5 Joshua 1
>What should the people do if they are to take the land?

Study 6 Hebrews 4:1-13
>What does Jesus do that Joshua can only foreshadow?

Study 7 Judges 21:15-25
>What do the people of God need?

Part Six – Kings to exile – Bible passages to read
Study 1 1 Samuel 16:1-13 and 17: 42-53
>What does God do for David?
>What do the people get from David's victory?

Study 2 1 Samuel 22:1-2 and 2 Samuel 23:8-39
>What kind of men does David gather to himself?

>What does he turn them into?

Study 3 2 Samuel 7:1-29
>What does God promise David's Son?

Study 4 1 Kings 8:1-21

Why do they build a temple?

Study 5 2 Kings 24:20 – 25:21
Why does the exile occur (refer to the last chapter)?

Study 6 Luke 1: 26-38
Who fulfils the promise of 2 Samuel 7?

Study 7 Acts 13:16-43
How is Jesus greater than David?

Part Seven – The Latter prophets – Bible passages to read
Study 1 Jeremiah 7:1-15
What is the false hope of Israel and what causes the exile?

Study 2 Jeremiah 31:1-14
After the exile what does God do for His people?

Study 3 Jeremiah 31:21-40
What does God promise to give His people?

Study 4 Isaiah 11:1-12
What is the new Davidic King like?

Study 5 Ezekiel 37:15-27
What will the new Davidic King do?

Study 6 Isaiah 65:17-25
What is the land God promises like?

Study 7 Isaiah 40:1-11 and Matthew 3:1-12
Who announces the end of the true exile?

Part Eight – The writings – Bible passages to read

Study 1 Psalm 22 and Hebrews 2:9-12
Who is speaking in Psalm 22?
What can we learn?

Study 2 Psalm 146
Who are we to put our trust in?
Who are we not to put our trust in?

Study 3 Job 19:13-29
What does Job know?
Where is his help found?

Study 4 Proverbs 8
What can the person 'Wisdom' do for you?

Study 5 Song of Songs 5:1-6 and Revelation 3:14-22
What are the parallels between these passages?

Study 6 Daniel 7
>What kingdoms look all powerful?
>Which kingdom will last?

Study 7 1 Chronicles 1
>How does Solomon understand the temple?

Part Nine – The gospels – Bible passages to read
Study 1 Matthew 1
>What stands out in the introduction to this book?

Study 2 Mark 1
>What stands out in the introduction to this book?

Study 3 Luke 1:1-17
>What stands out in the introduction to this book?

Study 4 John 1:1-18
>What stands out in the introduction to this book?

Study 5 John 20:19-31
>Why was the Gospel of John written?

Study 6 Luke 24:36-53
>What does Jesus tell us about understanding the Old Testament?

Study 7 Matthew 28:16-20
>What comes next?

Part Ten – Acts and the church – Bible passages to read
Study 1 John 14:8-21
>Who will Jesus leave for the believer?
>What will this person do for the believer?

Study 2 John 15:26 – 16:15
>What does the Holy Spirit do in the unbeliever?

Study 3 Acts 1:1-11
>What are the disciples to do?

Study 4 Acts 2:14-36
>What does Peter use to explain that Pentecost is from God?

Study 5 Acts 2:42-47
>What does God form from Pentecost?

Study 6 Acts 20:13-38
>How does Paul see the church?
>What is the greatest danger it faces?

Study 7
>Who is the Holy Spirit?
>What does He do?

Part Eleven – The church in Revelation – Bible passages to read
Study 1 Revelation 1:9-20
  What is so great about churches like the one you attend?

Study 2 Ephesians 3:1-13
  What is so special about church?

Study 3 Ephesians 1:1-14
  Who is involved in forming the church?

Study 4 Galatians 5:13-26
  How is the church to be different from the world?

Study 5 Philippians 3:12–4:3
  Where does the church belong and how should this affect our behaviour?

Study 6 Revelation 20:11-15
  What happens on Judgment day?

Study 7 Revelation 21:1- 22:5
  What does the new heavens and the new earth remind you of?

Appendix 4
Old Testament quotations in the New Testament

Matthew 1:23	Isaiah 7:14
Matthew 2:6	Micah 5:2
Matthew 2:15	Hosea 11:1
Matthew 2:18	Jeremiah 31:15
Matthew 2:23	Numbers 6:1-21
Matthew 3:3; Mark 1:3; Luke 3:4-6; John 1:23	Isaiah 40:3-5
Matthew 4:4; Luke 4:4	Deuteronomy 8:3
Matthew 4:6; Luke 4:10-11	Psalm 91:11-12
Matthew 4:7; Luke 4:12	Deuteronomy 6:16
Matthew 4:10; Luke 4:8	Deuteronomy 6:13
Matthew 4:10; Luke 4:8	Deuteronomy 10:20
Matthew 4:15-16	Isaiah 9:1-2
Matthew 8:17	Isaiah 53:4
Matthew 9:13	Hosea 6:6-7
Matthew 10:35-36	Micah 7:6
Matthew 11:10; Mark 1:2; Luke 7:27	Malachi 3:1
Matthew 12:18-21	Isaiah 42:1-4
Matthew 13:14-15; Mark 4:12; Luke 8:10; John 12:40; Acts 28:26-27	Isaiah 6:9-10
Matthew 13:35	Psalm 78:2
Matthew 15:4; Mark 7:10; Ephesians 6:2-3	Exodus 20:12
Matthew 15:4; Mark 7:10; Ephesians 6:2-3	Exodus 21:15-17
Matthew 15:4; Mark 7:10; Ephesians 6:2-3	Deuteronomy 5:16
Matthew 15:8-9; Mark 7:6-7	Isaiah 29:13
Matthew 18:16; 2 Corinthians 13:1	Deuteronomy 19:15
Matthew 19:5; Mark 10:7-8; 1 Corinthians 6:16; Ephesians 5:31	Genesis 2:24
Matthew 21:5; John 12:15	Zechariah 9:9

Matthew 21:9; Luke 13:35;19:38; John 12:13	Psalm 118:26
Matthew 21:13; Mark 11:17	Isaiah 56:7
Matthew 21:13; Mark 11:17	Jeremiah 7:11
Matthew 21:16	Psalm 8:2
Matthew 21:42; Mark 12:10-11; Luke 20:17; Acts 4:11; 1 Peter 2:7	Psalm 118:22-23
Matthew 22:24	Deuteronomy 25:5
Matthew 22:32; Mark 12:26; Acts 7:32	Exodus 3:6
Matthew 22:37; Mark 12:30; Luke 10:27	Deuteronomy 6:5
Matthew 22:37; Mark 12:30; Luke 10:27	Deuteronomy 10:12
Matthew 22:37; Mark 12:30; Luke 10:27	Deuteronomy 30:6
Matthew 22:39; Mark 12:31; Romans 13:9; Galatians 5:14; James 2:8	Leviticus 19:18
Matthew 22:44; Mark 12:36; Luke 20:42-43; Acts 2:34-35; Hebrews 1:13	Psalm 110:1
Matthew 26:31; Mark 14:27	Zechariah 13:7
Matthew 27:9	Zechariah 11:12
Matthew 27:35; John 19:24	Psalm 22:18
Matthew 27:46; Mark 15:34	Psalm 22:1
Mark 9:44	Isaiah 66:24
Mark 10:6	Genesis 1:27
Mark 12:29	Deuteronomy 6:4
Mark 15:28; Luke 22:37	Isaiah 53:12
Luke 1:17	Malachi 4:6
Luke 2:23	Exodus 13:2
Luke 2:24	Leviticus 12:8
Luke 4:18-19	Isaiah 61:1-2
Luke 23:30	Hosea 10:8
Luke 23:46	Psalm 31:5
John 2:17; Romans 15:3	Psalm 69:9
John 6:45	Isaiah 54:13
John 10:34	Psalm 82:6
John 12:38; Romans 10:16	Isaiah 53:1
John 13:18	Psalm 41:9
John 15:25	Psalm 69:4
John 19:36	Psalm 34:20
John 19:36	Exodus 12:46
John 19:37	Zechariah 12:10
Acts 1:20	Psalm 69:25
Acts 1:20	Psalm 109:8

Acts 2:17-20; Romans 10:13	Joel 2:28-32
Acts 2:25-28; 13:35	Psalm 16:8-11
Acts 3:22-23; 7:37	Deuteronomy 18:15-19
Acts 3:25; Galatians 3:8	Genesis 22:18
Acts 3:25; Galatians 3:8	Genesis 26:4
Acts 3:25; Galatians 3:8	Genesis 28:14
Acts 4:25	Psalm 2:1-2
Acts 7:3	Genesis 12:1
Acts 7:7	Genesis 15:14
Acts 7:7	Exodus 3:12
Acts 7:27-28	Exodus 2:14
Acts 7:33	Exodus 3:5
Acts 7:34	Exodus 3:7-8
Acts 7:40	Exodus 32:1
Acts 7:40	Exodus 32:23
Acts 7:42-43	Amos 5:25-27
Acts 7:49-50	Isaiah 66:1-2
Acts 8:32-33	Isaiah 53:7-8
Acts 13:22	1 Samuel 13:14
Acts 13:22	Psalm 89:20
Acts 13:33; Hebrews 1:5; 5:5	Psalm 2:7
Acts 13:34	Isaiah 55:3
Acts 13:41	Habakkuk 1:5
Acts 13:47	Isaiah 42:6
Acts 13:47	Isaiah 49:6
Acts 15:16-17	Amos 9:11-12
Acts 23:5	Exodus 22:28
Romans 2:6	Psalm 62:12
Romans 2:6	Proverbs 24:12
Romans 2:24	Isaiah 52:5
Romans 3:4	Psalm 51:4
Romans 3:10-12	Psalm 14:1-3;
Romans 3:10-12	Psalm 53:1-3
Romans 3:13	Psalm 5:9
Romans 3:13	Psalm 140:3
Romans 3:14	Psalm 10:7
Romans 3:15-17	Isaiah 59:7-8
Romans 3:15-17	Proverbs 1:16
Romans 3:18	Psalm 36:1
Romans 3:20	Psalm 143:2

Romans 4:3,22; Galatians 3:6; James 2:23	Genesis 15:6
Romans 4:7-8	Psalm 32:1-2
Romans 4:17	Genesis 17:5
Romans 4:18	Genesis 15:5
Romans 7:7	Exodus 20:17
Romans 7:7	Deuteronomy 5:21
Romans 8:20	Ecclesiastes 1:1-2
Romans 8:22	Jeremiah 12:4
Romans 8:27	Psalm 139:1-2
Romans 8:31	Psalm 118:6
Romans 8:33	Isaiah 50:8-9
Romans 8:36	Psalm 44:22
Romans 9:7; Hebrews 11:18	Genesis 21:12
Romans 9:9	Genesis 18:10
Romans 9:9	Genesis 18:14
Romans 9:10	Genesis 25:21
Romans 9:12	Genesis 25:23
Romans 9:13	Malachi 1:2-3
Romans 9:14	2 Chronicles 19:7
Romans 9:15	Exodus 33:19
Romans 9:17	Exodus 9:16
Romans 9:20	Isaiah 29:16
Romans 9:20	Isaiah 45:9
Romans 9:25	Hosea 2:23
Romans 9:26	Hosea 1:10
Romans 9:27-28	Isaiah 10:22-23
Romans 9:29	Isaiah 1:9
Romans 9:31	Isaiah 51:1
Romans 9:33; Romans 10:11; 1 Peter 2:6	Isaiah 28:16
Romans 9:32; 1 Peter 2:8	Isaiah 8:14
Romans 10:5; Galatians 3:12	Leviticus 18:5
Romans 10:6-8	Deuteronomy 30:12-14
Romans 10:15	Isaiah 52:7
Romans 10:18	Psalm 19:4
Romans 10:19	Deuteronomy 32:21
Romans 10:20	Isaiah 65:1
Romans 10:21	Isaiah 65:2
Romans 11:3	1 Kings 19:10
Romans 11:3	1 Kings 19:14
Romans 11:4	1 Kings 19:18

Romans 11:8	Deuteronomy 29:3-4
Romans 11:9	Psalm 69:22-23
Romans 11:26-27	Isaiah 59:20-21
Romans 11:34-35; 1 Corinthians 2:16	Isaiah 40:13-14
Romans 12:19; Hebrews 10:30	Deuteronomy 32:35
Romans 12:20	Proverbs 25:21-22
Romans 14:11	Isaiah 45:23
Romans 15:9	2 Samuel 22:50
Romans 15:9	Psalm 18:49
Romans 15:10; Hebrews 1:6	Deuteronomy 32:43
Romans 15:11	Psalm 117:1
Romans 15:12	Isaiah 11:10
Romans 15:21	Isaiah 52:15
1 Corinthians 1:19	Isaiah 29:14
1 Corinthians 1:31; 2 Corinthians 10:17	Jeremiah 9:24
1 Corinthians 2:9	Isaiah 64:4
1 Corinthians 3:19	Job 5:13
1 Corinthians 3:20	Psalm 94:11
1 Corinthians 5:13	Deuteronomy 17:7
1 Corinthians 9:9; 1 Timothy 5:18	Deuteronomy 25:4
1 Corinthians 10:7	Exodus 32:6
1 Corinthians 10:26, 28	Psalm 24:1
1 Corinthians 10:26, 28	Deuteronomy 10:14
1 Corinthians 14:21	Isaiah 28:11-12
1 Corinthians 15:27; Hebrews 2:6-8	Psalm 8:4-6
1 Corinthians 15:32	Isaiah 22:13
1 Corinthians 15:45	Genesis 2:7
1 Corinthians 15:54	Isaiah 25:8
1 Corinthians 15:55	Hosea 13:14
2 Corinthians 4:13	Psalm 116:10
2 Corinthians 6:2	Isaiah 49:8
2 Corinthians 6:16	Exodus 29:45
2 Corinthians 6:16	Leviticus 26:12
2 Corinthians 6:16	Jeremiah 30:22
2 Corinthians 6:16	Jeremiah 31:1
2 Corinthians 6:16	Jeremiah 32:38
2 Corinthians 6:16	Zechariah 8:8
2 Corinthians 6:16	Ezekiel 37:27
2 Corinthians 6:17-18	Isaiah 52:11
2 Corinthians 6:17-18	Jeremiah 31:9

2 Corinthians 8:15	Exodus 16:18
2 Corinthians 9:9	Psalm 112:9
Galatians 3:10	Deuteronomy 27:26
Galatians 3:11	Habakkuk 2:3-4
Galatians 3:13	Deuteronomy 21:23
Galatians 4:27	Isaiah 54:1
Galatians 4:30	Genesis 21:10
Ephesians 4:8	Psalm 68:18
Ephesians 4:25	Zechariah 8:16
Ephesians 4:26	Psalm 4:4
Ephesians 5:14	Isaiah 60:1
Philippians 2:10-11	Isaiah 45:23
Hebrews 1:5	Psalm 2:7
Hebrews 1:5	2 Samuel 7:14
Hebrews 1:7	Psalm 104:4
Hebrews 1:8-9	Psalm 45:6-7
Hebrews 1:10-12	Psalm 102:25-27
Hebrews 2:12	Psalm 22:22
Hebrews 2:13	2 Samuel 22:3
Hebrews 2:13	Isaiah 8:17-18
Hebrews 3:7-11, 15; 4:3, 5, 7	Psalm 95:7-11
Hebrews 4:4	Genesis 2:2
Hebrews 5:6, 10; 7:17, 21	Psalm 110:4
Hebrews 6:14	Genesis 22:17
Hebrews 8:5	Exodus 25:40
Hebrews 8:8-12; 10:16-17	Jeremiah 31:31-34
Hebrews 9:19-20	Exodus 24:8
Hebrews 10:5-7, 8-9	Psalm 40:6-8
Hebrews 10:30	Deuteronomy 32:36
Hebrews 11:4	Genesis 4:3-10
Hebrews 11:5	Genesis 5:21-24
Hebrews 11:7	Genesis 6:13-22
Hebrews 11:8-9	Genesis 12:1-8
Hebrews 11:11	Genesis 17:9
Hebrews 11:11	Genesis 18:11-14
Hebrews 11:11	Genesis 21:2
Hebrews 11:12	Genesis 15:5-6
Hebrews 11:12	Genesis 22:17
Hebrews 11:12	Genesis 32:12
Hebrews 11:13	Genesis 23:4

Hebrews 11:13	Psalm 39:12
Hebrews 11:16	Exodus 3:6, 15
Hebrews 11:17	Genesis 22:1-10
Hebrews 11:18	Genesis 21:12
Hebrews 11:20	Genesis 27:27-40
Hebrews 11:21	Genesis 47:31
Hebrews 11:22	Genesis 50:20-24
Hebrews 11:23	Exodus 1:22
Hebrews 11:23	Exodus 2:2
Hebrews 11:24	Exodus 2:10-15
Hebrews 11:27	Exodus 2:15
Hebrews 11:27	Exodus 3:6
Hebrews 11:27	Exodus 24:9-11
Hebrews 11:27	Exodus 33:11
Hebrews 11:28	Exodus 12:21-30
Hebrews 11:29	Exodus 14:21-31
Hebrews 11:30	Joshua 6:12-21
Hebrews 11:31	Joshua 2:1-21
Hebrews 11:31	Joshua 6:22-25
Hebrews 11:33	Daniel 6
Hebrews 11:34	Daniel 3
Hebrews 11:35	1 Kings 17:17-24
Hebrews 11:35	2 Kings 4:25-27
Hebrews 12:5-6	Proverbs 3:11-12
Hebrews 12:12	Isaiah 35:3
Hebrews 12:20	Exodus 19:13
Hebrews 12:21	Deuteronomy 9:19
Hebrews 12:26	Haggai 2:6
Hebrews 12:29	Deuteronomy 4:24
Hebrews 13:5	Deuteronomy 31:6-8
Hebrews 13:5	Joshua 1:5
Hebrews 13:6	Psalm 27:1
Hebrews 13:6	Psalm 118:6
James 4:6	Proverbs 3:24
1 Peter 5:5	Proverbs 3:24
1 Peter 1:16	Leviticus 11:44-45
1 Peter 1:16	Leviticus 19:2
1 Peter 1:16	Leviticus 20:7
1 Peter 1:24-25	Isaiah 40:6-8
1 Peter 2:22	Isaiah 53:9

1 Peter 2:24	Isaiah 53:5
1 Peter 3:10-12	Psalm 34:12-16
1 Peter 3:14	Isaiah 8:12
1 Peter 4:8	Proverbs 10:12
1 Peter 4:18	Proverbs 11:31
1 Peter 5:7	Psalm 55:22
2 Peter 2:22	Proverbs 26:11
Jude 9	Zechariah 3:2
Revelation 1:17	Isaiah 41:4
Revelation 1:17	Isaiah 44:6
Revelation 2:23	Jeremiah 17:10
Revelation 2:27	Psalm 2:9
Revelation 3:7	Isaiah 22:22
Revelation 7:16	Isaiah 49:10
Revelation 21:23	Isaiah 60:20-21